The Changing Face
of Reference

**FOUNDATIONS IN LIBRARY AND
INFORMATION SCIENCE, Volume 37**

Editors: Thomas W. Leonhardt, *Director of Library Technical Services, Bizzell
Memorial Library, University of Oklahoma*
Murray S. Martin, *University Librarian and Professor of Library Sciencle
Emeritus, Tufts University*

Foundations in
Library and Information Science

Edited by **Thomas W. Leonhardt**, *Director of Library Technical Services, Bizzell Memorial Library, University of Oklahoma* and
Murray S. Martin, *University Librarian and Professor of Library Science Emeritus, Tufts University*

The Changing Face
of Reference

Edited by: **LYNNE M. STUART**
University Libraries
Pennsylvania State University
DENA HOLIMAN HUTTO
E.V. Hauser Library
Reed College

 **JAI PRESS INC.**

Greenwich, Connecticut   London, England

Library of Congress Cataloging-in-Publication Data

The changing face of reference   /   edited by Lynne M. Stuart, Dena Hutto.
      p.   cm. — (Foundations in library and information science   :   v. 37)
   Includes bibliographical references and index.
   ISBN 0-7623-0217-8
   1.   Academic libraries–Reference services–United States.
   2.   Academic libraries–Reference services–United States–Data
processing.   I. Stuart, Lynne M.   II. Hutto, Dena.   III. Series.
   Z675.U5C44   1996
   027.7–dc21

                                                      96-45479
                                                      CIP

Copyright © 1996 JAI PRESS INC.
55 Old Post Road, No. 2
Greenwich, Connecticut 06836

JAI PRESS LTD.
38 Tavistock Street
Covent Garden
London WC2E 7PB
England

ISBN: 0-7623-0217-8

Library of Congress Catalog Number: 96-45479

Manufactured in the United States of America

CONTENTS

FACING CHANGE:

REFERENCE SERVICE IN THE COMING AGE

Lynne M. Stuart and Dena Holiman Hutto

Reference librarians know that rapid and profound changes are transforming the environment in which they work. The most obvious changes
are the result of new information technologies used to produce, store,
and locate information. By the 1980s, electronic bibliographic information in the form of online catalogs and bibliographic database services
was commonplace in libraries. In the last half of the 1990s, the prolifera-
tion of Internet-accessible information services is exceeded only by public enthusiasm about the prospect of being able to find anything—anything
at all—on the World Wide Web. Full-text searching, manipulation of
numeric and geographic data, and organization of information in a hypertext environment are all useful skills for reference librarians today. As formidable as the technological challenges are, other challenges are just as

daunting. The population of the country as a whole is becoming increasingly diverse, and librarians are called upon to assist groups of users for whom traditional assumptions about library organization and service may not hold true. And all services, whether traditional or emerging, must be offered by libraries with stagnant funds and diminishing staff.

By 1986, Barbara J. Ford believed that the changes in academic libraries were so profound that the concept of the reference desk, which has been synonymous with reference services for generations of librarians, had outlived its usefulness.[1] In 1995, Kevin Ewing and Robert Hauptman were willing to take this idea much further, asserting in a *Journal of Academic Librarianship* "Symposium on Reference Service" that "…traditional academic reference service, until now held to be a key element within higher education, does not need to be rethought or reconfigured, it needs to be eliminated."[2] They identify the inadequacy of "human mediation" between the users of libraries and increasingly numerous and complex resources as a central cause of what they term the demise of reference librarianship.[3]

The editors of this volume believe that while reference service may be undervalued, it is far from obsolete. They agree with Lori Goetsch, who states in response to Ewing and Hauptman that it is the "…popular notion of reference services as 'reference librarians answering questions at a reference desk' that puts reference services in danger."[4] The most familiar image of reference service may be of a librarian answering questions from behind a desk, over the phone, or via electronic mail. However, answering questions and locating materials for library users is only one aspect of reference librarianship. Selecting and providing access to reference materials, creating guides and menus to help patrons use resources effectively, and conducting classes and workshops for students or the general public are just as much a part of reference service as answering specific questions. In all of these activities, reference librarians facilitate access to traditional collections and electronic resources alike.

To condemn reference service because librarians can be directly approached and questioned by library users during a modest portion of their working hours is to ignore its most essential function. In 1983, Rolland Stevens and Joan Walton wrote, "The reference librarian is the link between materials in the reference collection and the user who needs them."[5]. Today, the most obvious result of information technology is that librarians are more necessary than ever as a human link between information sources and library users—a human face to library service. They welcome, explain, encourage, listen, and share the joy of a successful conclusion to an information search. In doing so, they provide an irreplaceable, human dimension to library services. The greatest challenge facing librarians is the problem of extending this human dimension, perhaps through system interfaces or World Wide Web pages, to patrons who never need or want to come into a library building.

The Changing Face of Reference seeks to identify and describe the causes and effects of changes that have forced librarians to reexamine reference service. Its contributors see these changes as opportunities to create new ways of providing assistance and instruction, to reach out to new groups of library users, and to embrace new technologies, exercising skills and technological expertise traditionally considered to be outside the boundaries of the library profession. They recognize that in the face of change, library patrons continue to need help; indeed, the introduction of new technologies means that they require more kinds of help than ever before. The central role of reference services is to fill this continuing need of patrons. Contributors to this monograph recognize that because libraries are moving from a collection-based to a service-based orientation, they are in a unique position to redefine the role and function of libraries in the larger information environment.

The first section of this monograph, "Changing Approaches to Reference Service," presents ways of making sense of the changes that sweep reference librarianship today. In an historical analysis, Inga Barnello demonstrates how reference librarianship of the past century has never known a time of stability; rather, librarians have constantly faced and responded constructively to changing technologies and philosophies. For example, the invention of the electric light bulb and the telephone had an impact on libraries, just as computers have today. Major technological changes stimulate librarians to be creative and develop new ways of providing reference to patrons. Barnello encourages librarians to understand librarianship's past so that they can effectively change references services to meet current and future challenges.

Gary Thompson applies a manager's customer service approach to the problem of fulfilling both patron and librarian expectations when the two meet in the reference encounter. He discusses how librarians and patrons should behave in the reference setting in order to make reference interactions more successful. This chapter stimulates librarians to rethink their behavior at the reference desk. Treating patrons differently may not seem like a significant change, but it can increase customer satisfaction, making patrons feel more positive about libraries and librarians.

As changes in individuals' behavior can affect reference services, so can alterations in organizational structure. Barbara Alexander, Jessica George, and Kathleen Conley present a case study of how changes in staffing and bibliographic accessibility made it both possible and desirable to combine a federal documents collection and a general reference and information department into a dynamic new reference department. The authors describe how such a reorganization can energize a staff to become more knowledgeable and productive.

The idea that reference librarians can provide a human interface to information resources is based at least in part on the assumption that librarians are familiar with and able to understand the patron's point of view. This familiarity can be difficult to achieve when the patrons using library resources come from backgrounds that are racially, linguistically, or even generationally different from those of the librarian. In the section of this monograph entitled "Reference Services for Changing User Populations," contributors demonstrate how their libraries have shaped services in response to specific groups of patrons.

Two of the chapters in this section focus on reference services for a rapidly growing segment of the U.S. population: Hispanic Americans. María de Jesús Ayala-Scheuneman and Roberta Pitts discuss the problems of mostly white, non-Hispanic librarians in serving a majority Hispanic student body at Texas A&M University at Kingsville. They note that students are often more comfortable approaching a reference desk staffed by members of their own cultural group. Their library has made an effort to diversify as new staff are hired, but they have found that very few professional librarians come from Hispanic backgrounds. Reference librarians have responded to this challenge by cultivating awareness and sensitivity toward Hispanic culture, in part by participating in an intensive language and culture course sponsored by the university. Librarians focus on offering services and collections tailored to the needs of Hispanic students.

In a companion piece, Robert Mowery describes the problems of attempting to provide access to Mexican American resources using Anglo-American library practices. He shows how Library of Congress Subject Headings and other controlled vocabulary and classification systems perpetuate outmoded, English-language terminology and ways of thinking about library material by and about Mexican Americans. As a result, students and researchers who are knowledgeable about this subject area but unaware of its peculiar history in library practice can easily miss valuable library resources through ineffective searching. In such situations, reference librarians must learn to fill the gap between library practice and patron information needs. It is also important for them to share these frustrations with their technical service colleagues in order to improve subject cataloging, indexing, and classification of these materials.

The concluding chapters in this section focus on the special needs of two groups of students who may be less visible than other populations of patrons who use academic libraries. Mollie Lawson writes of the critical role her library plays in the McNair Central Achievers Program at Central Missouri State University. This program supports first-generation university students through their first four years of college and on to graduate studies. Librarians are integrally involved with the students' progress, from conducting a series of seminars on information literacy delivered early in the program to serving as library mentors who, with a team of writing and faculty mentors, support each student through the successful completion of the program.

Catherine Lee's contribution is a provocative view of what most librarians might consider typical college students: "Generation Xers." Lee shows how these students have views, characteristics, and information needs distinct from those of previous generations of college students. She offers suggestions for how librarians can modify instruction and reference services to better meet the needs of the current generation of undergraduate library users.

The most frequently identified source of change in libraries is undoubtedly electronic and networking technology. "Impact of Changing Technologies on Reference Service" presents contributions by reference librarians who have experienced and used electronic information technologies in their work. Vivienne Monty and Peggy Warren-Wenk provide an intriguing look at how academic use of the Internet has changed the scholarly research process in which academic reference librarians are inextricably involved. In their study of Internet use by scholars, Monty and Warren-Wenk found that scholars use the Internet in all aspects of their work. The authors challenge librarians to find methods of providing reference services for these Internet users.

While many scholars conduct research through the Internet, others are looking for an emerging category of library collections: instructional software. Carol Wright describes the challenges of helping patrons find and use software, courseware, multimedia, high-quality World Wide Web sites, and appropriate software authoring tools. Her chapter provides concrete information for librarians seeking application user groups, electronic publishers, multimedia products, and Internet sites that will help provide the link between patrons and these new types of materials.

This section of the monograph concludes with two chapters that demonstrate how librarians with programming skills are able to bring their technical knowledge to bear on the problem of designing information systems to supplement traditional reference service. Stephen Sottong's contribution shows how custom computer applications can be designed by librarians to meet the information needs of a busy reference service point. The author describes the creation of a ready reference database that replaced a ready reference card file. This chapter describes how reference librarians can create a customized database using new and relatively friendly programming tools.

Programming skills can solve problems as well as create products. Lisa Blankenship and Jane Smith tell how a disruptive library renovation project prompted them to create an online reference service. They describe a test program that allowed patrons to find answers to frequently asked questions, learn catalog searching tips, and use an online reference question service. The authors share the process, pitfalls, and outcomes of their effort.

The concluding section of *The Changing Face of Reference* explores the provision of reference services beyond the traditional boundary of library walls. Pamela Snelson defines remote access and describes how it has changed over time. She demonstrates that with the growth of remote access, users have replaced libraries at the center of the information universe.

In a companion chapter, Sally Kalin shows how libraries must evolve in the changing information environment from place-bound institutions into customer services that provide helpful, human mediation to users of all kinds of electronic information systems. She provides examples of the problems that remote users encounter and services that librarians can create to solve them.

Lucia Snowhill writes about her experience in providing reference service to a group of users who are often reluctant to approach the traditional library reference desk: university teaching faculty. Instead of waiting for the faculty to visit the library, she established regular office hours in their department. Access to the library's online catalog and bibliographic databases through the campus network allowed her to carry out many reference functions without the benefit of the library's traditional collections. Her experience shows that librarians can play a more active role in both the research and instructional activities of academe when they find creative ways of establishing a presence outside library walls.

In the final chapter, the librarians of Orange County Library System, Florida contribute a study of how they successfully transformed a problem—the inability of a busy public library reference desk to respond to telephone inquires in a timely manner—into a model remote access reference service. Key to their success is their recognition that a large and growing number of users in their community wanted and needed library services, but were unwilling to visit a busy urban library facility. In response, the library system dedicated staff and resources to create a separate, centralized telephone reference unit. This chapter provides an interesting example of how information can be managed effectively within a large library organization.

Collectively, the thoughts and experiences of the contributors to *The Changing Face of Reference* show that, contrary to the many negative predictions found in recent library literature, reference service is in no danger of becoming obsolete. In fact, there are many reasons for reference librarians to be optimistic about their continuing role in the emerging information environment. In a world of full-text, hypertext, and interrelated databases, the need for organization and accessibility is clear. Yet computing and networking specialists can only go so far in offering levels of organization and accessibility needed for users to be able to make sense, let alone make effective use of information technologies. It is the function of reference librarians to introduce and explain information resources. Their specialty is to take the broad view of how myriad networks, systems, and printed reference tools fit together to fill the information needs of each patron.

In a recent article about how technology is transforming reference service, Michael G. Enyart and Rebecca A. Smith observe that "...technology cannot take the place of personal service. Information seekers will look to librarians to shepherd them through the maze of electronic services that are being promised."[6] While reference librarians cannot assume that the general public will look to them for guidance, the contributors to *The Changing Face of Reference* show that opportunities for librarians to demonstrate their usefulness are abundant. They can and should set aside fears about their own obsolescence and get on with the business of shaping an exciting future for themselves and for library patrons.

NOTES

1. Barbara J. Ford, "Reference beyond (and without) the Reference Desk," *College and Research Libraries* 47, no. 5 (Sept. 1986): 491-494.

2. Keith Ewing and Robert Hauptman, "Is Traditional Reference Service Obsolete?" *Journal of Academic Librarianship* 21, no. 1 (1995): 3.

3. See note 2.

4. Lori Goetsch, "Reference Service Is More Than a Desk," *Journal of Academic Librarianship* 21, no. 1 (1995): 15.

5. Rolland E. Stevens and Joan M. Walton, *Reference Work in the Public Library* (Littleton, CO: Libraries Unlimited, 1983): 17.

6. Michael G. Enyart and Rebecca A. Smith, "Reference Services: More than Information Chauffeuring," *Special Libraries* 87, no. 3 (summer 1996): 160.

PART I

CHANGING APPROACHES TO REFERENCE SERVICE

THE CHANGING FACE OF REFERENCE:
A HISTORY OF THE FUTURE

Inga H. Barnello

ABSTRACT

Change is a constant in the provision of library reference services. This chapter provides a historical review of both conservative and liberal approaches to reference services over the last century, from Samuel Green's ideas about "reader's assistance" to "hyperlearning" in the Lewis Perelman's knowledge age. Both ideological and technological changes that have an impact on the information services environment are discussed, as are the development of teaching and consulting models of reference service.

INTRODUCTION

The telltale signs of change and chaos are clearly present in librarianship today. Librarians' words speak of their transformation as they struggle to apply current management theory to the problems of providing library services: *alternative, differentiated service, restructuring, reconfiguring, new paradigms, new protocols,* and *strategic visions,* not to be confused with *new visions*. The language of change has librarians tongue-tied, unable to put their teeth into their future. As they rethink and re-engineer their way to some understanding of where they are going, librarians are questioning their approach to their service work. Librarians are re-examining the interrelationships between themselves and their clients, paraprofessionals, and their more technically oriented colleagues in the computer center.

The language also speaks of chaos: *virtual* (nearly real), *burnout* (near collapse), and *downsizing* (nearly fired). The changes seem subject to no law or order. The Internet epitomizes two things that make librarians twitch: lack of control and inconsistency. Outsourcing is another disconcerting element of the present state of affairs in libraries. Information technology has presented librarians with a steep learning curve and technostress. No longer solely assistants to readers, nor reference desk attendants, librarians must continue to develop channels of service to their peripatetic patrons.

Although there is something quite disquieting about being turned on one's head, there is some positive fallout in all this turmoil in libraries. There is nothing healthier for a collective community, as small as a family or as large as a nation, than to come together and question its approach and face its quandaries. There is much disagreement among librarians on the direction of their profession. The most that they can agree on is that they are always learning, and that they are not learning fast enough.

Many of those in the library profession today experienced the advent of computer applications over the last two decades. They know about change and steep learning curves. People know intellectually of industrial revolutions, technological change, and moveable type and how they changed the world. But do librarians know of where they stand in their own history? None are old enough to have experienced the wave of change that librarians confronted nearly one hundred years ago. Are there connections between the past and the present? The baseball player Satchel Paige admonished his fans never to look back because something might be gaining on them.[1] Nostalgics wax and whine about the good old days; academics speak of past as prologue. Librarians are so caught up in the present that time spent in a review of one hundred years of their profession may not seem like top priority. The value of such a review becomes clear, however, once the similarities start to surface. The value approaches that of a mirror—revealing, reflective, and suggestive.

The historical process is more than a series of events senselessly succeeding one another in time. Toynbee writes that history conforms to regular and recurrent cycles of change. Although his sweeping overview of history is criticized as inaccurate by narrower specialists, it is thought by his proponents to be the only way to see rhythms and patterns.[2] With the long view of history in place, librarians enter the foray of historical examination knowing that much is left out, and that there is no value-free history. An historian's observations are limited by what he knows and by what he believes to be important.

A reading of the history of reference librarianship cannot make reference work less stressful, nor tell librarians how to redesign it. But as an exercise in putting change in perspective, a historical glance can, at the very least, help contemporaries realize that others have struggled before them, and faced some of the same issues. It may also lay a foundation for building and forecasting the future. Librarians cannot effectively address the question "Where are we going from here?" without looking back on how they have progressed to this point. History may provide that deep, cleansing breath librarians need to discuss how they are to most effectively interact with their patrons as reference librarians in the future.

ORIGINS OF REFERENCE SERVICE

It may be impossible to construct a time line of the history of reference. How does one draw an oblique blur? The history of reference service is part event and part attitudinal change. It is part the history of the growth of a profession and part the history of education. Reference service developed interconnectedly with forces from within and without.

Samuel Rothstein wrote that "the beginnings of reference service are lost in antiquity."[3] In fact it was lost, but librarians have him to thank for unearthing the origins of reference from the minutes of academic library committees and the proceedings of professional associations. The beginnings of reference are both tentative and contentious. Reference was not initially a part of librarianship. It began in the public libraries as a response to patron needs for assistance in interpreting the card catalog.

The accepted benchmark of the origin of reference service, Samuel Green's 1876 article, "Personal Relations between Librarians and Readers," speaks to the need to assist readers in their use of the nonfiction collection. His article is a hesitant, somewhat elitist call to librarians to bolster patrons' ability to select appropriate nonfiction titles. However, later generations must give Green credit for taking librarians from the role of gatekeeper of the archives and putting them on the front lines responding to patron inquiries. He characterized "assistance to readers," as reference service was first called, in this way. "A hearty reception by a sympathizing friend, and the recognition of some one at hand who will listen to inquiries, even although he may consider them unimportant, make it easy for such persons to ask questions, and put them at once on a home footing."[4] It is interesting to note the didactic nature of his examples of encounters with patrons. He felt that patrons, scholars as well as novices, should be taught. "Be careful not to make inquirers dependent," he warned, "teach them to rely on themselves."[5]

The development of reference service moved more slowly in academic libraries. Not until Melvil Dewey advocated his "modern library idea," at Columbia in 1885 did academic libraries have reference librarians and reference departments. On increasing appointments of reference librarians, he wrote, "we have learned that no system of catalogues, indexes, and bibliographies can possibly take the place of personal help."[6]

Dewey's "modern library idea" was a fresh approach to service which left the closed stacks and elite patronage behind and opened up libraries as laboratories of learning to all. Dewey had the revolutionary idea of doubling service hours and opening libraries during vacations and holidays. He wrote, "The work to be done by an ideal library is threefold. First, it should make more readers than ever before….Second, it should teach its readers better methods….Third, it should teach them to read better books."[7] These words sound familiar today, but Rothstein writes that Dewey was far ahead of his time in offering a different brand of public service. He was excited about the prospect of doing more for patrons, of teaching them, of reaching out to a wider circle. Dewey's ideas caught on slowly, and it would not be until World War I that reference became a regular service in academic libraries.[8]

SPURS OF CHANGE

The transformation of higher education propelled the advancement of academic libraries near the turn of the century. Arthur Bestor wrote of "the transformation of American Scholarship" and, specifically, the emphasis on the value of learning by inquiry as the catalyst for the development of academic libraries and their fledgling assistance to readers.[9] Until this period, academic libraries lay in a state of underdevelopment.

Rothstein describes the sad shape of academic libraries during the last two decades of the nineteenth century by noting that Boston Public Library had a collection the size of the libraries of Brown, California, Cornell, Columbia, Michigan, Pennsylvania, Princeton, and Toronto put together.[10] The staffing levels were atrocious, and the service hours for students approached five hours per week. There was no scholarship through research. Faculty thought of themselves as teachers, not scholars or specialists. There was no perceived need for library collections or librarians except as guardians of collections.

Bestor traces the development of research, professional societies, and librarianship and finds that they developed interdependently.

> The new professionalized attitude toward scholarship manifested itself in one other new type of organization, the publications of which also swelled the collections of scholarly libraries. This was the new learned society, devoted to a well-defined special field, and composed largely of college professors working within that field....The output of the new university scholar contributed in a far from negligible way to the contents of the growing university library.[11]

Once scholars required access to enhanced library collections, endowments began to grow. University collections became research libraries, and librarianship came into its own. The American Library Association was formed during this era as were the American Chemical Society, the American Historical Association, and the Modern Language Association. Not to idealize this era, these developments did not occur overnight or without stops and starts. In fact, John Cotton Dana was still complaining in 1911 about the quality of the university and its students when he wrote: "Colleges have lamented much that their students cannot write. It would be well if they concerned themselves first over the fact that their students cannot read."[12]

Academic librarians were faced with growing collections and larger library buildings, reflecting the different disciplines of scholarship. Scholars subdivided themselves into subject areas, and librarians subdivided their collections as well. Changing responsibilities for librarians were at hand. For Dewey, the changing nature of the work of academic librarians was connected with the issue of status. Taking the lead again, he called for a corps of specialists in academic libraries who could be best defined as faculty. He wrote, "It is certain that reference work must be closely divided if it is to be of high value. It is also certain that a library faculty can do the work much better than the professors in the same subjects in the university, because library questions refer to the literature of the subject, while the professor deals with the subject itself."[13] He clearly delineated the difference between the work of librarians and faculty while calling for collegial recognition among specialists both within and outside the classroom.

Along with changes in academe, technological innovation made an enormous impact on libraries. From the invention of electric lighting, the telephone, the telex, computers, and photocopiers to the advent of tele-facsimile machines, optical storage, and fiber optic cable, librarians have transformed their role in reference service, from that of desk attendant to information technology consultant. The telephone's prospects for providing greater access and a widening service front were to the nineteenth century, what computer networks are to the twentieth century. John Cotton Dana shared Melvil Dewey's enthusiasm for the telephone as revolutionizing service. Dana referred to it as the "great leveler" that "adds a million strong threads to that great social fabric which we are all trying to weave."[14]

In the Internet, librarians will discover either a great divide between them and their patrons or the port of call for reference service. Regardless, patrons will believe that they have discovered an omniscient leveler that provides all the information they need to obtain. Public policy and economic conditions will determine the place of libraries and librarians in the global network and the ultimate usefulness of the Internet. Librarians have not added a strong, effective voice to public policy debates. A failure to seize an opportunity to further libraries' place in the National Information Infrastructure (NII) may render libraries as service-poor archives once again.

Just as Dewey and Dana were situated at a pivotal point at the beginning of a new century, so are librarians in the 1990s. As their predecessors seized opportunity at a time of great change, so must today's librarians. Librarian leaders know that access is not everything. Patrons seeking information from global electronic libraries will need librarians even more than in the past. With each new technology librarians have been able to expand services. With the invention of the electric light bulb, library hours were extended into the night. The telephone allowed librarians to serve patrons remotely. Over time, these innovations created greater demand for service. They have imposed both a burden of instruction and a growing dependency on librarians. The complexities of today's ever-changing library environment requires that librarians be ready either to instruct patrons on how to find information or to find information for them.

Information technology presents a challenge to the definition of the profession. The virtual community of the future will witness an altered function and structure of librarianship. Essentially, the service front is widening again, and the result may be a crushing demand for librarians.

The development of research and the corresponding transformation of academic libraries occurred within the context of the economic and social developments of the late-nineteenth century. The nation changed from a rural to an urban industrial economy. The public library movement was in full swing, and the modern academic library movement finally took hold once universities emphasized research and graduate study. Collections increased exponentially. Today, with the change from an industrial economy to an information economy, education and libraries must change as well. Librarians, by virtue of their special skills, are well-positioned, to meet the challenges of the information economy.

LIBRARIAN AND PATRON: THE INTERPERSONAL DIMENSION

As the collection of nonfiction titles of Samuel Green's day grew to include reference books and access tools like bibliographies and periodical indices, patrons needed help in this increasingly complex environment. Librarianship responded by defining and developing reference service. The goal of this service in the late-nineteenth and early-twentieth centuries was staunchly conservative. Academic librarians guided students to use library resources entirely on their own. The conservative theory of reference service held that the prime responsibility of librarians was not to find answers, but to organize collections well enough so patrons could be taught to seek and educate themselves.

An early critic of the conservative service philosophy, James Ingersoll Wyer, in his 1930 textbook on reference work, capsulized the preceding fifty years of service as an effort to "provide the books and keep out of the way of readers as much as possible."[15] With one eye on the future and what technology might bring and one eye on contemporary developments in classification and cataloging, Wyer cautioned against neglect of the human factor. "Mechanical marvels" could not take the place of the librarian as intermediary and interpreter.[16] To Wyer, reference service existed because it was impossible to make libraries self-service facilities. He writes, "It seems unbelievable that the time can ever come when the general public will be so well instructed, so easy and effective in its use of its own libraries, that it will relieve the reference staff altogether, or even in large measure, from the actual work of fact-finding and of search."[17]

Wyer believed in a liberal service philosophy of providing patrons with the needed information without taking the patron's time to explain how or where it was found. Until the latter half of the twentieth century, the "maximum service" philosophy remained an ideal that few other than Wyer and special librarians celebrated. Even he saw it as an ideal rather than a policy ripe for implementation. He believed librarians should simply provide patrons with the desired information. Wyer made practical political arguments for the liberal theory of unlimited or maximum service. He writes that it is "poor practical policy" for a library to "withhold its utmost service." To do so is to "invite reproach and lack of financial assistance."[18] He further warns against the infringement of commercial interests ready to serve where libraries fail.[19]

In this century, conservatives and moderates have prevailed in academic libraries. Academic librarians have liberalized their service by going beyond their own libraries through referrals, interlibrary loan, and networks. In keeping with the traditional conservative philosophy of empowering their patrons, however, academic librarians have embraced the library instruction movement.

Librarians have developed two distinct philosophies of reference service. Today, both are in operation in varying degrees depending on the librarian and the type of question. There are no standard procedures for performing reference work. The closest the profession has come is the American Library Association's Reference and Adult Services Division (RASD) guidelines, which were first developed in 1976, one hundred years after Green's article. The 1976 guidelines emphasize proximity of information services to the "main focal point of activity" and its physical location. Location was naturally a consideration in a time when collections were mostly in print and housed in libraries. Although these guidelines are based on a client-centered philosophy and mention library to library networking, they are still naturally bound by contemporary limits of locale and space.[20] In contrast, the 1990 revision of the guidelines calls for libraries "to support state-of-the-art communications methods for access to information resources for users whether within or outside its building."[21]

Over time, librarians have become more sensitive to the psychological and sociological aspects of reference work. The current ideas about counseling models and appointment-based service began forty years ago.

Marta Dosa cites "counselor librarianship" as a term frequently used in the literature in the 1950s.[22] In addition to culling the literature for the evolution of the counseling service model, Dosa sets a standard of her own by identifying the common characteristics of counseling among the fields of social work, adult education, and librarianship. She lists the following thirteen elements that are essential for the development of an information counseling or client-centered program of service:

- Assessment of potential information needs
- Consideration of economic factors, cost, budget, or fees
- Establishment of objectives, policies, and plans guiding the counseling process
- Assessment of available information resources
- Construction of a directory file of resources and access to it
- Development of client-practitioner relationships
- Client interview and need assessment
- Research on the background of the problem or need
- Information giving (service)
- Referral to source where answer is most likely to be found
- Follow-up
- Collection of data and feedback information
- Reassessment and evaluation of the process[23]

   In the past twenty-five years, librarians have become increasingly interested in the reference interview. This body of research shows that verbal and non-verbal behavior by reference librarians is a determining factor in patron satisfaction,[24] patrons cannot distinguish from among the employees in a library who work at other service desks,[25] that reference librarians are effective only 55 percent of the time,[26] and that librarians infrequently conduct reference interviews.[27] Yet librarians have not been able to synthesize this information. The reference desk seems anachronistic today in a service environment that is increasingly interactive. Librarians place themselves, retail style, at their service counters as if on-the-spot help is all that most patrons want or need. Cash-and-carry was the approach to reference service in the nineteenth century, when gaslights lit library hallways, but it is inadequate today.
   While changes in service models have been suggested in library literature for decades, a concrete example did not emerge until 1990, when Brandeis University eliminated its reference desk and established a

"research consultation service" in its place.[28] Graduate students at an information desk handle the bulk of inquiries while referring more complex questions to librarians serving as counselors in this appointment-based service. Although staffing difficulties were the driving force behind this redesign of reference service, Brandeis sought to design an environment in which more in-depth questions could be handled without giving them short-shrift.

Brandeis' reference model is not a new idea. Differentiation in service was described by Rothstein as a division in level of reference service that developed between branch and central libraries a century ago. Central libraries developed into centers for research, while the branches handled simpler reference work. In her 1944 textbook, Margaret Hutchins suggests such a division within a reference department. She calls for a division of the services offered by reference librarians as a way to handle more in-depth questions.

> Separating and referring to an inner desk the persons whose requests are likely to take a long time to answer will also clear the outer desk for quick reference work. In large libraries an information desk serves this purpose. In libraries without separate desks...the same idea may be carried out by dividing the work in a similar way between two or more assistants....[29]

Alternative staffing arrangements that utilize paraprofessionals and students at separate desks for reference and directional questions was William Miller's response to ineffective reference service.[30] William Whitson called for recognition of reference as a "composite of several different services, each of which needs to be structured, staffed, supported, and evaluated on its own terms." He suggested a division of reference service into five areas: directions and general information, technical assistance, information lookup, research consultation, and library instruction.[31]

The conservative philosophy of reference service has had a strong foothold. Academic librarians have increasingly advocated a teaching role over the years. The history of reference service relative to the relationship between librarians and patrons resembles a game of hide and seek. Since the stacks opened, librarians have been seeking patrons in order to help them use the catalog and find books. Librarians in Green's day began to accompany them to the catalog and into the stacks. Today, librarians are in the classroom. Outside of class, teaching moments are sought in the reference area. Yet amidst this seeking, librarians have insisted on hiding behind the reference desk. There is no doubt that librarians want to help patrons, but mostly on librarians' terms. The desk has stood as a bulwark through decades of change. In spite of the desk, librarians have become increasingly interactive with patrons over time. This interaction has evolved from the cautious approach of Green of pointing the way, to the sage on the stage at the height of the bibliographic instruction movement, to the implementation of appointment-based reference service.

LOOKING BACK, LOOKING AHEAD

The pattern of the history of reference service has been a movement of librarians toward patrons. Patrons have asked for services and librarians have responded with reference, telephone reference, and readers' advisory. The provision of each of these services has brought librarians and patrons closer together in an interpersonal sense. Each time new technologies and educational models have emerged, librarians have offered more services. In its first one hundred years, reference has evolved from a tentative, distant activity to a collaborative interaction that teaches and counsels.

In retrospect, historians can say that librarians emerged triumphantly from the metamorphosis in higher education at the turn of the century. It was their best moment. Thirty years later, they met the challenge of the adult education movement with readers' advisory. In the 1960s librarians began to tackle the construction of a national database and network, enabling them to guide patrons to resources beyond their local collections. Now, another thirty years later, there is a new wave of change. Fiber optic cable networks are connecting homes, libraries, schools, campuses, corporations, and the government. This tidal wave of technology is the ripple effect of the end of the information age and signals the onset of the knowledge age, according to Lewis Perelman, author of *School's Out.*[32]

Learning is entering another phase of metamorphosis. Perelman defines "hyperlearning" as a new degree of connectedness of people and machine in learning through case-based reasoning and simulation. Learning is no longer confined to the classroom, no longer an individualized, human process. Instead, it occurs within human and computer networks among teachers and students alike as a lifelong process. Teamwork and virtualizing will replace the linear instruction of the hierarchical classroom, according to Perelman.[33]

Librarians' skills have a natural place in Perelman's knowledge age. They will grow in prominence only when librarians liberalize reference service and begin providing information to learners. Academic librarians, whether serving the elite or basic skills students, must sharpen their technical skills and be strong generalists to provide their clientele with everything patrons will ask of them.

The college student will spend less time in the classroom and the library in the years ahead. Nontraditional educational delivery systems in the form of distance education already exist. Information technology challenges the traditional notion that students spend a certain number of hours in a specific place for a certain number of days in order to learn the material presented in a college course.

Should students in these college courses be able to obtain the information they need instantly from the librarian who keeps abreast of the discipline's literature and searching its databases? Or would students do better to spend their time synthesizing information rather than gathering it? Terry Ann Mood, advocate of the liberal philosophy of reference, describes an aging student body whose goal is to get a better job. She writes, "Research skills to them are a specialized knowledge area, not germane to their needs and something they can hire out for to get done."[34]

There is something uniquely positive in store for information providers in an age of information technology. If librarians take the user's point of view in reforming reference service and secure a place for libraries in the National Information Infrastructure, then their future is bright. Customers are continually forming and reforming what they want from libraries. If librarians still find themselves tentative about how to be reference librarians and do not listen to the calls for service modifications, their future may be bleak.

There are as many reasons to be optimistic about the future of librarianship as there are to be pessimistic. With the growing complexity of information technology come loud cries for help from both burned out librarians and frazzled patrons. Knowledge seekers will want a search partner. While poking around in campus networks and cyberspace, they will need help along the way either with a World Wide Web site, with a remote search of the on-line catalog, or with a Lexis-Nexis search. All will wish they had a knowledgeable person at their side.

For the most part, inquirers will not look for librarians at the reference desk in the next century. Librarians need to be at the opposite end of researchers' keyboards. Interactive workstations staffed by librarians, scheduled as needed, will be the essential element in the future structure of information service in higher education. The service front is widening again. In-person reference service will be retained in some form as dictated by the needs of our patrons, but electronic reference will develop into an interactive service that is integrated into on-line library systems. Conference searching where patrons will call librarians into their on-line searches when they need assistance will be a standard service.

In what promises to be a time of profound change and complexity, patrons continue to deserve a librarian in the role of research guide. An algorithm of artificial intelligence just will not make the grade. Hypertext guides and intelligent agents will serve only a limited number of patrons in the electronic community. For many patrons, there will be no effective reference service without the human factor. Although librarians need to enhance the interpersonal dimension of reference service they presently offer, even today's status quo of reference service is preferable to a mechanized system.

There will be a liberalizing of the reference service philosophy. Teaching will not occur in the reference encounter; however, librarians will do more for patrons. They will continue to provide reader's advisory services. The complexity of electronic information will make academic library patrons more dependent on librarians for their highly skilled searching techniques. Interactive electronic interfaces will allow learners to try for themselves the strategies and databases suggested by librarians. Others will request the information prepackaged.

This shift towards unilaterally and routinely doing all searching for patrons has already begun. Librarians in their daily rush to serve all comers are more likely to construct rather than teach search strategies for students. As librarians do this, they feel the need to teach the strategy as well. This impulse will fade without much damage done, as students focus on analysis and synthesis of information rather than finding information. Having the search done for them does not preclude learning through investigation. When students need help, they will ask. Librarians need to be there by being expert in obtaining all types of information and by being available on all fronts.

It makes sense that librarianship is in the throes of change at a time like this. If it were not changing, librarianship would be in an even more difficult position than it finds itself already. The debates that are raging over finding versus teaching are an important part of this period of redefinition of librarianship. Librarians must question everything they do and how they do it if they are to remain viable. They have to know their clientele, give them what they need, and fill that niche as they have done so many times before.

While librarians of late are left feeling a bit like Alice down the rabbit hole, interesting times are ahead. It is to be hoped that librarians will build a professional model that will serve their clientele as well as offer librarians the rewards of professional accomplishment. In these tumultuous times, librarians can take some solace in knowing that the past indicates that they are on the right track. If librarians can emerge from this era as well as their predecessors did, then it is a past deemed worth repeating.

NOTES

1.   Brendan C. Boyd and Fred C. Harris. *The Great American Baseball Card Flipping, Trading, and Bubble Gum Book.* (Boston: Little, Brown & Company, 1973), 48.

2.   William H. McNeill, "Some Basic Assumptions of Toynbee's *A Study of History,*" in *The Intent of Toynbee's History,* ed. E.T. Gargan (Chicago: Loyola University Press, 1961), 27-46.

3.   Samuel Rothstein, *The Development of Reference Service Through Academic Traditions, Public Library Practice and Special Librarianship,* ACRL Monographs, no. 14 (Chicago: Association of College and Research Libraries, 1955), 20.

4.   Samuel S. Green, "Personal Relations Between Librarians and Readers," *American Library Journal* 1 (October 1876): 74.

5.   Green, 80.

6.   Melvil Dewey, "The Faculty Library," *The Library* 2, no. 2 (1901): 238.

7.   Sarah K. Vann, *Melvil Dewey: His enduring Presence in Librarianship* (Littleton, CO: Libraries Unlimited, 1978), 199.

8.   Rothstein, *Development of Reference Service,* 34.

9.   Arthur Bestor, Jr. "The Transformation of American Scholarship, 1875-1917," *Library Quarterly* 23 (July 1953): 164-179.

10.   Samuel Rothstein, "An Unfinished History: A Developmental Analysis of Reference Services in American Academic Libraries," *Reference Librarian* 25/26 (1989), 371.

11.   Bestor, 173.

12.   John Cotton Dana, *Libraries: Addresses and Essays* (Freeport, NY: Books for Libraries Press, 1966), 165-166.

13.   Dewey, 240.

14.   Dana, 140.

15.   James Ingersoll Wyer, *Reference Work: A Textbook for Students of Library Work and Librarians* (Chicago: American Library Association, 1930), 3.

16.   Wyer, 5.

17.   Wyer, 9.

18.   Wyer, 10.

19.   Wyer, 11.

20.   Reference and Adult Services Division. American Library Association. "A Commitment to Information Services: Developmental Guidelines." In B. Vavrek. "Bless You Samuel Green!" *Library Journal* 101 (1976): 971-974.

21.   Standards and Guidelines Committee. RASD. "Information Services for Information Consumers: Guidelines for Providers," *RQ* 30 (1990): 262-265.

22.   Marta Dosa, "Information Counseling: the best of ERIC," *Information Reports and Bibliographies* 7, no.3 (1978): 7.

23.   Dosa, 5-6.

24.   Edward Kazlauskas, "An Exploratory Study: A Kinesic Analysis of Academic Library Public Service Points," *Journal of Academic Librarianship* 2 (July 1976): 130-134.

25.   Joan C. Durrance, "The Influence of Reference Practices on the Client-Librarian Relationship," *College and Research Libraries* 47 (January 1986): 57-67.

26.   Peter Hernon and Charles McClure, "Unobtrusive Reference Testing: the 55 Percent Rule," *Library Journal* 111 (April 15, 1986): 34-41.

27.   Mary J. Lynch, "Reference Interviews in Public Libraries," *Library Quarterly* 48 (April 1978): 119-142.

28.   Virginia Massey-Burzio. "Reference Encounters of a Different Kind: A Symposium," *Journal of Academic Librarianship* 18, no.5 (November 1992): 276.

29.   Margaret Hutchins, *Introduction to Reference Work* (Chicago: American Library Association, 1944), 22-23.

30.   William Miller, "What's Wrong With Reference: Coping with Success and Failure at the Reference Desk," *American Libraries* 15 (May 1984): 303-306, 321-322.

31.   William L. Whitson, "Differentiated Service: A New Reference Model," *Journal of Academic Librarianship* 21 (March 1995): 105.

32.   Lewis J. Perelman, *School's Out: Hyperlearning, the New Technology, and the End of Education* (New York: William Morrow, 1992).

33.   See note 32 above.

34.   Terry Ann Mood, "Of Sundials and Digital Watches: A Further Step Toward the New Paradigm of Reference," *RSR: Reference Services Review* 22, no.3 (1994): 30.

THE REFERENCE SERVICE ENCOUNTER:
WHAT CAN PATRONS AND LIBRARIANS EXPECT?

Gary B. Thompson·

ABSTRACT

A review of recent professional literature concerning customer satisfaction and customer expectations shows the growing emphasis on relationship marketing and the variables of service provider performance contributing to successful outcomes in service encounters. The library science literature reveals several models for studying how librarians best can deliver assistance to patrons. Comments from reference librarians subscribing to an Internet discussion group provide insights into how practicing librarians cope with patrons at the reference desk in different library settings. Based upon these findings, the author posits a extensive working model of what behaviors and attitudes patrons and librarians should expect from each other during the reference exchange. The conclusion lists implications for librarians and libraries that plan to adopt reference services built upon relationship marketing and maximal service provider performance during the reference service encounter.

INTRODUCTION

In this age of instantaneous information available through radio, television, and computer access to Internet Gopher and World Wide Web sites, reference librarians are facing competition as the public's main source of information. Reference managers everywhere are investigating new approaches to delivering information-related services. They are using information technologies such as CD-ROMs, local area networks, Internet routers, and Web browsers to increase the patron's capabilities to access and search for information. They are experimenting with different staffing patterns, using paraprofessionals and student aides, setting up information desks closer to library entrances, increasing referrals to subject specialists, and providing information consulting by appointment for research projects. They are reexamining the skills required to provide the best quality reference and information services.

This chapter explores a fundamental question affecting the entire reference process; namely, what patrons and librarians can expect from the reference service encounter. First, it explores general research findings about customer satisfaction, customer expectations, and the variables which affect the service encounter, that critical moment when the customer meets the service provider. Then it discusses the professional literature and comments from reference librarians about expectations surrounding the reference encounter. Based upon a review of the literature and more than twenty years of experience working as a reference librarian and reference manager, the author proposes a working model for what patrons and librarians can expect from each other in a reference encounter.

CUSTOMER SATISFACTION AND CUSTOMER EXPECTATIONS

This chapter fits broadly within the literature of customer relations and customer satisfaction. The author posits that libraries need to be consumer- or customer-based service organizations. Recent management and marketing literature suggest that strategies centered around customer satisfaction are distinct from strategies to improve quality control. Quality control is a long-term strategy, while providing customer satisfaction is more short-term. Quality control focuses upon the service providers and the delivery systems they develop. Customer service focuses upon the client and the services they receive. The aim of quality control is to improve library operations, while the goal of customer satisfaction is to ensure that services meet the expressed needs of the library's clientele in a way that is acceptable to the customers.

Libraries are service organizations which market and deliver service offerings in competition with other organizations now marketing information products. In his book *Relationship Marketing: Successful Strategies for the Age of the Customer*, Regis McKenna reflects upon the changing nature of marketing and customer service. The old way of developing products, testing the market, and then introducing the customer to the product is too linear and too static. The new way of marketing is more interactive, interconnected, and dynamic. It is a total organizational effort involving all employees and all operations, rather than simply a marketing plan or a public relations campaign. Foremost it centers around developing relationships with the most desired customers. McKenna writes that:

> Relationship marketing is essential in developing industry leadership, customer loyalty, and rapid acceptance of new products and services. Building strong and lasting relationships is hard work and difficult to sustain. But I believe that in a world where the customer has so many options, even in narrow product-market segments, a personal relationship is the only way to retain customer loyalty.[1]

In the 1995 March-April issue of the *Harvard Business Review*, B. Joseph Pine II, Don Peppers, and Martha Rogers discuss similar tactics for keeping customers coming back to service organizations or businesses: establish learning relationships with customers in order to know consumer needs and preferences and then customize services to meet these preferences.[2] They conclude by saying that if a business wants to expand its customer base, it must either cultivate new customers from the same or different pools, or find other products/services for the regular customers. Should the marketing of library services be considered from this perspective?

Librarians can benefit from studying the literature concerning customer-based enterprises. Ron Zemke, in his now famous books with titles such as *Delivering Knock Your Socks Off Service*, talks about making your service delivery "easy to do business with," or ETDBW. He explains that there is a moment of truth when the customer comes in contact with the organization and evaluates the service provider using these criteria:

- reliability, or the ability to provide what was promised;
- responsiveness, or willingness to help customers promptly;
- assurance, or the ability to convey trust, competence and confidence;
- empathy, or degree of caring and attention to customers;
- tangibles, or physical facilities and equipment and physical traits of the provider.[3]

Stephen Taylor, in a discussion of health care marketing strategies, refers to the classic model of customer satisfaction as being dependent upon "a level of service performance that exceeds customer expectations."[4] The consumer focuses upon certain salient attributes in determining whether service exceeds or falls short of expectations. These expectations are either confirmed or disconfirmed in each encounter that the consumer has with the organization. Customers assess both technical and functional qualities of the service provided.[5] A recent survey of 139,830 surgical patients summarized in *Nursing* revealed that while patients expect nurses to have the necessary technical skills, patients also demand that nurses manifest a caring posture by showing empathy, informing patients about procedures, and dealing with them as clients with special needs and preferences.[6] Library patrons evaluate librarians using similar yardsticks.

A. Parasuraman, Valarie A. Zeithaml and Leonard L. Berry have written extensively about customer satisfaction and customer expectations. Their research contends that customer satisfaction is dependent upon customers' expectations about both desired service, defined as "the level of service a customer believes can and should be delivered," and adequate service, or "the level of service the customer considers acceptable." Assessment of the performance of the service provider is linked to customer's personal needs, perceived service alternatives, self-perceived role in the provision of services, and past experience, as well as situational factors. While customer satisfaction is a transaction-based assessment, the customer makes a global assessment of satisfaction with the service through the cumulative assessment of a series of service encounters.[7]

Librarians are beginning to study customer satisfaction and customer expectations in more depth. In a 1995 *College and Research Libraries* article, Christopher Millson-Martula and Vanaja Menon suggest how librarians can avoid unrealistic service expectations first by building effective learning relationships with patrons, and then by "determining what is possible in the area of service delivery, communicating that service to students and faculty, and lastly delivering the service as promised."[8] In a study of reference service effectiveness, Jo Bell Whitlatch discovered that "feedback, service orientation, time constraints, and task-related knowledge have a significant effect on reference service outcomes."[9]

THE SERVICE ENCOUNTER

The moment of truth is the "service encounter," that juncture where provider meets client. This brief or extended exchange is essential to any service organization, whether it is providing medical, business, governmental, or library services. It is the time and place when the service provider translates the service philosophy into reality. It is the moment when the service provider and the client deal with the human component of the service exchange.

Measuring the success of the service encounter is an extremely difficult endeavor. There are environmental factors such as time and place. For instance, one recent article documents the obvious effect of waiting for service and delays in delivery on overall satisfaction with service.[10] There are client assessments of performance by the service provider and the service outcomes. Competing models of dependent, independent and intervening variables are being hotly contested for validity, explanatory power, and diagnostic use.

According to Bitner, Booms and Mohr, "service provider performance refers to service delivery skills and competencies as revealed in the service encounter, including those customers take for granted, those they can articulate, (i.e., expectations), and those that they do not articulate but that can lead to delight when used skillfully."[11] Mary Jo Bitner, Bernard H. Booms and Mary Stanfeld Tetreault studied over 700 favorable and unfavorable service encounters from airlines, hotels, and restaurants. They identified three clusters of critical factors relating to the service provider: response to service delivery failures such as slow or unavailable service, response to special customer requests and preferences, and unprompted service provider actions that exemplify attentive and extraordinary behavior under adverse or unusual circumstances.[12]

In further investigations, Bitner, Booms, and Mohr found that service providers and clients tend to attribute blame to each other for unsatisfactory service encounters. Service employees identified drunkenness, verbal and physical abuse, violations of policies or laws, and general uncooperativeness as common customer problems.[13] Service providers also pointed out their frustrations when service delivery systems fail. Service providers must have the authority and knowledge to deal in an effective manner with any set of minor or major problems or needs, regardless of their origin.

Price, Arnould, and Tierney have added to the literature by studying three specific aspects of the service encounter: duration, affect, and proxemics. They show that brief encounters are simpler and less stressful and that extended encounters are more open and subject to "emotional dissonance" and "script noncongruence"; that is, there is more opportunity for the disparate roles, emotions, and perspectives of the provider and client to come forth.[14] Likewise, affect, emotions and nonverbal communication clearly impact upon the service encounter and thus must be controlled and channeled. Environmental factors such as proxemics, the height of the service counter, the ease of eye contact, and perceived receptivity of the service provider impact upon the effectiveness of the service encounter. Price, Arnould and Tierney suggest that customer satisfaction is built upon responsible performance and authentic understanding by the service provider and extra services rendered beyond the call of duty. An intervening variable is whether the experience of the customer was pleasant or negative.[15]

The writings about service encounters make clear that with adequate training and experience in interpersonal relations, the service provider can control the situation to produce the optimum outcome. The service provider must establish a favorable climate so that the client senses a partnership and a shared sense of mission. "The service provider must oversee the emergence of shared customer-provider scripts. Providers must interpret service episodes, explain unexpected events to crystallize expectations, and then provide evidence that expectations are being met."[16]

The customer is directly involved in the outcome of the service and not only as an object, but as a participant whose actions determine whether the service offered ultimately will produce a benefit to the customer or not. David E. Bowen has identified three key issues which must be settled in order for customers to do their part in the service encounter:

1. Do they understand how they are expected to perform? Do they know who to contact or where to go? Do they understand the various functions of the units and types of personnel within the organization?

2. Are customers able to perform as expected? Do they have the minimal requirements necessary for utilizing the service offered at this organization? Have they received adequate orientation and instruction to perform their role in the service encounter?
3. Are there valued rewards for customers performing as expected? Do clients who "play the game" get the appropriate return upon their investment? Can clients clearly see that if they contribute, there is a mutual benefit for both parties?[17]

THE REFERENCE SERVICE ENCOUNTER: GLEANINGS FROM THE LITERATURE

The reference interview and the reference process involve a service provider, generically called a reference librarian, and a client, generically called a library patron. The interaction between the reference librarian and the library patron can be called the reference service encounter. First, consider the librarian's role.

There are several competing business and medical models for the librarian's role in the reference encounter. In comparing librarians to innkeepers and storeowners, Samuel Swett Green, an early proponent of modern reference service, implored librarians in 1876 to offer library patrons "a hearty reception by a sympathizing friend, and the recognition of someone at hand who will listen to inquiries, even although he may consider them unimportant"[18] and then "hold on to them until they have obtained the information they are seeking and showing a persistency [sic] in supplying their wants similar to that manifested by a clerk in effecting a sale."[19] His early philosophy of customer service sounds similar to the "relationship marketing" being espoused in 1996.

James Rice contends that "there has never been a greater need than now for a profession willing to help people with their information problems."[20] Using a provocative medical model, Robert Grover and Janet Carabell, two library scientists at Emporia State University, discuss the detailed process of diagnosing and treating an information need utilizing a strong client-centered approach. As they put it, "the role of any professional is that of diagnosing needs, prescribing or recommending a remedy which meets those needs, implementing that remedy, and evaluating the outcome of this interaction."[21]

As information consultants in the highly technological environment of today's libraries, librarians must recognize that they are not simply locating books and articles that patrons request, but are dealing with the much more complex world of information. Lanning writes that "we've failed miserably at convincing people that they don't want books or computers, they want information....The concept of the Information Age hasn't trickled down to the average person. People don't understand what information is, how or where it is stored, nor the processes used to find it."[22] Robert J. Marikangas calls upon his fellow librarians to chart the way "through our library bibliographic systems and assistance and instructional systems, which in turn are best used by readers who become mapmakers themselves, with our assistance, in that they create mental maps of our systems and devise pathfinding and problem-solving schemes by which they traverse the maps to the knowledge-places they seek."[23]

The exponential growth of listservs, Internet Gophers, and World Wide Web sites increase the need for the big information picture as opposed to the telescoped view of knowledge which is the domain of specialists. In his article "Shaking the Conceptual Foundations of Reference," Jerry Campbell suggests that reference librarians become "access engineers" who frequently reconnoiter the information landscape, chart paths, and analyze consumer information needs. They are power users who can transfer needed information to the consumer upon demand.[24] As a consultant to patrons wanting to use the various information technologies to gather appropriate data from the world's information networks, the librarian must assume a higher profile in terms of designing, implementing, interpreting, and explaining how to use the numerous interfaces required to take full advantage of these systems. Even so-called user-friendly systems require occasional intervention by librarians to assist patrons with higher-end if not basic functions.

Librarians need to recognize their key role as change agents with responsibility for diffusion of the continuous rounds of innovations occurring in the world of information technology. In order to assume this role, reference librarians must:

1. learn how to use recent technological innovations;
2. instruct potential users, either in the capabilities of the technology...or how to formulate informational questions which will access relevant data sources;
3. assess new technological developments in light of user needs;
4. repeat these steps each time a "new" database is made available...[25]

The librarian is only one-half of the reference service equation. The patron is the other half, and it is important to know what she wants, prefers, and expects. Connie Bacon's 1902 statement about the differing expectations of patrons still rings true today. She divided patrons into three groupings:

1. The select few who know just what they want, state their want with clearness and expect you to meet it. It is a joy to work with them.
2. The people who expect nothing of you, apologize for disturbing you, and break out into a fever of gratitude over the slightest assistance. These are amusing.
3. The people who expect you to do all their work for them. These are irritating.[26]

Bacon goes on to give a profile of the librarians' ideal reference patron for 1902 or 1996. The patron knows what information she wants and is willing to tell the librarian what she needs. She does not tell the librarian where certain information is when she doesn't know. Lastly, she is willing to use her own brains, instead of requiring that the materials be predigested.[27]

Librarians must recognize realistically that all patrons will not fit this mold and that they must accommodate different levels and kinds of patrons. Otherwise they may send the wrong message: "In their enthusiasm to create do-it-yourself patrons, librarians may inadvertently convey that asking for help is wrong."[28] David W. Lewis emphasizes how librarians must be more cognizant of the patron's point of view:

> Whether and how students and faculty use the services we offer should be the primary criteria for judging the value of these services and our success in providing them....These simple measures of investment and expected return are central to judging a library's success.

While more and more librarians are studying patron satisfaction, research studies of the patron side of the reference service encounter are limited. Jo Bell Whitlatch's user assessment of reference service effectiveness analyzes the dynamic interaction between patron and reference librarian in terms of outcomes.[30] Millson-Martula and Menon analyze the gap between patron expectations and services received and suggest strategies so that patron expectations conform more closely with the services being offered and so that patrons know what their role is and how to perform in a way that leads to successful encounters.[31] Bryce and Gillian Allen's study of the disparate cognitive abilities of academic librarians and patrons is a model for further studies of patron behavior which can be utilized to enhance the reference encounter. Allen and Allen found:

> that librarians had higher average logical and verbal comprehension abilities than students, and that students had higher average perceptual abilities than librarians....These findings may explain why students appear to do well with simple browse searching, and why librarians prefer more sophisticated search capabilities and interfaces utilizing Boolean combinations of keywords.[32]

In a discussion of the changing nature of academic research and knowledge warehouses in this age of electronic information, John R. Sack calls on academic libraries and computer centers to become more client-centered. He outlines the changing demands and expectations of users in this electronic information environment:

- Users focus on results, not procedures.
- Users demand speed, not deliberation.
- Users expect a seamless integration of the library's system with whatever other systems they use.
- Users expect electronic information to be malleable, and the library's system to be flexible.
- Users have little sense of library tradition and will not readily make a distinction between owned-by-library information and non-owned information or between traditional library materials and those not typically managed by libraries.[33]

In an important article entitled "Beyond the Chip: A Model for Fostering Equity," Delia Newman notes that information technologies must be both accessible and attractive for persons to want to use them. At the local level, librarians need to provide equitable access to both print and electronic resources. They should eliminate disparities in access to reference services, or at least be more cognizant of these disparities.[34]

Librarians must also provide equity in the practices that they follow to help patrons. Dopp and Smith pose the basic dilemma for librarians:

> It is not uncommon for academic libraries to distinguish between undergraduate and graduate students, faculty and researchers, administrators and staff....In many cases, such distinctions are made for practical purposes. However, the philosophical question is the basic principle of equality of access to information as a funda-

mental requisite for a democratic society. To what extent does the categorization of users and differentiation between groups conflict with that basic principle?[35]

Reference teachers and managers of the past have recognized the principle of differentiating among patrons based upon levels of knowledge and needs. Margaret Hutchins in her 1944 textbook states that "generally speaking, the smaller and less accustomed or obligated to self-help the patron is, the more time is devoted by the reference department to the needs of the individual" and the corollary that "in all libraries there are patrons who abuse their privileges and demand more than their share of attention. If possible, they should be prevented, firmly but tactfully, by the reference department from usurping time that should be given to other people."[36] A study of library science students finds that "reference users can moderate their requests based upon personal ethical standards that define the limits of equitable demands."[37] Reference departments must come up with strategies for dealing with demanding as well as reticent patrons.

A VIEW OF THE REFERENCE ENCOUNTER FROM THE PARTICIPANT OBSERVERS

In March 1995, David Kurz from the Washington County Public Library posed the provocative question "What is too much service?" to the Internet discussion group Ref-L.[38] It led to a lively debate among public, college and university librarians about the wide-ranging expectations of patrons who approach reference staffs for assistance, the appropriateness of librarians' responses to these inquiries, and the best means of managing dwindling staff resources to provide the greatest good for the greatest number at the reference desk. It provided an insight into the frustrations and difficulties that librarians face in their goal of providing fair and equitable service to all library patrons. Many of the respondents defined the appropriateness of the reference/information assistance according to the patron's input:

> I would say that the response of the library need not, and generally should not, be more than commensurate with the commitment indicated by the enquirer. A casual enquiry or demand need not elicit a fulsome response, though it may do if time, resources, etc. are available. But the concept of "too much service" just doesn't apply when the enquiry is serious—whether the enquiry is from a business researcher or a seven year old child.

—Ray Thomas, Faculty of Social Sciences, The Open University, Milton Keynes, England.

Most clients try to be decent, honest and fair about the use of a librarian's time. But as is true of all human interactions, a few clients are incredibly selfish. Part of my professional responsibility is to sometimes, say no to outrageous requests so that I can use my time to better help a greater number of clients.

—Linda Fortney, Montgomery College, Rockville Maryland.

Other respondents considered how much is too much service in terms of the role of the librarian:

So I will not do for some what I will not do for everybody. I try to weigh the needs of the user against what is appropriate for the situation. Sometimes I am teaching, sometimes I'm doing the research for somebody. Both are worthwhile endeavors, but I won't always do both for everyone. And if I do research for a student, I want it to be in such a way that I won't be burdened if I do it for everyone in the class. The twelfth person in a 35-student class needs to get what the first one did, not less.

—Ken Grabach, Miami University of Ohio

In our academic library the mission of the library is to assist students to become independent library users and researchers, therefore as librarians we teach them the different ways to locate information, and how to apply the search strategy to various class assignments. However, when a librarian "spoon feeds" the patron by doing all the research from A-Z without giving the patron the opportunity to discover the process of doing research, then this is too much service, which overall hardly benefits the patron. The librarian becomes a crutch for such patrons instead of a guide.

—Hope Young , City University of New York

Maybe we should be concerned about librarians and library staff who don't seem to care to lift a finger to help patrons; they concern me more than those who are running themselves ragged trying to solve patrons' every whim. I have travelled the country doing genealogy....And while I've run into a number of wonderful librarians, I've also run into a dismaying number who simply couldn't be bothered, who had to be pumped for information, etc....Our profession suffers because of such people.

—Warren Gray , Somerset Community College (Kentucky)

Then there are the respondents who recognized that in a customer service environment the patron defines how much is too much service while or after it is provided:

It is not "too much service" if the patron thinks the amount of service is OK. It can only be "too much service" when the patron doesn't want the service, i.e. if the patron asks where the genealogical books are, and the librarian locates each member of the patron's family tree for them.

—David King, University of Southern Mississippi

More service than the patron wants is too much service. I have observed reference librarians leading a patron around who has had enough "help" and is ready to do it themselves. I am one of those people. I like a short explanation then to be left alone to figure it out myself. I have also seen a patron left at a terminal who is confused and frustrated and needed some more help. I use to do this because I believed every patron was like myself. There are people who want you to take them through every step and maybe do that everytime they come in. Then there are those who want you to leave them alone until they ask for help.

—Victoria S. Chase, Quinnipiac College (Connecticut).

These comments from librarians working in a wide range of reference settings complement the theoretical writings on the reference service encounter with real-life examples and the viewpoints of practitioners dealing with patrons.

WHAT CAN THE LIBRARIAN EXPECT FROM THE PATRON IN THE REFERENCE ENCOUNTER?

As a service profession like nursing, law, teaching, and counseling, librarianship needs to better define the nature of its primary interaction with its clients. What can the patron expect from the librarian in the reference encounter? What can the librarian expect from the patron in the reference encounter? How can librarians make the patron more aware of her role and make her expectations more closely match the service that librarians expect to provide?

Experienced reference librarians asked to name characteristics of the ideal patron could quickly compile a list. Conversely, librarians could provide a long list of pet peeves about patrons. It is time for librarians to establish a professional code of ethics for the reference service encounter which spells out the rights and responsibilities of both patrons and librarians.

Here are six attributes that the patron should bring to the reference encounter in order to ensure a successful outcome:

1. The patron must be willing and able to articulate the nature of his/her information need.

This is a fundamental first step in the reference service encounter, paralleling the intake stage when a patient tells the physician what his/her ailments are. In order for the librarian to help the patron, the patron must be ready to tell the librarian what information is needed, in what context the information is needed, and how the information will be utilized. For instance, if information is needed for a school assignment, the student should tell the librarian what course is being taken, what is the assignment, and if the assignment is a term paper, what topic has been chosen. Librarians need to work with classroom teachers to ensure that students understand that librarians can help if students understand their assignments fully and can express their information needs clearly.

2. The patron must be willing to invest the time and energy required to accomplish the task that he sets out to do.

As with any professional service, reference service requires an investment of time on the part of the patron and the librarian. The time required may include a waiting period, whether at a reference desk waiting for the next available librarian or the interval spent waiting for an appointment with a reference librarian to discuss an information need. It includes time for the reference interview, during which the librarian and the patron define the nature of the information inquiry. It also includes time for the librarian to find the information needed or to put forth a strategy for doing the necessary research. Most importantly, the patron must spend the minutes, hours or days required to evaluate the sources, read the information, record the data, and evaluate and synthesize the information content.

3. The patron must have an active desire to learn.

The reference encounter is fundamentally an educational process requiring the transfer of knowledge. In order for the encounter to be successful, the patron must be in a learning mode, ready and eager to assimilate this transfer of knowledge in the most effective manner. The knowledge could be a simple piece of information, such as the address of a company, or specific applied knowledge, such as how to use a computer printer or how to locate a book, or a complex search strategy with many steps. The patron must recognize librarians as teachers.

4. The patron must be willing to establish a collaborative relationship with the librarian.

For the reference encounter to result in a successful outcome, the patron cannot be a passive recipient of information, expecting the librarian to supply the patron with reams of information about any topic requested without any action upon the part of the patron. Rather, the patron needs to be involved as a partner, contributing on a regular basis to a symbiotic relationship in which both patron and librarian move the process of discovery forward. Using this collaborative model, the patron can respond to each step along the journey, indicating whether the desired results are being produced. Patrons may also need to make adjustments in their research inquiries based upon the findings.

5. The patron must be prepared to take advantage of the learning opportunity.

In order for education to produce learning, the student must be prepared. This preparation includes obvious things, such as having the necessary educational utensils, like pencils, pens, paper, and computer diskettes. As a prerequisite, patrons are expected to have a certain basic level of knowledge of the subjects they want to research and of how libraries are organized. As we approach the twenty-first century, patrons are also expected to have basic computer literacy skills, including how to operate a computer keyboard, how to use a mouse, how to use a printer, and how to follow on-line instructions.

6. The patron must contribute actively to the research process

Depending upon whether the setting is an academic, public, or special library, the patron will be expected to assume a lesser or greater role in conducting the actual research in order to gather the information needed. The librarian serves as a guide or advisor, pointing the way for the researcher. The patron must define the parameters of the research, search for the information, evaluate the sources, and determine when the research has produced the desired results and can be terminated.

WHAT CAN THE PATRON EXPECT FROM THE LIBRARIAN IN THE REFERENCE ENCOUNTER?

In the competitive information industry of the 1990s, the reference librarian must meet the expectations of patrons in terms of access to information and service resulting in successful outcomes. These are eight attributes that the librarian should bring to the reference encounter:

1. The librarian must have a solid understanding of client needs, expectations and preferences.

Through surveys, focus groups, and other means, reference librarians need to acquire an in-depth understanding of the needs, wants, expectations and preferences of patrons using their libraries. Survey instruments need to go beyond traditional studies of who uses the library when and how to focus upon patron expectations and user preferences.

2. The librarian must demonstrate a sense of caring or empathy for the client.

Compared with other professional service encounters, reference encounters tend to be short and impersonal. Librarians must quickly gain rapport with their patrons. They must convey their commitment to the helping role with each patron. This may be difficult because of the continuous bombardment of questions at a busy reference desk. This is why many libraries are reconsidering the arrangement of reference assistance conducted from a single service desk.

3. The librarian must possess the interpersonal skills to manage the reference encounter so that patron and librarian operate with the same script in terms of the educational and research agenda.

Librarians are service professionals who must have the interpersonal skills to manage the reference encounter. Both must be moving together in the process so that the patron can achieve her end. It is essential that the librarian frequently verify that they are on the right research track, that the patron understands what the librarian is saying, and that the patron is responding accordingly with appropriate actions.

4. The librarian must be committed to a developmental model of learning.

Reference encounters should not be isolated and separate incidents, but rather progressive steps which foster learning and growth for the patron. If the patron does not learn , the encounter is a failure. If the patron does not become more competent in using the library and doing research, then the librarian has failed to perform her professional duties. A central goal of reference service must be to develop the patron's skills. This means that librarians must keep track of where the patrons are in their skill development and then plot a course for them to progress to higher levels of expertise in information gathering, analysis and synthesis.

5. The librarian must serve as educational mentor, technical advisor, and on-line consultant.

As advisor and consultant to the patron, the librarian must show that he is competent in using printed and electronic resources to find appropriate information. He must provide guidance and advice to the patron in doses that are easy to assimilate.

6. The librarian must facilitate open and equitable access to the full range of printed and electronic resources.

Librarians have a long record of professional commitment to serve as the "arsenal of democracy," ensuring free and equal access to information. The reference desk concept has provided for open and accessible help for anyone within the service parameters set by the institution. It is a concept which is most akin to the hospital emergency room. At the reference desk and in the hospital emergency room, staff must strive to provide each client with equitable service based upon the nature of the need and the time and resources available. No one should be denied service or be provided with lesser service based upon arbitrary criteria.

7. The librarian must have the authority and ability to deal effectively with unexpected problems to guarantee the best possible outcomes.

As direct service providers, reference librarians need to be empowered to do whatever is necessary in order to provide patrons with the best possible service. Patrons have rising expectations. They do not want excuses for why they cannot have what they need when they need it. It is true that librarians cannot always provide instant answers for every inquiry. Therefore, they must establish mechanisms for dealing with failures to deliver a quality product when the patron wants it. They must consult with other librarians and information providers to furnish leads for alternative sources. They must consult with automation specialists to solve technical glitches such as hardware, software, or network malfunctions. Finally, librarians must be willing to negotiate with library managers when bureaucratic roadblocks thwart patron requests. Empowered reference staff must serve as advocates for patrons.

8. The librarian must offer an attractive and rewarding service for the customer.

The reference encounter must be perceived as a attractive and rewarding alternative for the patron in search of a solution to her information problem. It must produce a positive outcome in the eyes of the patron or she will not return. In order to be rewarding, the reference encounter must provide timely service, meet and surpass the patron's service expectations, remove impediments to the patron achieving his learning objective, and respond to special needs. Unsolicited assistance beyond the call of duty makes the patron feel special.

IMPLICATIONS FOR REFERENCE SERVICES

How can this kind of relationship between librarians and patrons be introduced and fostered within the reference department? Libraries must change the organizational culture to become a customer-driven enterprise. Library priorities must change so that everyone working in all aspects of library operations asks these basic questions: What do patrons expect and prefer, and how can librarians find out what those expectations and preferences are? How can librarians best provide what patrons want? To start to build reference service based upon patron expectations, libraries must adopt these additional measures in planning reference services:

- *Regular studies of patron needs, expectations, and preferences, sponsored by local library organizations.* These studies would require use of patron observation, focus groups, and other qualitative analysis techniques to assess the diverse ways patrons seek, gather and evaluate information.
- *Services which advance the concept of relationship marketing and extended service encounters.* This model of library service would change the patron from an anonymous user to a person with a name, background and research interest. Librarians need to find ways of developing client files as other service professionals do so that they can provide enhanced services to their patrons. In the past, the issue of privacy has precluded many libraries from keeping records of patron profiles and patron interests. A system could be set up so that patrons could voluntarily submit such information if they want enhanced service.
- *Organization structures and procedures for dealing with human or technical service delivery problems.* Many patrons feel frustrated by the barriers imposed by bureaucratic library procedures and technical system failures. Library bureaucracies must be streamlined and humanized if libraries are to become user-centered and customer-based organizations. Libraries need to borrow ideas from other customer-driven organizations about how to obtain patron suggestions and complaints and respond in a positive and proactive way.
- *Service philosophies and practices that make the difference between delivery of adequate and desired service levels as perceived by patrons.* Collectively the reference staff must sustain a long-term commitment to outstanding service. The philosophy and practices must encourage veterans as well as newcomers to the staff to practice the utmost care and nurturance with each and every patron that is encountered. The success must be measured by the patrons' evaluation of the service through survey instruments.

- *An educational environment which encourages patrons to assume a more active and sophisticated role in the reference encounter.* Librarians must explore various kinds of learning environments for reference/information service to determine which environments enhance active learning, discovery, and creative and critical thinking.
- *Outreach and promotional activities.* Libraries and librarians must do a better job of marketing themselves as competent and caring information providers, expert information consultants, dedicated teachers, and the guarantors and advocates of free and open access to information.
- *Professional standards which define the levels and kinds of reference services which libraries should support.* Divisions within the American Library Association and the Association of College and Research Libraries responsible for reference and public services need to develop new standards relating to customer service and satisfaction. Specifically these standards must address the rights, responsibilities and roles of both librarians and patrons in the reference service encounter. Criteria need to be developed for measuring and assessing the provider's performance in the reference service encounter.
- *Formal and informal evaluation methods for assessing all of the above.* Librarians cooperatively must perform regular service audits to determine how well the profession is fulfilling the expectations and preferences of its customers.

This chapter puts forth a marketing/customer service approach to reference service. It suggests that reference librarians must be committed to understanding the expectations of patrons and interacting with patrons in a symbiotic relationship of mutual respect and collaboration. Patrons, for their part, must be committed to learning and willing to invest the time and energy required to discover the answers to their information inquiries. Reference managers must adopt a service strategy which guarantees responsive, quality, and equitable service to meet patrons' information needs. The library profession must establish standards of service that meet these criteria: (a) types of services offered must flow directly from a regular and systematic study of patron expectations and preferences; (b) customer-driven, outcome-oriented service goals and objectives must be established and results measured; (c) performance standards for evaluating individual staff must contain sections devoted to meeting patron expectations about adequate and exceptional service, developing extended teacher-learner relationships with patrons, and overcoming roadblocks to providing quality service; (d) services provided must be rewarding to patrons, when compared with services offered by competitive organizations in the information industry; (e) services must be attractive to the wide diversity of real and potential customers of libraries.

NOTES

1.   Regis McKenna, *Relationship Marketing: Successful Strategies for the Age of the Customer* (Reading, MA: Addison-Wesley, 1991), 102.

2.   Joseph B. Pine II, Don Peppers, and Martha Rogers, "Do You want to Keep your Customers Forever?" *Harvard Business Review* 72 (March-April 1995): 103.

3.   Kristin Anderson and Ron Zemke, *Delivering Knock Your Socks Off Service* (NY: AMACON, 1991).

4.   Steven A. Taylor, "Distinguishing Service Quality from Patient Satisfaction in Developing Health Care Marketing Strategies," *Hospital and Health Services Administration* 39 (summer 1994): 224.

5.   Taylor, "Distinguishing Service Qualities," 227.

6.   Beverly P. Giordano, "Nineties-style Nursing: Offering Customer Service," *Nursing* 24 (July 1994): 79.

7.   A. Parasuraman, A., Valarie A. Zeithaml and Leonard L. Berry, "Reassessment of Expectations as a Comparison Standard in Measuring Service Quality: Implications for Further Research," *Journal of Marketing* 58 (January 1994): 112.

8.   Christopher Millson-Martula and Vanaja Menon, "Customer Expectations: Concepts and Reality for Academic Library Services," *College & Research Libraries* 56 (January 1995): 43.

9.   Jo Bell Whitlatch, "Reference Service Effectiveness," *RQ* 30 (Winter 1990): 205.

10.   Shirley Taylor, "Waiting for Service; The Relationship between Delays and Evaluations of Service," *Journal of Marketing* 58 (April 1994): 56-59.

11.   Linda L. Price, Eric J. Arnould and Patrick Tierney, "Going to Extremes: Managing Service Encounters and Assessing Provider Performance," *Journal of Marketing* 59 (April 1995): 84.

12.   Mary Jo Bitner, Bernard H. Booms and Mary S. Tetreault, "The Service Encounter: Diagnosing Favorable and Unfavorable Incidents," *Journal of Marketing* 54 (January 1990): 74.

13.   Mary Jo Bitner, Bernard H. Booms and Lois A. Mohr, "Critical Service Encounters: The Employee's Viewpoint," *Journal of Marketing* 58 (Octpber 1994): 98.

14.   Price, Arnould, and Tierney, "Going to Extremes," 85.

15.   Price, Arnould, and Tierney, "Going to Extremes," 91.

16.   Price, Arnould, and Tierney, "Going to Extremes," 86.

17.   David E. Bowen, "Managing Customers as Human Resources in Service Organizations," *Human Resource Management* 25 (fall 1986): 378-381.

18. Samuel S. Green, "Personal Relations between Librarians and Readers," *Library Journal* 118 (June 15, 1993): s4 (reprinted from *Library Journal* October 1, 1876).

19. Samuel S. Green, "Personal Relations between Librarians and Readers," s5.

20. James Rice, "The Hidden Role of Librarians," *Library Jounal* 114 (Jan. 1989): 58.

21. Robert Grover and Janet Carabell, "Toward Better Information Service: Diagnosing Information Needs," *Special Libraries* 86 (winter 1995): 2.

22. Scott Lanning, "What does a Reference Librarian do?" *Public Library Quarterly* 11(4) (1991): 27.

23. Robert J. Marikangas, "Theory and Practice of Library Client Interaction," *Reference Librarian* 16 (1987): 301.

24. Jerry D. Campbell, "Shaking the Conceptual Framework of Reference: A Perspective," *Reference Services Review* 20 (winter 1992): 32-33.

25. Diane R. Callahan, "The Librarian as Change Agent in the Diffusion of Technological Innovation," *Electronic Library* 9 (February 1991): 14.

26. Connie Bacon, "Reference Work from the Librarian's Point of View," *Library Journal* 116 (June 15, 1991): s26 (reprinted from *Library Journal* November 1902).

27. Bacon, "Reference Work from the Librarian's Point of View," s26.

28. Patricia F. Stenstrom, "Our Real Business," *Journal of Academic Librarianship* 16 (May 1990): 78.

29. David W. Lewis, "A Matter of Return on Investment," *Journal of Academic Librarianship* 16 (May 1990): 80.

30. Whitlatch, "Reference Service Effectiveness," 205-220.

31. Millson-Martula and Menon, "Customer Expectations," 33-47.

32. Bryce Allen and Gillian Allen, "Cognitive Abilities of Academic Librarians and their Partners," *College & Research Libraries* 54 (January 1993): 72.

33. John R. Sack, "Open Systems for Open Minds: Building the Library without Walls," *College & Research Libraries* 47 (November 1986): 542-543.

34. Delia Neuman, "Beyond the Chip: A Model for Fostering Equity," *School Library Media Quarterly* 18 (Spring 1990): 158-164.

35. Richard E. Dopp and Linda C. Smith, *Reference and Information Services: An Introduction* (Englewood, CO: Libraries Unlimited, 1991), 39.

36. Margaret Hutchins, *Introduction to Reference Work* (Chicago: American Library Association, 1944), 177.

37. Gayle J. Hardy and Judith S. Robinson, "Reference Service to Library School Students: A Crucible for Ethical Inquiry," *RQ* 30 (fall 1990): 82-87.

38. The comments on the next pages are the result of a question posed to the Reference Listserv (Libref-L@Kentvm.Kent.edu) during the spring of 1995.

COMBINING DISPARATE UNITS, BUILDING EFFECTIVE TEAMS, INTEGRATING FEDERAL DOCUMENTS:
A CASE STUDY AT ILLINOIS STATE UNIVERSITY

Barbara B. Alexander, Jessica George, and
Kathleen M. Conley

ABSTRACT

In 1992, Illinois State University in Normal, Illinois embarked on the integration of the General Information and Reference department and the Federal Documents collection. The reorganization resulted from sudden personnel changes and the desire to empower a general reference department located in a subject divided library by adding a unique collection to its area. After three years of experimentation, reorganization, changes in staffing patterns, and teambuilding, the members of the newly integrated General Reference and Documents department have emerged with self-confidence, clearly defined mission statement and goals, and the knowledge that they offer a new and improved type of public service.

INTRODUCTION

As funding dwindles and the demand for public service in academic libraries increases, the issue of the decade becomes effective use of that most important of resources, human beings. In today's climate of change, libraries are more than ever forced to face new arrangements of human and material resources in order to make the best use of disparate collections, or to promote little used collections such as federal depositories. Both the literature in the field and informal discussions show that libraries increasingly choose to integrate collections such as federal depositories that may have more selective use with more centralized and heavily manpowered areas such as central reference. In recent years, discussion newsgroups such as Govdoc-L[1] and LibAdmin[2] have provided a forum for informal discussions of this topic; articles in journals such as *Documents to the People*[3] and *Journal of Government Information*[4] and American Library Association (ALA) programs such as the one presented by the Government Documents Roundtable of ALA (GODORT) in Miami Beach also focused on this issue.

Combining documents with another unit and/or integrating that collection into the mainstream can be a challenging task. Witness the title of the ALA GODORT program, "Shotgun Weddings and Amicable Divorces: Integration vs. Separation of Government Documents and Reference Services." Not only was the tone negative, but the presentations did not include any successful "weddings," only amicable divorces, philosophic thought, and a survey of current situations. In part this may be due to the territoriality of librarians, and not just documents librarians. In a discussion held by the GODORT Education Committee a year prior to this ALA program, the majority of those attending related tales of how their units had separated from subject or general reference units because of frictions. Beverly Norton of Brigham Young University, who was present at that meeting, documented her experience in an article in the September 1995 issue of *Documents to the People*,[5] illustrating how her unit separated, combined, and then happily separated again.

ILLINOIS STATE UNIVERSITY AND
THE MOVE TO INTEGRATION

Separation of collections and reference services is not the only successful solution, however. Illinois State University (ISU)[6] combined its general reference unit with federal documents in 1992. The newly combined unit became General Reference and Documents (GRD). The impetus for a change in the documents arrangement and the realignment of unit responsibilities began in the summer of 1990. Illinois State University has a central library, arranged into four subject floors and a general reference unit, which is on the second, or main floor. For years, the federal documents had been located on the fifth floor, along with science and technology, health, and home economics. The decision to place documents on the fifth floor dates back to 1976 and the move to a new building. Subject distribution called for a special collection to be established on each floor, and documents, both state and federal, joined the science and technology floor. As time passed, the job of Documents Librarian fell to the head of that floor, who had expressed an interest in documents work.

In step with most of the larger library community, documents at Milner Library had always been viewed by library personnel and administrators as a discrete collection of complex materials. It was perceived that proper use of the collection required the expertise of one librarian who saw and processed practically every piece and title accessed by the department. Documents processing remained separate from the rest of library procedures, and for all intents and purposes, it was possible for most in the library to ignore that documents, apart from space considerations, even existed. Adding to this isolation was the reputation of federal documents as a "free" collection. The administration's philosophy about federal depository status was that the library should provide information of potential value while contributing little more than personnel hours and shelf space. Because the investment in the collection was minimal, very little effort was spent on making documents visible, improving their accessibility to patrons, or training staff in their effective use.

Administrators were also concerned that the main floor general reference unit had not achieved the stature of the subject floors. When the present building was opened in 1976, the main floor's special collection was developed as a General College Library, holding a mini-collection of general monographs and a reference area that duplicated materials on other floors. As the library profession as a whole began to question the need for duplicates, so did ISU, and the main floor monographs were dispersed to other floors. The unit managed all popular current periodicals, circulating them much in the manner of a reserve desk. Four microform reader/printers, as well as nine microfilm and five microfiche readers located near the General Reference desk, required constant attention.

The floor held the largest number of on-line public access terminals (seventeen) as well as four InfoTrac[7] stations. Main floor librarians were encouraged to refer all but the most general questions to the subject floors, and phone questions were limited to some degree. Administrators and some staff believed that the lack of a subject area resulted in low self-esteem among the general reference librarians, who had no responsibilities for identified subject areas or account lines for purchasing materials. The unit was often seen as a training ground for new librarians who then moved on to other positions in the library.

CHANGES LEADING TO DOCUMENTS REORGANIZATION

The most important circumstances contributing to the integration of documents and reference were personnel changes. In 1990, the head of the documents and science floor retired on the same day as the Library Technical Assistant (LTA) III who had provided much of the processing support for the federal depository collection. Responding to pressure from science faculty who wanted more periodicals on the fifth floor, and to the need to fill documents personnel vacancies, the library's administrators took a serious look at the integration of the documents collection with another unit in order to provide better accessibility and utilization of staff. It is important to note that the administration's decision to move the documents collection to the main floor and the general reference unit had nothing to do with economics; positions were not eliminated, nor were individuals reassigned. Therefore, moving the documents to another unit meant a group of people who had previously not had the opportunity to work with documents were suddenly responsible for them. This relocation proved to be an interesting challenge.

ISU'S PLAN TO MOVE FEDERAL DOCUMENTS

These ideas for the evolution of the main floor reference unit were confirmed when consultant Susan Bekiares, Head of the Documents Library at the University of Illinois at Urbana-Champaign, recommended moving Milner's documents collection to the main floor. In an in-house feasibility study, staff developed a lengthy and involved plan, including a step-by-step blueprint to effect the change.

Based on the studies and on the observations and goals of the administrators, several objectives emerged. Library administration expressed a particular need to locate the collection where it might be more heavily used. The collection up to this point was perceived very much as the property of a documents librarian, and few were comfortable overstepping those bounds in order to make use of federal publications. The organization and lack of access to depository materials prevented general use, whether in house or by library customers. Only five percent of the materials appeared in the on-line public access catalog. Pamphlet-type materials were locked in filing cabinets and did not circulate. The entire unit was three floors away from the library's entrance, a situation that did not encourage community use or a reasonable level of visibility.

Coinciding with the exit of personnel in the documents unit, the head of General Reference also retired in 1990. Following these personnel changes, formal consultations and actual planning for the reorganization, the search began in 1992 for the new head of the General Reference floor. The job announcement made no reference to documents, but by the time the candidates arrived for interviews, the decision had been made to move the collection. One of those recruited to interview came from Texas A&M University, where she headed the Documents/Maps Department at the Sterling C. Evans Library. After being offered and accepting the position, she arrived in Illinois to see a very different arrangement than when she visited. The new head brought much needed documents experience and training in management and leadership to the new division.

The new division head arrived in August 1992, one week before school started, to find the unit in the midst of putting up new shelving, getting new carpets, and attempting to address how inexperienced staff would answer documents questions. Since 1990 one of the general reference librarians had managed the documents collection. She possessed documents expertise, and consequently the rest of the staff, because of their self-perceived inadequacy in this area, seldom attempted to answer questions. The division head, while aware of the value of the interim documents librarian's knowledge and experience, also recognized the need for all General Reference staff to become documents, or better yet, integrated librarians, and began making plans toward that eventuality.

Training sessions for traditional documents resources such as Census materials, the *Federal Register*, and the *U.S. Statutes at Large* were developed by the General Reference and Documents librarians, and were open to all library staff. Even though Milner is a subject divided library, all faculty rotate at the General Reference desk on Saturdays and Sundays during the fall and winter semesters. Good referrals result from a knowledge of what is actually on those floors, and opening up documents training sessions to everyone allowed for increased knowledge and better referrals. The real bonus, however, went to those preparing and giving sessions. Rather than calling on experts, as is often the pattern in this and other libraries, the training was distributed so everyone could learn through teaching.

A significant change to the organization of the unit that impacted how the librarians and staff dealt with the documents integration was the development of a documents processing unit in the Acquisitions Department. The removal of the processing responsibilities from GRD was received with mixed feelings from the librarians in the department. Some felt that the absence of a sense of touching the materials as they arrived, seeing them daily, and knowing the quirks and foibles of the depository system deprived them of a sense of ownership, and distanced them from the intimate knowledge needed to do proper documents reference. Another reaction came from the library's deeply ingrained professional/paraprofessional stratification. Some librarians experienced anxiety that the documents processors had become de-facto documents librarians by virtue of their daily activities.

As time has progressed, as the documents teams of both librarians and support staff have taken shape and begun to work together, and as all members of the staff have become more comfortable in their documents roles, a well-honed working relationship has developed between the documents processors and the librarians. Since the two documents staff members attend all the GRD meetings, serve on various working groups within the unit, and take regular reference desk shifts, these positions have become an integral part of the work flow in the department. The librarians rely on the documents staff in all aspects of maintaining the depository collection, congressional information, and the electronic products, and the professional and support positions complement each other in an enviable fashion. Collection development decisions and complex reference work could not happen without the problem solving skills of the librarians, and the collection would not be accessible without the organizational skills of the processors.

Organization of the General Reference and Documents unit into teams introduced a new viewpoint toward documents. Taking the approach that the collection is one to be managed so as to best meet the public's needs requires a commitment from all members of the unit. Rather than separate and divide responsibilities into discrete areas, whether according to a Superintendent of Documents (SuDoc) or federal agency breakdown or by specific jobs such as reference or microforms, the division head separated the workload into two arbitrary units, each of them staffed with three or more individuals. One team, the Documents Traditional Management Team, addresses the collection as it now is, evaluating the reference collection, the arrangement of materials for public visibility, collection development, and weeding, and problem solving related to the curiosities of working with federal publications. The Documents Electronic Management Team considers the promotion of CD-ROM's, Internet options such as GPO Access, Gopher and World Wide Web, and selection of appropriate commercial indexes, working closely with the library's Systems Unit to select, install and develop these materials. The General Reference Collection Development Team makes the traditional decisions on purchase and maintenance of the general collection for the unit.

A PATTERN FOR SUCCESSFUL INTEGRATION: CONFIDENCE BUILDING ACTIVITIES

The integration of the documents collection into the general reference collection has been effective in several ways, primarily and most obviously in the increased knowledge of the library staff who assist users at the reference desk. This increased improvement in reference service has not been effortless. The librarians' growing confidence has resulted from a philosophical commitment to incorporate documents resources into the reference repertoire, to consult with colleagues in order to answer questions accurately and efficiently, and to use appropriate handbooks and guides while working at the reference desk.

Paired staffing at the General Reference desk provides an opportunity for staff to share knowledge and work cooperatively when answering questions. Because most members of the department are not completely comfortable at this point with all aspects of documents reference, a second opinion is often necessary. Also, proximity to the collection from the service desk provides the opportunity to use the collection. With two librarians at the desk, it is not an inconvenience to leave the desk to assist patrons who might be unfamiliar with the SuDoc classification system or need extended one-on-one assistance to use the collection successfully.

All but one of the thirty-seven librarians in Milner, whether assigned to technical or public service, share weekend rotations at the General Reference and Documents desk. They are offered training in the location and use of government documents. Although in the past the training has been only one to two hours in length, it has provided at least a cursory introduction to this part of the collection. This familiarity encourages referrals from the subject floors to the central reference and documents collection, a departure from the supposition that almost all referrals would be made from the main floor to the subject areas. This two-way flow of reference assistance negates the former unspoken but all too frequently accepted assumption that "easy" questions are answered at the General Reference Desk and "hard" questions need to be forwarded to another department. The enhanced reference configuration also greatly improves assistance to patrons, who now have access to a central reference desk staffed six days a week until either 9 or 10 p.m. with a reference librarian who is knowledgeable about both the general collection and government documents.

All librarians, either alone or working in tandem with other librarians from the department or Milner subject librarians, are encouraged to provide library instruction to classes that require extensive understanding and use of government documents. Such classes have included Political Science, Marketing, and Criminal Justice. Through teaching experiences, GRD librarians gain self-esteem and confidence by interacting with teaching faculty at a more advanced level.

PERSONNEL CHANGES AND A NEW DEPARTMENTAL MISSION

The hiring patterns of the last three years proved to be particularly important. (The evolution of job assignments from 1991 to 1995 can be found in Appendix A.) Retirements and resignations led to a large turnover of the GRD faculty. By the third year of the documents integration, four new professional librarians had taken their place in the department. The hiring process brought to the department the issue of what qualifications are required of incoming librarians. In selection of candidates for each of the entry-level positions, attention was given to experience with documents, whether in a professional setting or through coursework. It was considered important that documents not be a mystery to each new librarian. A certain comfort level with and enthusiasm for documents was seen as a definite asset to the position. Willingness to learn, creativity, and flexibility were considered equally, if not more important than expertise.

With the original integration of documents and General Reference, several members of the department approached the new demands of becoming documents librarians with considerable trepidation. The General Reference and Documents staff has had to embrace the documents collection, learn its service capabilities and limitations, and most importantly, learn to approach the depository with a positive and unintimidated attitude. The new librarians have been an important link in that process. Enthusiasm, courage, and a positive attitude can have an important and contagious effect in a working group, and since the influx of new staff, this department has developed a strong sense of mission, a well-formed service attitude, and an effective working relationship.

The first GRD retreat occurred in the fall of 1995. As the new head of the department had recognized three years earlier, it would take until this point in time for a synthesis of the documents and general reference collections to allow for a truly productive working group to emerge. The day-long retreat revealed that the new department had meshed. The focus of the retreat was to reach consensus on the direction of the service mission of the department and to structure the various departmental responsibilities and teams to support that mission. At the retreat, ideas were generated in a brainstorming process that produced a solid and concise mission statement for the department and a panoply of achievable goals. (See Appendix B for the text of the GRD mission statement.)

The mission statement was intended as an expression of GRD's commitment to Illinois State University. It also serves as a statement to the rest of the library that the department is willing and ready to assume responsibility as a central reference station. Because of the main-floor location of the GRD desk, and in light of the new service offering tewnty-four-hour service five days per week on the main floor, the department is increasingly the busiest reference point in the building. The staff's increasing confidence with documents and its enthusiasm for service has led to the department's answering more difficult reference questions which in the past may have been prematurely referred to the subject floors. In light of the established working relationship and the philosophical agreement among the staff, the mission statement proved to be a natural voicing and merging of individual and common thought.

THE ESSENTIAL INGREDIENT: TEAMWORK

One of the most important aspects of the new face of Milner's General Reference and Documents department is the commitment to the team or working group approach. Collaboration has been an essential element in establishing the staff members' confidence with the variety of reference challenges facing an integrated documents/general reference desk. Group work is also proving to be essential in some of the most important responsibilities of the department, namely, development of its general reference collection, selection and maintenance of the depository collection, and management of electronic resources. Documents CD-ROMs, traditional bibliographic databases, multi-media, and Internet sites impact all aspects of GRD reference work.

The fall 1995 retreat provided an opportunity to organize the staff into effective work groups based on individual interest, expertise, or past experience with the issues at hand. It also allowed for the reassignment of responsibilities in a long list of duties needing attention, assuring that the tasks would be assigned to individuals who were most motivated by those aspects of the department. Besides assignment to the established and ongoing teams mentioned above, teams of two or three staff members were formed for documents and general reference weeding, shelf reading, and profiling for the new Marcive, Inc. cataloging tapeloads set to begin in 1996. The staff members came away from the retreat full of enthusiasm and with a sense of control over their work schedules and responsibilities for the coming school year.

The success of the team approach relies on the nature of the individuals involved and on the confidence of the division head that this arrangement will not only succeed but will produce a participatory ambiance. Historically, the GRD unit had experienced more turnover than any other unit in Milner Library, in part because that unit had more temporary or year-to-year appointments than tenure track positions. Over the past three years, two of the three year-to-year appointments have been transferred to tenure lines, and the hiring of flexible, proactive individuals into these positions has resulted in the productive teams which eagerly began the fall of 1995. With four of the librarians in the department untenured, work load distribution must be carefully planned to support tenure-track activities and collaborative professional efforts.

This commitment to cooperation and the realization that complex reference questions are now rightfully in the department's purview serves to bolster self-esteem and contributes to a sense of empowerment and community among both librarians and support staff. Furthermore, the department's goal is to have all librarians view themselves as General Reference and Documents librarians. In order to do so, they must commit to taking active roles in the comprehensive management of the collection. They must become involved beyond Milner Library in the larger community of reference and documents librarians by reading, networking, and attending workshops, meetings and conferences, sharing their discoveries and knowledge. There is no room in this reference model for a single documents librarian who serves as the guardian of government knowledge and to whom all patrons must be referred. In addition to serving as an excuse for the rest of the staff to remain woefully ignorant of much of the collection, the presence of one documents librarian in the department is impractical at a busy reference desk and antithetical to concepts of collaboration, support, and empowerment.

THE CHALLENGES OF TRAINING AND TECHNOLOGY

The training sessions on specific, commonly used government documents which took place early in the integration process provided further strengthening of reference skills both for those who taught and for those who attended. However, only two General Reference and Documents librarians of the eight who participated in the training sessions are currently employed in the department. The formal training sessions and enlarged focus session on new products and means of access should soon be repeated.

A formidable challenge to the provision of efficient reference service is the lack of uniform bibliographic access to the documents collection. Few of the documents holdings are available in the on-line catalog. Locating a particular title or issue often entails consulting separate shelf lists for paper and microforms, the computer or card-file systems, or the on-line catalog for check-in information. It is often necessary to consult the holdings of the Illinois State Library (the state's regional depository library) or a current *List of Classes of United States Government Publications* in order to determine a SuDoc number. More tenacity and commitment may be required to physically locate an item than to answer the reference question that necessitated the search.

Because the documents processing and check-in functions are located in another department, the two clerks responsible for these functions, although part of GRD, spend a great deal of time out of the reference and documents area. Their efficiency and knowledge about the collection contributes a great deal to the ongoing success of the merger. However, accessibility to materials would be improved if the documents processing and check-in functions were located in GRD or if documents check-in records were available electronically. Plans to implement Marcive, Inc.'s shipping list service, along with the cataloging tapeloads, should provide such vital information library-wide. With administrative support, these cataloging and processing activities are being addressed by a team composed of the heads of GRD, Cataloging and Processing, in consultation with both librarians and support staff as appropriate. Eventually these processes and procedures will be addressed by multi-unit work groups.

Another challenge facing the remodeled unit is the increase in government information provided in CD-ROM and other electronic formats. Time to preview, provide documentation, train both staff and students, and understand and obtain the hardware necessary to access information in this format present many obstacles to effective reference service. Furthermore, technology has increased use of the documents collection. Patrons can now search the *Monthly Catalog of U.S. Government Publications* and *PAIS Decade* on the Milner On-line catalog terminals via FirstSearch.[8] Students bringing their printouts from these databases to the service desk for guidance often are not specifically looking for government documents but the information contained therein. Serendipitous discovery of federal publications on the part of the students presents an opportunity for those in the library to become aware of and assist in the use of documents.

To promote new technologies or services, GRD is planning a departmental newsletter, in order to inform and encourage use of the library and collaborative efforts with its librarians. Informal "Docs Walks" around the department to introduce patrons to government resources are also planned.

CHALLENGES OF THE CHANGING LIBRARY CULTURE

In 1992, when the GRD Division Head arrived, only four faculty at Milner Library were untenured, with five librarians in year-to-year appointments. By the fall of 1995, half of the thirty-seven faculty members were untenured and there are now only two librarians with year-to-year contracts. Such radical changes in staffing have brought a different mentality to the organization. For instance, ten members of the new faculty formed a support group which is preparing an Internet/remote access use survey to be distributed spring 1996. Tenured faculty who continue to publish in the field work together with untenured faculty on publications. In 1995, Milner staff presented eight poster sessions at the Illinois Library Association Annual Conference and three at the American Library Association Annual Conference. All of the latter presenters were invited to publish their presentations. In the fall of 1995, eight new librarians submitted papers for second year probationary reappointment. Rather than being competitive with their colleagues as has often occurred in the past, they worked on their papers together for consistency and for support.

This type of proactive community spirit, combined with the success of mastering depository materials, providing well-received library instruction, and publishing and presenting work-related material, has driven out much of the pervasive insecurity often felt within the library profession. The GRD librarians have a clear concept of themselves as librarians, are proud of their profession, and actively work to promote it. It is interesting to note that only one of the current GRD staff chose federal documents as a career path. The others accepted the responsibility because documents meant an opportunity for advancement, an offer for employment, or a means of expanding their expertise. The GRD staff is confident, self-motivated and professional because they have met the challenge of documents and have repudiated the territoriality often clung to by both subject and documents librarians.

The reorganization of the general reference unit meant moving from a pattern of answering directional questions, referring reference questions, and deferring to subject librarians into one which finds each individual providing in-depth reference, using all of the technologies and tools at hand as well as the complex and challenging federal publications collection. GRD boasts more on-line public access terminals than any other floor in the building. It serves as the internal, and on occasion statewide, beta test site for new electronic products, and it views change as challenging and exciting. Such self-confidence and pleasure in daily exchanges with university and community patrons has resulted in a positive shift in the unit and in how staff members perceive themselves.

Likewise, the technology itself presents great implications for the cross-disciplinary reference that can be offered at one location. It is no longer practical nor necessary, especially in the undergraduate environment, to send students to two or more floors in order to find the materials they need. Furthermore, the current situation in Milner Library presents students with one computer workstation which offers the on-line book catalog; IBIS (Illinois Bibliographic Information Service), a database of thirteen periodical indexes; FirstSearch, with its fifty-plus databases; and Internet access. The multiplicity of databases, indexes and other options can be overwhelming to both undergraduates and graduates in large libraries. Working with students, and often with faculty, may require starting at the beginning and assisting library users through many steps in the research process. Directing patrons to other units where they must establish several new working relationships in one day may cause frustration with the complete process.

CONCLUSION

During the three-year transition to a newly integrated General Reference and Documents department at Milner Library, personnel have learned important lessons about creating new working relationships while improving reference service. Clearly, combining units and enhancing reference service requires teamwork and careful planning of departmental duties. Most importantly, improving reference service requires creativity, initiative, and the constant expansion of professional vision and adaptability to new resources. The success of the integration and the development of working teams has required great energy from the individuals involved and a strong commitment to make the reorganization work. The General Reference and Documents department has learned that a mindset must be established that this is not a documents nor a general reference department, but a central service unit representing the best the library has to offer in electronic resources and reference assistance, as well as unique public resources to serve the community in a broad capacity. GRD sees itself in a ground-breaking leadership role for the library, and in a sense, for the university. The integration of the documents collection has been a powerful catalyst in establishing a de-facto centralized reference system. The department firmly believes that through both improved service and increased professional confidence of the entire staff, it is better able to serve its community than ever before.

Appendixes
Follow

APPENDIX A
General Reference and Documents
May 1994
Job Responsibilities

Librarian
Division Head
Tenure-track

Unit management
Weekly desk schedule
BI's
Liaison with other library units
Desk - 8 hrs/week

Librarian
Tenured

Desk - 13 hrs/week
English 101BI's
Science/Technology floor - 20 hrs/week
Collection Development Team (with two librarians, non-tenure track), make decisions as to general reference selection, monitor funding

---

Librarian
Tenure-track

Desk - 13 hrs/week
BI's, both English 101 and federal documents
Collection development for documents
Weeding project/documents

Librarian
Administrative Professional*

Desk - 13 hrs/week
Liaison with local community college/half-time
BI's (primarily local community college and English 101)
External committee responsibilities, Local Reference Round Table, Alliance Library System Board

---

Librarian
Administrative Professional*

Desk - 13 hrs/week
Desk coverage, approximately 13 hrs/week, including one evening
BI's
General Reference Collection (manager)
FirstSearch Coordination
Browsing Book Collection

Librarian
Administrative Professional*

Desk - 13 hrs/week
BI's (scheduling, contacting instructors, follow-up)
Phone book collection (make selection, get replacements)

Librarian
Administrative Professional*

Desk - 13 hrs/week
BI's
Collection Management Team (with two other librarians)
Data Times Consultant
Internet notebook

Librarian Technical Assistant I

Desk - 8-10 hrs/week
Supervise GRD students
Oversee check-in and processing of newspapers and periodicals
Provide support for librarians
Manage statistics for dept.
Word processing, spreadsheet expertise for dept.
InfoTrac technology

Library Clerk III
Primarily Documents Processing

Desk - 8-10 hrs/week
Hire, train, supervise documents processing students
Supervise Clerk II, documents processing
Oversee check-in and processing of documents
Deal with difficult document questions related to check-in and processing
Manage statistical databases for documents

Library Clerk II

Desk - 8-10 hrs/week
Check in and process documents
Oversee documents student check-in
Manages weeding

*Year to year contract

57

APPENDIX B

MILNER LIBRARY'S GENERAL REFERENCE AND DOCUMENTS MISSION STATEMENT

We actively participate in the educational mission of Illinois State University by using and promoting information resources in order to provide dynamic library service.

We recognize our responsibility as the central reference desk of Milner Library to insure patrons receive the information, assistance, and instruction they need.

We believe in the value of library instruction and are committed to ongoing development of those programs and services, both formal and informal.

We dedicate ourselves to personal and professional growth, to networking, to outreach, and to a far-reaching perspective.

We are guided by our commitment to the profession.

APPENDIX C

General Reference and Documents

Fall 1995

Unit Responsibilities

The organizational chart remains as it was in 1994. Public service desk time is not included.

BI's (General) All librarians

BI's (Documents) All librarians

BI Committee Librarian (Tenure Track)

BI Scheduling Librarian (Tenure Track)

Browsing Books Librarian (Administrative Professional)/Clerk II

Conferences/Meetings/Workshops All GRD staff

DataTimes Librarian (Tenure Track)

Documents Electronic Resources Management Team Librarian (Tenured/Division Head), Librarian (Tenure Track), LTA I, Clerk II

Documents Processing: Clerk III, Clerk II

Documents Stacks Maintenance, LTA I, Clerk III

Documents Traditional Resources Management Team Librarian (Tenure Track), Librarian (Tenure Track), Librarian (Administrative Professional), Clerk II

Documents Weeding Librarian (Tenure Track), Librarian (Tenure Track), Librarian (Tenure Track), Librarian (Tenure Track)

Education Committee Librarian (Tenured/Division Head), LTA I

FirstSearch Librarian (Tenure Track), Librarian (Administrative Professional)

General Reference Periodicals Librarian (Tenure Track), LTA I

General Reference Collection Development Librarian (Tenure Track), Librarian (Tenure Track), Librarian (Administrative Professional), LTA I

General Reference Processing LTA I, Clerk II

General Reference Weeding Librarian (Tenured/Division Head), Librarian (Tenure Track), Librarian (Administrative Professional)

GRD Desk Scheduling Librarian (Tenured/Division Head)

GRD Desk Reference Pamphlet File Librarian (Administrative Professional)

GRD Shelf Reading Project Librarian (Tenure Track)

Handouts Librarian (Tenure Track) Coordinator; All

Hours Message Clerk II

Information Cardfile Librarian (Tenure Track)

InfoTrac Task Force Librarian (Tenured/Division Head), LTA I

LegiSlate Librarian (Tenure Track)

Liaison with Cataloging LTA I, Clerk II

Marcive Profiling Librarian (Tenure Track)

MERC (electronic access) Committee Librarian (Tenure Track), Librarian (Tenure Track), Librarian (Tenure Track)

Microforms Maintenance Librarian (Tenure Track), Clerk II

Newspaper Collection Maintenance/Task Force Committee Librarian (Tenure Track), Clerk II

PhoneDisc/Phonebook Collection Librarian (Administrative Professional)

Preservation Committee LTA I

Printing Task Force Librarian (Tenured/Division Head)

Research Committee Librarian (Tenure Track)

Storage Maintenance Clerk II

Student Training LTA I, Clerk III

Tax Forms Ordering and Display LTA I

Terminal Maintenance/"Cleaning" Clerk II

ACKNOWLEDGMENT

This chapter is based on B.B. Alexander, and S.K. Naylor, *Merging Federal Documents with General Reference: A Transformation in Usage and in Librarian Stature.* In *Continuity & Transformation: The Promise of Confluence: Proceedings of the Seventh National Conference of the Association of College and Research Libraries Held in Pittsburgh, Pennsylvania 29 March-1 April 1995,* edited by Richard AmRhein, 95-100. Chicago: Association of College and Research Libraries, A Division of the American Library Association, 1995.

NOTES

1. Govdoc-L is a moderated listserv addressing issues of importance to federal depository libraries and other interested individuals and organizations. The list address is govdoc-L@psuvm.psu.edu and the subscription address is listserv@psuvm.psu.edu.

2. LibAdmin is a moderated listserv addressing issues of importance to library administrators and other interested individuals and organizations. The list address is libadmin@list.ab.umd.edu and the subscription address is listproc@list.ad.umd.edu.

3. B. Norton, "Documents Reference," *Documents to the People,* 21 (1993): 154-156.

4. A.R. Rawan and J. Cox, "Government Publications Integration and Training," *Journal of Government Information,* 22 (1995): 253-266.

5. Norton, 154-156.

6. Illinois State University, Normal, IL, is one of the premier undergraduate universities in the state. It has an enrollment of 19,000, and offers Master's and Ph.D. programs in selected fields. Milner Library is a subject-divided library with thirty-three public and technical service librarians and four administrators. The Milner Librarians are all accorded faculty status with the majority of the positions tenure-track.

7. InfoTrac, an information retrieval service offered by Information Access Company.

8. FirstSearch is an information retrieval service offered by OCLC, Inc., Columbus, OH.

PART II

REFERENCE SERVICE FOR CHANGING USER
POPULATIONS

THE ROLE OF REFERENCE SERVICES IN A MULTICULTURAL UNIVERSITY LIBRARY

María de Jesús Ayala-Schueneman and Roberta Pitts

ABSTRACT

This chapter explores multiculturalism as it affects reference services at the Jernigan Library, Texas A&M University-Kingsville (TAMUK), a majority Hispanic institution in South Texas. Minorities are a growing part of the United States population, and in some areas the minority is rapidly becoming the majority. This trend will have an impact on reference services in libraries. This chapter will focus on ways that library reference services have been developed at TAMUK to meet the challenge of a multicultural academic community. Diversity in staffing and collections is examined, as well as the cultural sensitivity necessary for any library that desires to serve a multicultural community.

INTRODUCTION

The fact that academic institutions in the United States are becoming increasingly multicultural in nature is a widely acknowledged phenomenon. The literature abounds with demographics and population statistics that predict a multiethnic future. But for many academic libraries, the future is not all that distant. Institutions with large minority populations and high international student enrollment are already grappling with issues of cultural awareness and diversity. Hardly a professional journal exists that has not touched upon the subject of a diverse workforce and the library's role in a multicultural world.

The term"multiculturalism" has many interpretations. The Oxford English Dictionary defines it as simply "pertaining to a society consisting of varied cultural groups."[1] Lorna Peterson points out the problems inherent in defining the word when she speaks of the careless language that surrounds use of the term. Does it refer to racial minorities, equity, or simply cultural differences? She cautions that libraries need to clarify their meaning before developing diversity plans.[2] For the Jernigan Library at Texas A&M University-Kingsville (TAMUK) the term "multi-cultural" refers to the fact that two distinct cultures exist in South Texas, and that the resulting differences must be addressed to ensure a success-ful library program.

A significant role of libraries is to prepare individuals for meaningful participation in economic and social responsibilities in a multicultural environment. Such preparation is not possible if libraries themselves are not prepared.[3] As they move toward the predictions of the future, librar-ies are challenged to change old practices and develop new ones to ensure that diversity is incorporated into all areas of library services. Such changes include not only diverse collections and new approaches to ser-vices, but attitudes as well.

It is normal for people to view the world through the lens of the society in which they were raised. However, in the case of a culture that domi-nates the entire world as no previous culture has done, it becomes espe-cially difficult to think in terms of any other culture. The Western culture of Europe, the United States, and Canada have been dominant for half a millennium. Western methods of warfare, styles of clothing, scientific thought, cars, computers and machines of all kinds have swept the world and exert a tremendous influence on disparate societies. Some authors have suggested that a recent Western fashion of blaming the West and extolling the Third World is itself based on ideological trends that origi-nate and are controlled in the West.[4] This viewpoint expresses a pro-found skepticism that Westerners can ever escape their own background and environment. A more usual and optimistic view is that their viewpoint can be transcended, though the road to understanding is always difficult. Such understanding is perhaps rare and never complete.

For libraries, the key to such understanding and subsequent change often rests at the initial point of contact for most students: reference services. It is at this juncture that cultures meet as students and librarians deal with each other. Because of the nature of reference work, this contact is often brief. Misconceptions, whether they are due to language or other cultural differences, may be dismissed or not even recognized.

Students from different cultures view the librarian from their own perspectives. From experience some patrons appear to prefer to work with male librarians. They also seek librarians from their own part of the world. At TAMUK, one Hispanic librarian has been mistaken for an Iranian or Indian; indeed, those who thought so were hopeful that this was the case because they were happy to find a familiar cultural presence. Some students are very reticent about approaching the desk and asking for help. With these students, the reference interview takes on a special significance, and a librarian trained to be sensitive to these factors assures a more successful outcome. In general, libraries must recognize that reference desk services are key in ensuring that cultural differences are addressed.

Institutions like TAMUK where diversity is highly evident can serve as pathfinders for those who are searching for ways to incorporate cultural awareness and a multicultural perspective into their institutions. Academic libraries across the United States are developing equally innovative ways to meet the needs of their diverse student populations. At the University of Michigan, a Peer Information Counseling Program was developed as a minority student support program. The program uses trained student volunteers who help other minority students with term paper research or general instruction in the use of the library. A welcome letter that explains available services is sent to all undergraduate first-year minority students. Newsletters and testimonials from students who have used the program are part of a well-developed publications package.[5]

Another approach to serving minority students is to dedicate a position to minority services. The University of California at Santa Cruz opted to halt a search for a business reference specialist and changed the position to a Multicultural Services Librarian. The decision came after library faculty attended a minority student group meeting and faced the realization that they were not serving a large portion of their student body as well as they might. The new Multicultural Services Librarian takes the library message into dormitories and other campus areas. In addition the library was heavily involved in the university's Summer Bridge Program which helps incoming students who need special tutoring.[6]

Yoshi Hendricks at the University of Nevada, Reno, realized some cultural awareness was necessary when students from their Japanese campus in Tokyo began arriving in Reno. Language was obviously a major obstacle in bibliographic instruction, but just as important was a lack of cultural understanding. For example, a Japanese student might nod while listening. To an American, a nod indicates that the student understands, when in fact it is simply a part of listening behavior in Japanese society. Hendricks' discussion of culture-bound assumptions is useful in helping staff become alert to cultural differences.[7]

MINORITY DEMOGRAPHICS

The United States Census Bureau projects that the Hispanic population in the United States may double in the next thirty years. Hispanic Americans have been identified as the newest and fastest growing group of users.[8] California and Texas will continue to have the largest Hispanic populations, followed by New York, Florida, and Illinois. In Texas, the number of Hispanics is projected to increase from 4.9 million to 10.3 million by the year 2020.[9] In 1993, Karen Downing observed that "High minority teen birthrates, financial pressures, poor academic preparation, lack of family or other role models, and other social circumstances contribute to low college progression and low graduation rates among minority youth."[10] This statement is perhaps more true of Hispanics than any other minority group. Nationally, about 61 percent of Hispanics were high school graduates compared to 75 percent of blacks and 83 percent of whites. Although their graduation rates are improving, Hispanic students drop out of high school more often than either blacks or whites. Hispanics who primarily speak English at home are more likely to stay in high school.[11] The number of Hispanics who have completed college is low; and in Texas, only 8 percent of Hispanics have college degrees. Retention rates for Hispanic student populations indicate that as many as 80 percent leave their undergraduate institution without receiving a degree.[12]

Texas A&M University-Kingsville is one of the few institutions of higher education in the United States that is majority Hispanic, specifically Mexican American. Located in South Texas, its multicultural campus has an enrollment of approximately 6,500 students from thirty-one states and fifty foreign countries. The Hispanic student population is about 62 percent and the total minority population is approximately 65 percent. Of the 368 faculty members, Hispanic faculty members represent approximately 14 percent of that number. Black faculty members represent just under 3 percent. TAMUK provides 70 percent of the bilingual teachers in Texas, and it consistently ranks among the country's top ten producers of Hispanic engineers.

South Texas is heavily Hispanic and has traditionally been an area of low economic and educational opportunities. Within this area, Kingsville, home of TAMUK, is located 120 miles north of the Mexican border. Ranching and agriculture are prominent. Though politically it has been Democratic, it is a very conservative and traditional part of the United States. Economically, South Texas lags behind the rest of the state and the United States. The per capita income was only $9,580, compared with the Texas figure of $12,904 and the U.S. figure of $14,420. The state legislature recognized this in 1993 and responded by developing the South Texas Initiative, a program to improve and expand educational opportunities in this economically underdeveloped area.

The university is dedicated to serving an ethnically and culturally diverse population. A primary mission is to foster the growth of a middle class in South Texas. University President Manuel Ibañez identified this mission in a vision statement created with the participation of a number of groups on campus. The goal at TAMUK is to provide an intellectually challenging education while maintaining a selectively open admissions policy. "Selectively open" means that the university will admit students conditionally even though the students have not met the minimum admission requirements.

Because Hispanics were the dominant group on campus, librarians wanted to know what problems these students might face when they enrolled in the university. Understanding the library's clientele is a continuous process and a necessary one to ensure quality reference service. Through discussion and observation librarians have begun to develop a profile of these students. Many are the first generation in their family to attend college. Language skills can present problems. These students speak English, but often it is not the language spoken in the home. The finer nuances of comprehension that are so important at the university level may create extra burdens for the students whether they are taking notes in class or explaining to the librarian what information they need.

Over 80 percent of the students receive financial aid, which means they are working and going to school. Finally, while many freshmen may feel a sense of separation from family, the Hispanic student is especially vulnerable. The family is one of the strongest social institutions in Mexican society, and the lack of proximity to large extended families has been identified as a factor in the failure to retain Hispanic students.[13]

LIBRARY SERVICES

The student populations at TAMUK pose a number of challenges in the provision of library reference services. The university's selectively open admissions policy and its mission to foster the growth of a middle class encourages enrollment of first-generation college students. Over 27 percent of TAMUK students are part-time, over 46 percent are commuters, and over 36 percent are twenty-five or older. A number of classes are offered at off-campus sites to accommodate the needs of non-traditional students in rural areas. These groups often come from backgrounds where there has been less exposure to current technology and limited access to libraries and other resources.

Special programs offered by the university expand the library's clientele beyond the primary focus of university faculty and students. The Upward Bound Bridge Program sponsors first-generation high school seniors in college courses. The University's Migrant Education Program and the nursery school bring elementary school students to the library. Recently, the university developed a high school program to serve public school students. The university also sponsors Elderhostels that bring older citizens to campus.

The library's primary goal is to meet the information needs of the university's diverse groups and cultures. In order to meet this goal, librarians at TAMUK have identified six objectives. These are to:

- establish a workplace which reflects the composition of the diverse environment
- ensure that librarians and staff have opportunities to enrich their knowledge about cultures different from their own
- participate in various cultural and ethnic festivals to increase cultural awareness and promote library services
- develop ways that staff can share culture-related materials and ideas

- actively recruit minorities to the library profession with local scholarships or other support
- build an atmosphere of approachability at the reference desk.

In her article on diversity within the reference department, Deborah Curry explains the need for staff and collections that reflect society as a whole. As society changes demographically and minorities approach one-third of the population, so must the library change, if only to properly represent its diverse clientele. Reference service must mirror the change or risk losing relevance for a third of the population. Curry's specific goals include the hiring of more non-white librarians, innovative use of non-white student workers, the creation of a task force to evaluate the services offered by the library, and the development of a reference collection that supports the concept of multiculturalism.[14]

STAFFING FOR DIVERSITY

For Jernigan Library, the first challenge was to increase the diversity of its reference staff. Experience has shown that often minority students are more comfortable approaching another minority person for help in the library. However, in a 1992 article, Otis Chadley noted that minorities are still under represented in library science graduate schools. Hispanic librarians represented only 2 percent of the total library work force, and among the 10 percent of ACRL librarians that are minorities, only 15 percent are Hispanic.[15] The latest figures indicate that there is no improvement in sight. In fact, the number of minorities entering the profession is declining.[16] A Hispanic reference librarian at TAMUK was one of the few minority students who attended the masters program in library science at San Jose State University in the late seventies. She recalls that even then the American Library Association was concerned with the lack of minority enrollment, and during their accreditation visit to the school, minority recruitment was an issue. She was recruited by the Library Science Department to make a video demonstrating that while not numerous, minorities benefited from and were valued by San Jose State.

The lack of minority enrollment was seen as a crisis in the late seventies, and it has not improved in the years since. Chadley cites low pay and previous experience requirements as barriers minorities face in entering the library science field.[17] However, it may be inaccurate to identify problems that apply to all library science graduates as being special problems for Hispanics or other minorities. For example, low salaries certainly are a problem that all library professionals face. Another identified barrier is the seeming reluctance of minority professionals to relocate. TAMUK's Career Services has identified this as a problem as well.

Minorities must be attracted to the idea of serving in the information industry. As Margaret Myers says, librarians must use their "vision for the future to promote [their] profession actively and strategically."[18] One way to do this is to emphasize the power of information. Not only are many minority neighborhoods and third world countries materially poor, they are also information poor. One librarian's experience with the Benjamin Franklin Library (USIS) in Mexico City was the determining factor in her decision to seek a career in the library world. Partly this was because the power of information was amply demonstrated. Libraries must energize minorities with the vision that librarianship will be a power profession in the twenty-first century.[19]

TAMUK is fortunate to have a comparatively large number of Hispanic librarians and staff. The library's reference team was able to assign two Hispanic librarians, three Hispanic staff members, and two Hispanic graduate students to the reference desk. This is an attempt to bring individuals with different experiences, cultures, and backgrounds to the reference desk. Their common bond is a desire to serve library patrons. The reference staff strives to be aware of the culture and ethnicity of patrons and to have respect for their individuality.

Some aspects of diversified reference services are obvious. Language readily stands out. It is not possible to have library staff who know all the languages they might encounter, but it is possible to have reference librarians with basic skills in a prominent second language. This is especially important in an area like South Texas, where Spanish is spoken by a significant majority of the population. Certainly most transactions are in English, but the need for Spanish does arise. While it is not always possible to know a patron's native tongue, the reference librarian can show sensitivity toward the patron's culture. Sometimes this can be as easy as knowing a little history and keeping up with current events. International students are very impressed when the librarian displays a knowledge of their country. These are minor things, but they can help create an atmosphere of trust.

As minorities are recruited into the library profession, care should be taken within the library staff itself to avoid stereotyping. For example, many Hispanics would hate to be solely identified with mariachi music. How many librarians are aware of the strong classical music tradition in Mexico? No one would consider identifying country music as the only expression of United States music, but often in cultural matters like music, literature, and food, non-Hispanics see only a narrow or preconceived view of the Mexican-American. Care must be taken to ensure that Hispanics and other minorities are not stereotyped into certain jobs. For example, it is easy to assume that Hispanic librarians would be ideal for positions dealing with Spanish language materials. Certainly it may be the case, but it might not. A better effort to recruit minorities must be made on the basis of how a diverse library staff can enrich the entire mission of the library.

At TAMUK reference librarians have been provided with the opportunity to increase their awareness of the culture in which they work. Both minorities and nonminorities have participated in a Transculturation Project that seeks to familiarize faculty and staff with Mexican-American culture. Transculturation involves a movement of acceptance on the part of two different ethnic groups toward one anothers' languages and cultural identities. This differs from the usual concept that all movement of acceptance of culture and language must be on the part of the minority group. Though aimed at the Mexican-American culture, developing an appreciation and value for one culture broadens the entire staff's multicultural perspective.

The transculturation project at TAMUK began in 1989 with a three-year grant from the Fund of the Improvement for Postsecondary Education (FIPSE) under the U.S. Department of Education. A total of about 90 faculty have participated over the last five years. Led by Dr. Rosario Torres-Raines from the Department of Psychology and Sociology and Dr. Ward S. Albro, III from the Department of History, the semester-long course includes weekly three-hour seminars with nationally recognized Hispanic scholars. These experts present materials on the Mexican-American population, touching on history, demographics, culture, and identity. These transcultural experiences are designed to produce changes in attitudes, values, and beliefs about a culture other than one's own. The program culminates at the end of the semester with a two-week stay in Cuernavaca, Mexico with intensive Spanish language instruction.

The transculturation experience helps participating faculty and staff recognize and understand Hispanic biculturalism and bilingualism, and by doing so, incorporates this recognition and understanding into their teaching and interactions with students at TAMUK. The objectives are better performance and higher retention rates and recruitment levels for both minority students and faculty.[20] About 60 percent of the library faculty have participated in the program. Another benefit of the program is the development of a greater sensitivity to all cultures with which public service librarians come into contact. The experience of living in a foreign land with languages and cultures not well understood mirrors the experience of many international students.

Sometimes at the reference desk, librarians and staff face language and cultural problems. Language problems are obvious, but cultural problems are sometimes harder to define. In some cultures, for example, women usually do not work outside the home. Therefore, it is difficult for some international students to relate to women in a workplace. It is also difficult for some non-Hispanics to relate to Hispanic librarians, just as it is difficult for some male Hispanics to relate to women librarians. The sensitivity gained from the FIPSE program helps librarians understand that respect, understanding, and knowledge are valuable assets in dealing with people from other cultures.

INSTRUCTION

A library staff that understands diversity is better equipped to fulfill the information needs of the university's diverse community through instruction and collections, as well as reference. At TAMUK, library orientation and research skills are offered through a college success course called College I which all freshmen are required to take. One goal of the program is to increase the retention of minority and other students. Because the university's mission is to create a middle class in South Texas, there is a clear goal of ensuring that these students remain in school and complete a degree. The services within the College I program include an Academic Rescue Program, which is a mentoring program that pairs freshmen with upper-class division students, and a Student-to-Student Development program. College I provides academic skills workshops through the Academic Skills Lab, the Reading Lab and the Writing Skills Center. Developmental courses in reading, writing and math are also available.

Before a formal library skills program was developed, faculty assigned to teach the College I course requested a tour of the library and brief bibliographic instruction for their classes. It became clear from the students' subsequent use of the library that these brief encounters were not effective. Librarians at TAMUK took the advice of Downing, McAdam and Nichols, who write about the need for a stronger library presence on campuses. They write:

> College and university libraries affect students at all levels and across all academic disciplines. Sooner or later most students pass through the library' s doors. The library is in a singular position to have an impact on a large segment of the campus population. Here is an opportunity for librarians to take a proactive stance and to help set the pace, not only for other libraries, but also for the larger institutions they serve.[21]

In 1994, the reference librarians developed a bibliographic instruction program and presented it to the coordinators of College I who fully endorsed the library's participation. Within this program, reference librarians are assigned sections of the College I success course and teach library skills to freshmen students for two class meetings. A basic premise of the course is that students need to feel successful about their library experience. Through means of a class assignment, reference librarians introduce library and research skills to over thirty sections of freshmen students with approximately twenty-five students in each section.

MULTICULTURAL COLLECTIONS

Developing collections to meet the needs of culturally diverse populations is another area of concern. Richard Chabrán noted almost a decade ago that he could already see an increasing sophistication in multicultural materials available for patrons. He predicted, and rightly so, that this trend would acquire new urgency by the year 2000 when Latinos would become the largest ethnic group in the United States.[22] Multicultural materials are available and librarians must take the initiative to insure that these materials are added to the collection in a systematic fashion. Without such a plan libraries risk failing to provide relevant collections to a significant number of patrons. TAMUK offers both a masters and doctoral program in bilingual education and courses in numerous disciplines that feature Hispanic cultures, folklore, history, literature, and politics. Because the library's mission is to support collections in all disciplines, TAMUK is committed to building a strong multicultural collection and in particular relevant Hispanic resources. Collection development teams which include both librarians and appropriate faculty work together to insure these materials are present.

It is essential for academic libraries to collect popular journals and newspapers for minority groups. This is especially true if the minority actually comprises a majority of the student body, as is the case at TAMUK. The Jernigan Library has tried to meet these needs by subscribing to popular magazines like *Hispanic,* as well as political opinion journals from Mexico like *Proceso* and *Este País,* and newspapers like *El Norte* which is also published in Mexico. Sometimes there are specific journals in academic areas that deal with minority concerns. *Latin American Music Review* and *The Hispanic Journal of Behavioral Sciences* are two examples of such journals. These materials are not used solely by Hispanic patrons. *El Norte,* besides supporting Hispanic culture generally, is an important journal for the Political Science Department at TAMUK. Other departments, including Business and Language, and Literature, have expressed a desire for multicultural journals.

The Jernigan Library has also undertaken the task of collecting most Latino fiction. In order to build this collection, it has tried to identify and obtain the output of important publishers and authors in this area. Access to this material must be provided through indexes and bibliographies such as the *Chicano Index, Hispanic American Periodical Index* (HAPI), *Handbook of Latin American Studies,* and *Fichero Bibliográfico Hispanoamericano.* Multicultural reference materials must also be added to library collections. It is certainly gratifying to see many more published reference sources concerning minorities, such as the works that Gale has published on the literature of blacks and Hispanics. These areas were often neglected in the past.

The library at TAMUK has a Bilingual Collection containing materials on bilingual and bicultural education, Spanish language juvenile books, and similar materials. The Bilingual Collection was opened in June 1976 to meet the growing need for a comprehensive collection devoted to library materials in the field of bilingual-bicultural education. The University provides 70 percent of bilingual teachers in Texas, and an Ed. D. in Bilingual Education has been offered since 1976. One of the collections' strengths is materials relating to the educational needs of Mexican Americans and other Spanish-speaking minorities. The collection now numbers about 15,000 items and includes materials in the following areas: English as a second language, English as a foreign language, Spanish language and literature, the culture of Spain and Hispanic America, Spanish American history, and all areas of linguistics. The types of materials include doctoral dissertations, unpublished research reports, monographs and reports produced by conventions and other professional meetings, bibliographies, reference works, textbooks, juvenile literature, teaching aids, and curriculum guides.

Another way to enhance understanding of diverse cultures across campus is to provide opportunities for cultural enrichment. Students from diverse cultures are proud of their heritage, and the library can encourage that pride through displays and special events. In cooperation with the Department of Language and Literature, the library hosted a program featuring two Hispanic authors from Arte Público, Juan Bruce Novoa and Beatriz Rivera. A recent display case prepared by a graduate student highlighted Latino literature in the United States. National Library Week banners carried the double theme, "Libraries Change Lives—Bibliotecas Cambian Vidas!"

A LOOK TOWARD THE FUTURE

The librarians and staff at TAMUK continue to strive to fulfill the goals they have set. Assessment of services shows that they have had some success. Figures from the annual Texas Academic Libraries Survey indicate that reference transactions for a typical week rose by 468 percent in the past two years. The Spring Customer Satisfaction Survey shows that 57 percent of TAMUK patrons rated the staff as extremely or very helpful. Librarians reached over 5,000 students through freshmen orientation, research skills classes, and Internet training. The program has brought renewed interest in the Bilingual Collection, and the library is working with the College of Education to strengthen this collection.

The reference unit itself has undergone dramatic changes in the past two years. The reference staff has grown from one professional librarian to a team of four, two of whom are Hispanic. Two additional librarians are enrolled in the FIPSE transculturation project this semester and three staff members elected to take Spanish courses this year. As a result, reference services has strengthened both its ability to serve the academic community, and its sensitivity to other cultures, particularly the Hispanic culture. A small minority of patrons still seek out a male to help them. Because all four librarians in the reference unit are female, they can only compensate with an awareness of this cultural preference. The library seeks to ensure that all patrons receive competent assistance regardless of their cultural background.

The library's most immediate goal is to strengthen the program with more outreach services. The library now participates in Senior Day, an activity that brings over 600 high school seniors to the campus. The library, along with academic departments, sponsors a booth displaying materials that inform potential students about the services it offers. A large majority of these students who elect to attend TAMUK have had a positive introduction to the library.

Librarians want to reach more non-users and believe the faculty is the key to reaching these students. With flyers and information alert bulletins, the library tries to ensure that all faculty are aware of its bibliographic instruction program. In all library classes students are encouraged to go to the reference desk for help.

The program of services for off-campus learners also needs to be expanded. A state-wide program called TexShare has helped in this endeavor. TexShare is a cooperative agreement among the fifty-two public universities in the state to share electronic resources and provide reciprocal borrowing privileges. One off-campus site, located two hours from the main campus, is able to borrow books from another state university located nearby. Students are able to access shared databases over the Internet in computer labs available at all sites.

Multiculturalism represents a way of looking at the world. The library, and especially reference services, must view the new cultural demands of an increasingly diverse society as a challenge not only to be met and dealt with, but welcomed. Libraries have always been multicultural to some extent. Now they are called upon to serve as a repository of knowledge and to provide an environment that supports human differences.[23]

Texas A&M University-Kingsville has made a start on this road. However, it would be inappropriate of the library to claim that it has reached its goal of becoming a multicultural library. As Irene Hoadley writes, success is a "continuum rather that a constant state…Success is a process which needs to be nourished, expanded, and diversified to be realized."[24] The reference services that are provided to any library's diverse group of users must always be nourished, expanded and diversified.

NOTES

1.   *Oxford English Dictionary*, 2nd ed. CD-ROM. s.v. "multiculturalism."

2.   Lorna Peterson, "Multiculturalism: Affirmative or Negative Action?" *Library Journal* 120 (July 1995): 30.

3.   Carla J. Stoffle and P.A. Tarin, "No Place for Neutrality: The Case for Multiculturalism," *Library Journal* 19 (July 1994): 46-49.

4. Pascal Bruckner, *The Tears of the White Man: Compassion as Contempt* (New York: Free Press, 1986).

5. For more information about Michigan's Peer Information Counseling Porgram see Karen E. Downing, B. McAdam, and D.P. Nichols, *Reaching a Multicultural Student Community; A Handbook for Academic Librarians* (Wesport, CT: Greenwood Press, 1993).

6. Allan J. Dyson, "Reaching for Outreach," *American Libraries* 20 (November 1989): 952-954.

7. Yoshi Hendricks, "The Japanese as Library Patrons," *College & Research Libraries News* 52 (April 1991): 221-225.

8. Robert P. Haro, *Developing Library and Information Services for Americans of Hispanic Origin.* (Metuchen, NJ: Scarecrow, 1981), 454.

9. Bureau of the Census, Paul R. Campbell, *Population Projections for States, by Age, Sex, Race, and Hispanic Origin: 1993 to 2020,* by Paul R. Campbell, Current Population Reports, P25-1111. (Washington, DC: GPO, 1994): xvii.

10. Downing, McAdam, and Nichols, *Reaching a Multicultural Student Community,* 14.

11. American Council on Education, Minorities in Higher Education, (Phoenix, AZ: Oryx Press, 1994), 11.

12. V. Scott Solberg, J. Valdez, and P. Villareal, "Social Support, Stress and Hispanic College Adjustments: Test of a Diathesis-Stress Model," *Hispanic Journal of Behavioral Science* 16 (August 1994): 230-239.

13. Haro, 82.

14. Deborah Curry, "Assessing and Evaluating Diversity in the Reference Department," *The Reference Librarian* 38 (1992): 114.

15. Otis A. Chadley, "Addressing Cultural Diversity in Academic and Research Libraries," *College & Research Libraries* (May 1992): 207.

16. Rosemary Ruhig Dumont, L. Buttlear, and W. Canyon, *Multiculturalism in Libraries.* (Westport, CT: Greenwood Press, 1994), 59.

17. Chadley, 207.

18. Kathleen de la Pena McCook and P. Geist, "Diversity Deferred: Where Are the Minority Librarians," *Library Journal* 118 (November 1 1993): 118, 38.

19. Vicki Anders, C. Cook, and R. Pitts, "A Glimpse Into a Crystal Ball: Academic Libraries in the Year 2000," *Wilson Library Bulletin* (October 1992): 39.

20. Texas A&M University-Kingsville, Transculturation Seminar & Syllabus and Calendar. (Kingsville, TX: Department of Sociology, 1994).

21. Downing, 15.

22. Richard Chabrán, "Latino Reference Arrives," *American Libraries* 24, no. 5 (May 1987): 386.

23. James Fish, "Responding to Cultural Diversity: A Library in Transition," *Wilson Library Bulletin* (1992): 66, 34-37.

24. Irene Hoadley, "Guest Editorial: Defining Success," *College & Research Libraries* (1994): 100.

ACCESSING LIBRARY MATERIALS ABOUT MEXICAN AMERICANS

Robert L. Mowery

ABSTRACT

This chapter surveys and evaluates the effectiveness of general and special-ized indexes and resources to assist patrons in finding library materials and information about Mexican Americans. The first section discusses the access that is provided by Library of Congress subject headings, the Library of Congress and Dewey Decimal Classification systems, general periodical indexes, and newspaper indexes. The second section identifies various specialized indexes and reference tools, including the *Chicano Database on CD-ROM*. The third section highlights the specific problem of subject access to the fiction and poetry of individual Chicano authors. The final section offers recommendations for improved access to these collections.

The subject cataloging and periodical indexes used by college and univer-sity libraries in the United States and Canada pose various problems for patrons who are seeking library materials about ethnic and minority groups. Patrons who use Library of Congress (LC) subject headings must cope with the problem of varying entry words; though the words "Asian American(s)," for example, are the entry words in the headings "Asian

American students" and "Asian Americans in business," they are buried in the subdivisions of the headings "American drama—Asian American authors" and "American fiction—Asian American authors." Patrons must use certain dated headings, such as "Afro-Americans" and "Indians of North America." Patrons must also contend with meticulous but cryptic distinctions between subject headings, such as "Afro-Americans," which is used for Blacks born in the United States, and "Blacks—United States," which is used for Blacks from other countries living in the United States.

Patrons may be confused by the fact that different indexing systems use different terms for the same subject. Although *InfoTrac Expanded Academic Index*, for example, has adopted the heading "Native Americans," LC subject headings and *Readers' Guide Abstracts* continue to use the heading "Indians of North America." Patrons may not realize that terminological change makes it difficult to maintain the currency of headings used in indexing systems. While *Readers' Guide Abstracts* refers to African Americans as "Blacks," *Readers' Guide to Periodical Literature* used the heading "Negroes" until 1977.

Although the LC Classification (LCC) and Dewey Decimal Classification (DDC) systems classify works by subject, both systems tend to scatter works about ethnic and minority groups. For example, books about Japanese American art, Japanese American poetry, and Japanese American authors are typically assigned to three or more different class numbers, all of which differ from the class numbers for general books about Japanese Americans. Given the common library practice of shelving material by format, books about an ethnic or minority group are not shelved with videos and other media materials about that group. Periodicals may be shelved in one location, and terminals providing access to electronic resources such as full-text databases, the World Wide Web, and other electronic resources may be housed in yet another location. It is not surprising that many users fail to discover more than a fraction of the resources on ethnic and minority studies available in their libraries.

This chapter focuses on the question of access to library materials and information about Mexican Americans. More than fifty colleges and universities have undergraduate majors in Mexican American or Chicano studies,[1] and a number of these campuses offer graduate programs in these areas. Over 400 campuses have programs in Hispanic American studies or bilingual/bicultural education,[2] while other campuses offer one or more courses on Mexican American life and culture. The syllabi of many contemporary American literature courses include novels and poems by Chicano authors, and many college courses in history, sociology, and other disciplines have sections on Mexican Americans. Reference librarians must be prepared to guide users through the maze of controlled vocabulary and classification systems to relevant information and materials.

GENERAL RESOURCES

Library users can access books, periodical articles, and other materials about Mexican Americans by using such mainstream tools as LC subject headings, the LCC and DDC systems, general periodical indexes, and general newspaper indexes. The LC subject heading "Mexican Americans" may have many topical subdivisions, such as "Mexican Americans–Civil rights," "Mexican Americans–Economic conditions," and "Mexican Americans–Social conditions." "Mexican Americans" is often geographically subdivided, as in the headings "Mexican Americans–California" or "Mexican Americans–Rio Grande Valley." The entry words "Mexican Americans" also occur in phrase headings such as "Mexican Americans and libraries" and "Mexican Americans in motion pictures."

The adjectival form "Mexican American" is used in such headings as "Mexican American architecture," "Mexican American college students," and "Mexican American women." The term "Mexican American" occurs as a subdivision of some headings, such as "American literature–Mexican American authors," and as an inverted heading in other headings, such as "Short stories, Mexican American (Spanish)." Reference librarians may need to help patrons to discover such headings.

The function of Library of Congress subject headings is to help patrons find the works on a single subject, even if the terminology about the subject varies or changes over time. Many works which have been assigned LC subject headings containing the words "Mexican American(s)" have titles containing the terms "Chicano" or "Chicana." LC subject headings do not use these terms, preferring instead the term "Mexican American(s)." For example, a USE reference under the entry "Chicano poets" in *Library of Congress Subject Headings* (*LCSH*) directs readers to the heading "Mexican American poets," while a USE reference under the entry "Chicano poetry (English)" directs users to "American poetry–Mexican American authors."[3] Online catalogs which support keyword searches will naturally support searches for titles containing "Chicano" or "Chicana."

Material about Mexican Americans often appears in works that have been assigned subject headings which do not contain the words "Mexican American(s)." Relevant material may appear, for example, in general works about Hispanic Americans. Such works are often assigned headings like "Hispanic American art" or "Hispanic Americans—Suffrage" that contain the term "Hispanic American(s)," a term used by LC to refer to United States citizens of Latin American descent.[4] LC subject headings do not employ the term "Latinos." Material about Mexican Americans may also appear in works assigned such general headings as "American literature—Minority authors," "Education, Bilingual" or "Multicultural education." Reference librarians may need to suggest the potential relevance of such headings to persons searching for material about Mexican Americans.

Many librarians are unaware of the fact that there is a Spanish language subject heading list called *Bilindex. Bilindex* subject headings, published by the California Spanish Language Data Base in 1984 with supplements in 1986 and 1992,[5] provide Spanish equivalents of English language LC subject headings. Library of Congress cataloging does not include *Bilindex* headings, but many public libraries that serve Spanish-speaking populations in Florida, the Southwest, California, and Illinois add them to their cataloging records.[6] An academic library that has been especially active in adding *Bilindex* headings to cataloging records is the library of Texas A&M University—Kingsville. *Bilindex* headings provide a helpful alternative for library patrons who are more comfortable using Spanish than English subject headings.[7] Even though many libraries are interested in providing this type of access, *Bilindex* headings appear in only a fraction of cataloging records.

Many articles about Mexican Americans can be found using general indexes such as *Readers' Guide Abstracts, Education Index,* and *Social Sciences Index.* In these indexes the adjectival term "Mexican American" provides the entry words for headings like "Mexican American literature" and "Mexican American women," while the phrase "Mexican Americans" provides the entry words for headings like "Mexican Americans—Education" and "Mexican Americans—Political activities." *Readers' Guide Abstracts* and *Social Sciences Index* use the heading "Mexicans—United States" to refer to Mexicans in the United States. This heading is apparently equivalent to the heading "Mexicans in the United States" in the *Education Index.* The term "Mexican American" occurs in a few inverted headings like "Art, Mexican American." Librarians may need to remind patrons that material about Mexican Americans may be included in articles indexed under the broader heading "Hispanic American(s)." Cross references in these indexes direct users from headings beginning with the words "Chicanos" and "Latinos" to headings containing the terms "Mexican American(s)" and "Hispanic American(s)," respectively.

The words "Mexican American(s)" appear in the subject headings of various other periodical indexes. *InfoTrac Expanded Academic Index* has several dozen headings that begin with the plural term "Mexican Americans," like "Mexican Americans–employment" and "Mexican Americans–ethnic identity," and a shorter list of headings that begin with the adjectival form "Mexican American," like "Mexican American art" and "Mexican American leadership." This index also uses various subdivisions of the phrase heading "Mexicans in the United States" and various broader headings containing the term "Hispanic American(s)." Although many headings in *PAIS International* also contain the words "Mexican American(s)," the broader term in this index is not "Hispanic American(s)" but "Spanish American(s)." Besides the descriptor "Mexican Americans," the *Thesaurus of ERIC Descriptors* lists the broader descriptors "Spanish Americans," "Spanish Speaking," and "Hispanic Americans."[8]

Many newspaper indexes use the heading "Hispanic Americans" rather than specific headings like "Mexican Americans" or "Cuban Americans." The *Chicago Tribune Index*, the *Los Angeles Times Index*, *The Wall Street Journal Index*, and *The Washington Post Index* all contain "See" references which direct users from the headings "Mexican Americans," "Chicanos," and "Latinos" to the heading "Hispanic Americans." *NewsBank Index* also refers users from "Chicanos" and "Mexican Americans" to "Hispanic Americans," though the latter heading has the subdivision "Mexicans." *The New York Times Index*, however, avoids the heading "Hispanic Americans," preferring instead the heading "Spanish-Speaking Groups (US)." The heading "Mexican-Americans" appears in this index mainly in cross-references to such general headings as "Citizenship," "Education and Schools," and "Music."

Although the terms "Latinos," "Mexican Americans," and "Chicanos" do not occur as headings in these newspaper indexes, they regularly appear on the pages of these and other newspapers. Patrons who search the full texts of newspapers electronically can search by any of these terms. The term "Latinos" occurs more frequently than "Chicanos" or "Mexican Americans" in most of these papers. The term "Chicanos" occurs least frequently; it tends to be restricted to direct quotations and proper names, such as "National Chicano Council on Higher Education." Despite the prominence of the term "Hispanic Americans" as a subject heading in many newspaper indexes, this term occurs relatively infrequently on the pages of most of these newspapers.

The previous paragraphs have identified two distinct patterns. Although the term "Mexican Americans" appears in many LC subject headings, many headings in periodical indexes, and the pages of many newspapers, the broader term "Hispanic Americans" appears instead of more specific terms like "Mexican Americans" and "Cuban Americans" in many newspaper indexes. Reference librarians may need to assist users in making this terminological transition when moving from one type of index to another.

Librarians should also consider the access to library materials about Mexican Americans that is provided by the LCC and DDC systems. The LCC system provides the number E184 for minority groups, defined as "Elements in the population of the United States," and specific minority and ethnic groups are classed in alphabetical order within this number. Catalogers have classed many works about Mexican Americans in E184.M5 (the LCC number for Mexicans in the U.S. population) and many works about Hispanic Americans in E184.S75 (the LCC number for Spanish Americans in the U.S. population). Patrons who wish to browse the library shelves for materials about Mexican Americans and Hispanic Americans can be directed to these class numbers. But librarians need to caution patrons that many works about Mexican Americans in the context of other subjects have been classed in LCC numbers for those subjects, such as LC2680-2688 (education of Mexican Americans and Mexicans in the United States), N6538.M4 (Mexican American art), and Z1361.M4 (bibliography of Mexicans in the United States).

The Dewey Decimal system identifies ethnic or minority populations by appending a suffix for the specific group to the base number for the topic. For example, many books about Mexican Americans as an ethnic group are classified under the base number 305.8 (racial, ethnic, national groups), with the suffix −6872073 for Mexican Americans. But many works about Mexican Americans and other groups are scattered throughout other DDC numbers.

SPECIALIZED RESOURCES

The next step in a comprehensive search for Mexican American resources is to use more specialized finding aids. The outstanding bibliographic database covering Mexican Americans and Mexicans residing in the United States is the *Chicano Database on CD-ROM*.[9] Available since 1990, this database contains more than 45,000 entries dating from 1967 to the present.

Most of this database's entries have appeared in print in the *Chicano Periodical Index*, the *Chicano Index*, or one of the bibliographies published by the Berkeley Chicano Studies Library. The first two volumes of the *Chicano Periodical Index* covered twenty-three periodicals from 1967 to 1981, including such varied titles as *El Grito, Journal of Mexican American History*, and *Hispanic Business*. From 1982 to 1988 this index also selectively covered about 500 mainstream periodicals. The adoption of the name *Chicano Index* in 1989 signaled a broadening of the coverage to include not only periodical articles but also books, reports, articles in anthologies, and other types of material.

The *Chicano Database on CD-ROM* also contains the bibliographic data published in *Arte Chicano: A Comprehensive Annotated Bibliography of Chicano Art, 1965-1981*,[10] *Chicano Anthology Index: A Comprehensive Author, Title, and Subject Index to Chicano Anthologies, 1965-1987*,[11] and *The Chicana Studies Index: Twenty Years of Gender Research 1971-1991*.[12] The CD-ROM also contains the *Latinos and AIDS* database created at UCLA. It is anticipated that future editions will include the *Spanish Speaking Mental Health Database* developed at UCLA. The *Chicano Database on CD-ROM* can be searched by author, title, journal name, and various other access points, including not only controlled subject headings but also global keywords.

Although the *Hispanic American Periodical Index* (*HAPI*), published by the UCLA Latin American Center, focuses on periodical literature on Latin America, it indexes some articles on Hispanics in the United States. Relevant material appears under such headings as "Mexican Americans," "Mexican American literature," "Mexican-American border region" and "Hispanic Americans (U.S.)." *HAPI* is one of the indexes included in the *Latin American Studies* CD-ROM, which also includes the index of books from the Benson Latin American Collection at the University of Texas at Austin.

Several specialized newspaper indexes should be noted. The *News Monitoring Service* indexed articles about the Latino community that appeared in major United States newspapers from 1972 to 1980. *Chicanos in the Times* indexed articles about Chicanos in the *Los Angeles Times* from July 1985 to December 1986, and *Chicanos in These Times* covered 1987 to 1990. The *Ethnic NewsWatch* CD-ROM, which supports searches in either English or Spanish, provides full texts of articles in various ethnic and minority newspapers, including *La Opinion* (Los Angeles), *El Bohemio News* (San Francisco) and *El Sol de Texas* (Dallas).

The databases of the National Center for Bilingual Education (NCBE) provide information about the education of linguistically and culturally diverse students in United States public schools. Many entries focus on the education of Mexican Americans and other Latinos. The NCBE Bibliographic Database supplies bibliographic citations and abstracts of periodical articles, ERIC documents, and other material on this topic. The NCBE Resources Database offers profiles of research centers, professional associations, clearinghouses, and other organizations that provide services. A third database, the NCBE Publishers Database, identifies organizations involved with the development, publication, and distribution of material for linguistically and culturally diverse students. All of these NCBE databases can be accessed on the Internet. The Internet also provides access to the catalogs of the excellent Chicano studies and Mexican American studies collections at the University of Texas at Austin, Arizona State University, and campuses of the University of California.

Many reference books provide bibliographic and other information concerning Mexican Americans. Two specialized bibliographies deserving note are *Spanish-Language Reference Books: An Annotated Bibliography*[13] and *Latinos in the United States: Social, Economic and Political Aspects: A Bibliography*.[14] The subtitle of the *Hispanic Resource Directory, 1992-1994: A Comprehensive Guide to Over 6,000 National, Regional and Local Organizations, Associations, Agencies, Programs and Media Pertaining to Hispanic Americans*[15] indicates its scope. A more recently published resource is the third edition of *Hispanic Americans Information Directory*.[16] The *Statistical Record of Hispanic Americans*[17] offers more than 900 tables of data gathered from federal and other sources, while the more narrowly focused *Hispanic Databook of U.S. Cities and Counties*[18] reports 1990 census data. The *Hispanic-American Almanac: A Reference Work on Hispanics in the United States*[19] has chapters on twenty-five topics, including history, music, and sports.

Biographical and bibliographical information concerning Chicano writers can be found in *Chicano Literature: A Reader's Encyclopedia,*[20] *Chicano Writers: First Series,*[21] *Chicano Writers: Second Series,*[22] and *Hispanic Writers: A Selection of Sketches from Contemporary Authors.*[23] The handsome four-volume *Handbook of Hispanic Cultures in the United States* provides separate volumes with the subtitles *Literature and Art,*[24] *Anthropology,*[25] *History,*[26] and *Sociology.*[27]

CHICANO LITERATURE

Subject access to the fiction and poetry of individual Chicano authors represents a special problem. In a recent study, only thirty-six of 104 cataloging records for the novels and short stories of Chicano authors have LC subject headings that contain the term "Mexican American(s)," and only twenty-seven of seventy records for the poetry of Chicano authors have such headings. In contrast, many cataloging records for the anthologies and critical studies of Chicano literature have subject headings like "Mexican American women—Literary collections" and "Mexican American fiction (Spanish)—History and criticism." Many of these records also have headings like "American literature—Mexican American authors" or "Short stories, American—Mexican American authors."[28]

Some cataloging records for the fiction of individual Chicano authors have *Bilindex* headings like "Mexicano-americanos—Nuevo México—Novela" and "Cuentos estadounidenses—Autores mexicano-americanos," and some of the records for the poetry of these authors have headings containing "mexicano-americanos." Some of the records for collections and critical works have *Bilindex* headings like "Mexicano-americanos—Colecciónes literarias," and some have headings like "Literatura estadounidense—Autores mexicano-americanos," which contain the subdivision "Autores mexicano-americanos." But most cataloging records for both primary and secondary works of Chicano literature do not have *Bilindex* headings.

Anthologies and critical works tend to be classed in a series of LCC subject numbers scattered throughout subclass PS, "American literature," including PS153.M4 (history of Mexican American literature), PS508.M4 (collections of literature by Mexican Americans), and PS591.M49 (collections of poetry by Mexican Americans). Nowhere in subclass PS is there a single number or range of numbers for Mexican American literature. Literature by Mexican Americans in the Spanish language is classed under subclass **PQ**, "Spanish literature," while bibliographies of Mexican American literature are classed in Z1229.M48. The browser who discovers one of these class numbers is not likely to stumble upon the others.

Although anthologies of and critical works about Mexican American literature have their own LCC numbers, the works of individual Chicano authors do not have numbers which identify them as Chicano authors.. Works of individual Chicano authors who write in English or English and Spanish are assigned LCC numbers for authors of the English literature of the United States, where they are intermixed with the works of other United States authors. On the other hand, many Spanish language works of individual Chicano authors are classed with the Spanish language works of Cuban Americans and other Hispanic authors of the United States and Canada. When classed in this manner, the works of individual Chicano authors become an invisible collection scattered throughout the literature shelves. Indeed, the LCC system creates invisible collections of all ethnic and minority authors.

Most of the DDC numbers assigned to works of Chicano literature are general literature numbers which fail to associate these works with Chicano literature. Some English language anthologies and critical studies have been assigned DDC numbers like 810.986872073 that conclude with the distinctive seven-digit sequence −6872073 for Mexicans in the United States. However, many other anthologies and critical works have been given DDC numbers that are not explicitly associated with Mexican Americans. Most works of individual Chicano authors writing in English or English and Spanish have been assigned numbers for American literature in English, like 813.54, while works of individual Mexican American authors writing in Spanish are classed with Spanish literature. Such numbers obviously fail to identify these works as the works of Mexican American authors.

The Chicano Studies Library of the University of California at Berkeley has avoided many problems inherent in the LCC and DDC systems by creating an LCC subclass PX, which classes the English, Spanish, and English and Spanish works of individual Chicano authors in a single subclass reserved for Chicano literature. This subclass enables the staff of this library to give a direct answer to the question, "Where is your Chicano literature shelved?" Unfortunately, the PX schedules have never been published or used by other libraries. Other reference librarians who are determined to give visibility to their invisible collections of Chicano literature need to create library guides that identify and highlight the authors in their collections.

CONCLUSION

Reference librarians need to respond in a proactive manner to the problems faced by patrons who use LC subject headings and the headings in periodical and newspaper indexes to access materials about Mexican Americans. Besides providing personal assistance to patrons, reference librarians should create library pathfinders which identify the major relevant subject headings in each searching system, including important headings whose entry words are not "Mexican American(s)." These pathfinders should also identify key specialized resources available in the library.

Keyword searching in online catalogs and other databases helps to overcome some of the problems caused by the inadequacies of subject heading systems, because it enables patrons to employ their own terminology, such as "Chicanos," during searches. However, keyword searching has its limitations. Patrons who search only by keywords will fail to retrieve a wealth of relevant material available in their libraries.

LC subject headings fail to identify more than a fraction of the fiction and poetry of Chicano authors as works of Chicano literature, and both the LCC and DDC systems fail to provide satisfactory answers to the question, "Where is your Chicano literature shelved?" Reference librarians can actively respond to these needs by creating guides to their Chicano literature holdings.

Although this chapter has focused on questions of access to library materials about Mexican Americans, the greatest need in some libraries may be the need to develop and strengthen the collection of these materials. A book in the hand may be worth more to many patrons than a list of books and articles that can be obtained through interlibrary loan.

NOTES

1. James A. Jaramillo, "Current Mexican-American and Chicano Studies Undergraduate College Programs in the United States," *ERIC document ED380034* (1995).

2. Alan Edward Schorr, *Hispanic Resource Directory, 1992-1994: A Comprehensive Guide to Over 6,000 National, Regional and Local Organizations, Associations, Agencies, Programs and Media Pertaining to Hispanic Americans* (Juneau, AK: Denali Press, 1991), 131-148.

3. U.S. Library of Congress, Cataloging Policy and Support Office, Collections Services. *Library of Congress Subject Headings*, 18th ed., 4 vols. (Washington, DC: Library of Congress, Cataloging Distribution Service, 1995), 1:915.

4. Ibid, 2:2339.

5. *Bilindex: A Bilingual Spanish-English Subject Heading List: Spanish Equivalents to Library of Congress Subject Headings* (Oakland, CA: California Spanish Language Data Base, 1984). The supplements have the subtitles *Supplement I 1985-1986* (Berkeley, CA: Floricanto Press, 1986) and *Supplement II 1987-1990* (Encino, CA: Floricanto Press, 1992).

6. Robert L. Mowery, "Spanish Subject Headings in ILLINET Online," *Illinois Libraries* 77 (1995): 32-34.

7. Marielena Fina, "The Role of Subject Headings in Access to Information: The Experience of One Spanish-speaking Patron," *Cataloging & Classification Quarterly* 17 (1993): 267-274.

8. *Thesaurus of ERIC Descriptors*, 13th ed. (Phoenix: Oryx, 1995).

9. *Chicano Database on CD-ROM* (Berkeley, CA: Chicano Studies Library Publications Unit of the University of California, 1990-).

10. Shifra M. Goldman and Tomas Ybarra-Frausto, eds., *Arte Chicano: A Comprehensive Annotated Bibliography of Chicano Art, 1965-1981*, Chicano Studies Library Publications Series, no. 11 (Berkeley, CA: Chicano Studies Library Publications Unit, University of California at Berkeley, 1985).

11. Francisco García-Ayvens, *Chicano Anthology Index: A Comprehensive Author, Title, and Subject Index to Chicano Anthologies, 1965-1987*, Chicano Studies Library Publications Series, no. 13 (Berkeley, CA: Chicano Studies Library Publications Unit, University of California at Berkeley, 1990).

12. Bibliotecas para la Gente, Reference Committee, comp., *The Chicana Studies Index: Twenty Years of Gender Research 1971-1991*, Chicano Studies Library Publications Series, no. 18 (Berkeley, CA: Chicano Studies Library Publications Unit, University of California at Berkeley, 1992).

13. Bibliotecas para la Gente, Reference Committee, comp., *Spanish-Language Reference Books: An Annotated Bibliography*, Chicano Studies Library Publications Series, no. 15 (Berkeley, CA: Chicano Studies Library Publications Unit, University of California at Berkeley, 1989).

14. Joan Nordquist, *Latinos in the United States: Social, Economic and Political Aspects: A Bibliography* (Santa Cruz, CA: Reference and Research Services, 1994).

15. See note 2.

16. Charles B. Montney, ed., *Hispanic Americans Information Directory*, 3rd ed. (Detroit: Gale Research, 1994).

17. Marlita A. Reddy, ed., *Statistical Record of Hispanic Americans* (Detroit, Washington, London: Gale Research, 1993).

18. *Hispanic Databook of U.S. Cities and Counties* (Milpitas, CA: Toucan Valley Publications, 1994).

19. Nicolás Kanellos, *The Hispanic-American Almanac: A Reference Work on Hispanics in the United States* (Detroit, Washington, London: Gale Research, 1993).

20. Julio A. Martínez and Francisco A. Lomelí, eds., *Chicano Literature: A Reader's Encyclopedia* (Westport, CT: Greenwood, 1985).

21.   Francisco A. Lomelí and Carl R. Shirley, eds., *Chicano Writers: First Series*, Dictionary of Literary Biography, vol. 82 (Detroit: Gale Research, 1989).

22.   Francisco A. Lomelí and Carl R. Shirley, ed., *Chicano Writers: Second Series*, Dictionary of Literary Biography, vol. 122 (Detroit: Gale Research, 1992).

23.   Bryan Ryan, ed., *Hispanic Writers: A Selection of Sketches from Contemporary Authors* (Detroit: Gale Research, 1991).

24.   Francisco A. Lomelí, ed., *Handbook of Hispanic Cultures in the United States: Literature and Art* (Houston: Arte Público Press; Madrid: Instituto de Cooperación Iberoamericana, 1993).

25.   Thomas Weaver, ed., *Handbook of Hispanic Cultures in the United States: Anthropology* (Houston: Arte Público Press; Madrid: Instituto de Cooperación Iberoamericana, 1994).

26.   Alfredo Jiménez, ed., *Handbook of Hispanic Cultures in the United States: History* (Houston: Arte Público Press; Madrid: Instituto de Cooperación Iberoamericana, 1994).

27.   Félix Padilla, ed., *Handbook of Hispanic Cultures in the United States: Sociology* (Houston: Arte Público Press; Madrid: Instituto de Cooperación Iberoamericana, 1994).

28.   For a detailed discussion of the data, see Robert L. Mowery, "Subject Cataloging of Chicano Literature," *Library Resources & Technical Services* 39 (1995): 229-237.

SPECIAL STUDENTS, SPECIAL NEEDS, SPECIAL REFERENCE:
LIBRARY RESPONSE TO THE NEEDS OF STUDENTS IN THE RONALD E. MCNAIR CENTRAL ACHIEVERS PROGRAM

Mollie D. Lawson

ABSTRACT

The McNair Central Achievers Program (McCAP) at Central Missouri State University is one of ninety-six nationwide which has been funded through federal grants. Designed to encourage lower-income, first generation college students with academic promise to continue their education through to the doctoral level, an important component of the program is to assure the information literacy of each scholar. From the program's inaugural year at Central in 1991, members of the library faculty have actively participated by planning and conducting a series of seminars relevant to information literacy, attending group meetings with faculty departmental mentors and research/teaching mentors, and serving as library mentors for the individual scholars. As a result, a program of individualized reference service has been developed which is tailored to the research needs of each McNair scholar. Because many of the McNair scholars are also nontraditional students (ethnic minorities, disabled, older than age

twenty-four, or women), this model appears to be very effective in assisting
disadvantaged students to become successful library users.

INTRODUCTION

The population of today's college and university campuses is not as
homogeneous as it was in the 1960s. In the 1990s, it may be difficult to
describe what is the typical college student. Traditional college students
between the ages of eighteen and twenty-two are joined by nontraditional
students in their thirties and forties and even fifties. Enrollment projections suggest that the largest number of students during the next decade
will be those over the age of twenty-four and that most will be enrolled as
part-time students. Some will be returning to school and others will be
looking for opportunities to change careers.[1]

Female students enrolled in higher education increased by twenty-five
percent from 1982 to 1992. The increase in male students for the same
time period was 8 percent. This indicates that the number of female students is growing more quickly than the number of male students. The
enrollment of students twenty-five years old and over increased by 34 percent between 1980 and 1990. The numbers of students enrolling under
age twenty-five increased by only 3 percent. The National Center for Education Statistics projects that the rise in the number of persons over age
twenty-five enrolling in higher education between 1990 and 1993 will be
14 percent with a corresponding increase of 6 percent among those
under twenty-five.[2]

The numbers of minorities in American higher education is also
increasing. In 1992 the percentage of all minorities was 22.5 percent, an
increase from 15.7 percent in 1976. African-American students
accounted for 9.9 percent of the students in higher education in 1992.[3]
There are more women students than men, more disabled students than
in the past, and more people of varied racial and ethnic backgrounds
enrolled in higher education in the 1990s. Rebecca R. Martin's research
shows an increase in the number of multicultural students enrolled in colleges and universities following ten years of declining enrollments for
multicultural persons. Projections for multicultural students who graduate from high school indicate an anticipated increase from 22 percent in
1986 to 28 percent in 1995. However, the number of multicultural students who graduate from college is very low, especially in graduate education.[4]

At Central Missouri State University, the student population is still composed of a nearly homogenous group of males and females. In the fall of 1995 there were 5,023 men and 5,928 women enrolled in all classes including part-time, evening, and graduate classes. Of the estimated 9,439 undergraduates enrolled, 21 percent are over the age of twenty-four years which indicates a fair number of nontraditional students.[5]

Minorities comprise a small segment of Central Missouri State's student population. African-Americans made up the largest minority population with 737 students. Other minority populations include 109 Hispanic, 100 Asian/Pacific Islander, and 37 Native American. International students totaled 380 of the 10,951 total enrollment in the fall of 1995.[6] The number of disabled students was not officially recorded, but an unofficial estimate from the university's Office of Accessibility Services indicated that approximately 120 students made use of their services during the fall of 1995.[7]

Interest in the retention of college students is an important issue on college campuses. As funding for higher education becomes more competitive, institutions of higher learning are operating less like ivory towers and more like businesses. In order for colleges and universities to survive, it is critical that they attract and retain successful college students. Programs are being designed to encourage all students to remain in school and are directed, in some cases, toward students who have academic promise despite some inherent disadvantages that might interfere with their success.

Special programs and support services, including services from the library, have been identified as important to the educational success of multicultural students. There is a growing need for individuals to know how to find information necessary for success in college. It is rare, however, for librarians to be consulted as strategies are planned to address the needs of nontraditional students.[8] Librarians need to address these issues: What are libraries doing to meet the need for information literacy among multicultural clientele? How must the delivery of reference service change in order to prepare these students adequately?

FIRST GENERATION COLLEGE STUDENTS

In addition to the groups mentioned before, first-generation college students also form a large pool of the students enrolled in higher education.

These students, whose parents have not completed a bachelor's degree, bring with them characteristics which create unique challenges for them in their quest for a college education. Community colleges were the first institutions to recognize the first-generation college students as a student population with special needs. They actively recruit these individuals and work to develop mechanisms that increase students' chances for completion of their degree programs. Four-year colleges and universities have also acknowledged the influx of first-generation, lower-income, and non-traditional college students and their impact on higher education. At Central, an estimated 20 percent of all students are first-generation and low-income college students.[9] Although no official count of first-generation college students is maintained by the university, the *CMSU Facts 1995* reported that 8,465 students, or nearly 80 percent of the total student enrollment, received some form of financial aid.[10] It can be assumed that there are many first-generation college students who have academic promise and who are in need of various types of assistance in order to maximize their potential. Once these academically talented students have achieved an undergraduate degree, it is imperative that the best and the brightest be recognized and encouraged to pursue postgraduate education.

It is a commonly held opinion that ethnic minorities and the disabled are underrepresented in graduate education. In 1992, there were 2,092,000 graduate students who indicated they were white, whereas only 143,000 indicated they were black, and 62,000 identified themselves as Hispanic.[11] All undergraduate and graduate disabled students in 1986 amounted to only 1,319,229, or approximately 10.5 percent of the total student enrollment for that year.[12] Some four-year colleges and universities focus on programs that will help these students to earn a bachelor's degree and prepare for additional graduate studies.

A large majority of first-generation college students are members of working class families or ethnic minorities, and many are women. Frequently, these students are inadequately prepared for college study and may face more economic difficulties than students whose family members have earned college degrees. Their families and friends may not be supportive in their efforts to achieve a college education. They may confront an impersonal and bureaucratic environment which does little to encourage them to complete their undergraduate degrees, let alone encourage them to continue in graduate school. Studies have indicated that the level of integration of students within the educational institution is a more critical factor to their success and continued education than their ethnic or socioeconomic backgrounds. Alexander Astin states that "Student-faculty interaction has a stronger relationship to student satisfaction with the college experience than has any other involvement variable..."[13]

A variety of programs have been established to facilitate the integration of these nontraditional students into higher education. Occasionally, the role of the library and the librarian has been identified as an important component in the equation for retention of students and their successful completion of degree programs. Julia Boucher and Keith Lance identified three roles that libraries play in education. First is the teaching of information skills and technologies. Second, libraries provide access to information and ideas unimpeded by social, cultural, and economic constraints. Finally, libraries assist in preparing individuals to be lifelong learners and productive employees.[14] As more emphasis is placed on the expectation that students are able to continue to grow and learn once a degree is completed, the ability of the individual to learn independently and to find and evaluate information has become more important than ever.

REFERENCE SERVICE FOR SPECIAL STUDENTS

Around 1876, at about the same time as the beginning of the American Library Association, formalized reference service also was introduced. Librarians undertook the role of educator, not only that of collectors and storers of books, but as facilitators of their use as well.[15] Reference service was defined in 1915 by William W. Bishop as "the service rendered by a librarian in aid of some sort of study....It is in aid of research, but it is not research itself."[16] Hannelore B. Rader defined three levels of reference service: "personal assistance to users with information needs, formal and informal library use instruction designed to provide guidance and direction in pursuit of information, and indirect reference service which provides access to information and bibliographic sources through interlibrary loan and interagency cooperation."[17]

The standard brief reference encounter takes place between a librarian and a patron who know each other slightly, if at all. The library setting encourages a brief and impersonal exchange during which the patron obtains the information she sought. However, research indicates that most people prefer more personal reference service.[18] Joan C. Durrance's research with a group of citizen leaders as public library users indicates that these users were five times more likely to believe that the library was a valuable resource, two times more likely to have a successful quest for information, and five times more likely to be a frequent library client when they knew the name of the librarian.[19]

Like the public library users in Durrance's study, students are rarely satisfied by a brief reference encounter with an anonymous librarian. Students are required to do research, which demands detailed analysis of the problem and a thorough literature search. Students are then required to produce a paper that demonstrates that they have grasped the concepts of the research. Bergen concluded that the personal interaction also led to the "increase of the professional visibility of the librarian as an individual," resulting in greater job satisfaction for the librarian.[20]

What is the optimum method for providing reference assistance as well as information literacy instruction to these special groups of students? A trend which began in the 1960s was experimentation with individualized reference service. The decade of the 1960s was a time of great change on college and university campuses. The heterogenous groups seeking higher education dramatically illustrated the different needs of learners and researchers. Because library users had differing levels of expertise in using library resources and different styles of learning, many librarians implemented an individualized approach to teaching library skills. For example, the Personalized Library User Service at State University of New York at Oswego aimed at not just handing out information, but demonstrating library methods which could be used for other research needs.[21] A number of other academic libraries have established an individualized instruction model to assist with research for term papers. Various term paper assistance programs, frequently called term paper clinics or tutorials, have been described in library literature. Students who have an immediate need for specific, detailed, and in-depth information are most likely to appreciate this type of service.

First-generation college students who may be at a disadvantage for academic success have been identified as a group with special educational and research assistance needs. In research conducted with graduate students at Bowling Green State University in Ohio, Marilyn Parrish concluded that while faculty members may assume graduate students learned how to perform research in their undergraduate degree programs, in actuality, most students have difficulty with each phase of the research process. Many received no basic library orientation as undergraduates.

Even those with better research skills face the common problems of managing their time and accessing materials that are cross-disciplinary.[22]

MCNAIR CENTRAL ACHIEVERS PROGRAM

In an effort to channel academically talented first-generation college students into graduate education, Congress established the national Ronald E. McNair Post-Baccalaureate Achievement Program in 1989. The stated purpose of this program is "to prepare first-generation, low-income college students and students from groups underrepresented in graduate education for doctoral study."[23] By 1995, there were ninety-six programs nationwide.

Central Missouri State University has participated in the McNair program since November 1991. The fourth group of McNair Central Achievers Program (McCAP) scholars was selected in the spring of 1995. The goal of the original program was to identify at least twenty Central undergraduate students, preferably juniors or seniors, with at least two-thirds qualifying as first-generation and low-income students and the remaining one-third in the category of groups underrepresented in graduate education. The twenty students are required to have a minimum of 2.5 grade point average, a 3.0 grade point average or above preferred, and must seriously plan to pursue graduate studies at the doctoral level. Each student must be recommended by at least one faculty member who attests to the potential of that individual to succeed in post-baccalaureate graduate studies. The size of the groups of participants has grown from twenty-one in the first class in 1992 to the most recent group of twenty-seven in 1995.

Once selected, students participate in a series of workshops which cover the categories of foundations for graduate study, general information seminars, and library skills seminars. In the foundations portion of the curriculum, students take diagnostic tests to determine their academic strengths. They are tutored in high-risk courses and, when necessary, referred to specific classes and support services. The general information seminars include sessions on financial aid available for graduate study, how to prepare a quality dossier or resume for the application to graduate school, and field trips to visit campuses of other nearby institutions of higher learning.

Mentors are important in the McNair program at Central. Mentoring has been described as a tested and tried strategy for assisting students through a research experience. The existing talents of students are nurtured and expanded via the mentoring process.[24] At Central, each McNair Achiever is assigned three faculty mentors. One faculty mentor is from the department of the student's major and assists the student with the administrative portions of the program. A second faculty member is assigned to shepherd the student through the research activities of the program, particularly if the student applies for and receives a summer internship in the program.

With the acknowledgement that these students require special mentoring in the subject areas to enhance their chances for success, came the recognition that information literacy was imperative. Therefore, the third faculty mentor is a librarian who works with the student to ensure that a degree of information literacy is attained. This librarian may be the bibliographer/liaison for the department in which the student is pursuing a major, or may have special expertise in the literature of the subject to be researched by the student. In 1992, seven library faculty members were assigned as McCAP library mentors. By 1995 eleven librarians participated in the program.

LIBRARY INSTRUCTION IN MCCAP

Included in the group sessions for all McCAP scholars are workshops on "Introduction to Research" and "Academic Writing" mentioned previously as the Foundations sessions. In the information seminars, students are exposed to methods for educational planning, resources for financial aid for graduate studies, information regarding prospective graduate schools, and motivational discussions such as "Overcoming Barriers to Success" as well as the visits to other campuses.

The final formal segment is the Library Skills Seminar at which point faculty members from Library Services begin to work with the students. A coordinator, along with the other library mentors, conducts a series of three workshops in which basic library research skills are taught. Each seminar focuses on specific research tools, but includes general information as well.

The purpose of the first session, "Library Reference Resources and Indexes," is to review basic printed reference sources and indexes with the students, as well as assess their existing library research skills. In the second seminar, "Computerized Library Resources," students are exposed to several CD-ROM databases and other electronic research tools. Prior to the final classroom session, the students had to have practiced some of the skills learned in previous sessions, such as using reference materials, print indexes, and CD-ROM databases. The third and final seminar, "Information Literacy in a Subject Discipline," is designed to give the students an understanding of the literature and research tools specific to their subject areas.

With this initial instruction completed, each McCAP scholar is expected to work directly with his library mentor who determines whether the student has a basic understanding of library research. The completed assignments are evaluated by the individual mentors. In cases where the McCAP student appears to be experiencing difficulty, the library mentor works with the student, reviewing the information presented in the seminars and providing remedial instruction where needed. The library's component of the program applies a dual approach of group instruction for general research information and assistance to students on a one-on-one basis.

SUMMER RESEARCH INTERNSHIPS

The second major component of the McCAP program involves a competition among the McCAP scholars for summer research internships. The purpose of the internships is to provide an opportunity for students to carry out a specific research project under the guidance of the research mentor. Research proposals are evaluated by the directors of the McCAP program, and sixteen receive funding for their projects. A large portion of the funding for the McNair program is allocated for stipends for the students internships. Each student receives $2,400 for the summer plus an allowance for photocopying, research or laboratory materials, and other research-related expenses. Additional funds are set aside to allow students to attend conferences and present the results of their research. To date, sixty-eight summer research internships have been awarded for a total of $163,200.00. The interns received funding of $10,800 for supplies and $19,600.00 for travel to conferences.[25]

Working with the research mentor, each student selects a topic for research. The topics of research projects of past McCAP scholars have included such diverse subjects as the effect of junk food on the diet of rats, a study of the eating habits of young college women to identify potential candidates for eating disorders, and research into shopping habits in a high-crime city neighborhood. Other students have researched the success of rehabilitation programs among nurses with chemical dependencies, the degree of client satisfaction with home health nursing, and the characteristics of people who are victims of spousal abuse. The research mentor works closely with each student in developing a research plan and in monitoring the actual work.

The first task of the McCAP scholar is to prepare a research proposal which includes a bibliography of published background information on the topic. The work of the library mentor figures prominently at this stage as each student conducts a literature review to determine what information already exists on the chosen topic. In most cases, the librarian begins with an in-depth reference interview with the McCAP student to determine what the student expects to discover in the course of the proposed research. Some students already have an idea for a research topic before they attend the library skills seminars. In these cases, the library exercises are applied to the chosen topic. The student prepares a substantial bibliography on the research topic as a portion of the research skills learning process. This is encouraged by the library mentors, who believe that exercises which can be incorporated into chosen topics are more likely to be meaningful learning experiences than generic assignments. The library mentor meets with both the student and the research mentor to plan a strategy for background research needed for the topic. This interaction between library and academic department faculty members fosters a feeling of partnership which benefits the student.

The library mentor role in the McCAP program parallels Rader's view that the library user can be aided more effectively when the librarian adopts an active teaching role.[26] The reference role of the library mentor is to explore the literature of the research topic with the student. Depending upon the skills of the student, the library mentor advises and directs the student to possible resources. Because in all cases the primary focus is to teach the student how to perform research, the library mentor is charged to assure that the student is information literate.

The library mentors choose how they approach the instruction for each student. One approach that has worked well for those students who have poorer research skills is to work one-on-one with the student in locating finding aids pertinent to the subject matter. The student is directed to any listings of periodical literature that subject bibliographers have prepared for the discipline and a hands-on session with the student at CD-ROM workstations using appropriate indexing and abstracting tools completes the method of instruction.

As the student becomes more comfortable with the use of appropriate library resources, the mentor performs a less direct role and becomes a reviewer of the results. If a McCAP scholar experiences difficulty in locating information, the library mentor meets with the student to analyze the library research that the student has accomplished and provides further guidance. Before the student proceeds with the original research project with the research mentor, his bibliography of resources is evaluated by the library mentor. If either the library mentor or the research mentor believes further background research is needed, she directs the McCAP scholar towards additional sources of information.

Throughout the process good information-finding skills are taught, including the ability to locate relevant information from the resources owned by the library and in identifying sources of information that may be available from another library. Rader pointed out in 1980 that it would be mandatory for reference librarians to teach users about new developments such as computer literature searching and on-line catalogs in order for them to be able to know how to obtain information. The teaching component of reference service would become the most highly developed function of the library's services.[27]

Besides local resources, the library mentor teaches the student to navigate the Internet and find information at remote sites that are appropriate for her topic. Each McCAP scholar receives an E-mail account through the university and is encouraged to use it for communication with the three mentors and McCAP office personnel. The library mentor assumes responsibility for teaching the student about E-mail.

Over the course of their three-month research period, McCAP scholars are encouraged to continue working with their library mentors, who schedule regular meeting times and use E-mail as a communication tool. As needed, the library mentor helps the student locate additional print and electronic information resources, perform DIALOG searches, master E-mail usage, and learn the approved format of bibliographic citation for the research paper. Students may choose to work more independently at any point in the process, but this is at the discretion of the student.

The students normally meet with their research mentors on a weekly basis and often more frequently while working on their independent research projects. Most choose to meet with the library mentors approximately five times during the summer research project. As the student demonstrates improved information skills, the library mentor's role decreases. At the end of the independent research project, the library mentor reads the draft and final versions of the research paper produced by the student and makes editorial and bibliographic citation corrections. For the McCAP students, having an identifiable, known individual in the library to call upon for assistance is a tremendous advantage. These students feel that a librarian knows and cares about their needs.

Some of the McCAP students have been more cognizant of the librarian as a resource than others. Because the program is limited in size, the library mentors are able to provide one-on-one attention. The students are delighted to have a person who will work with them on any of their research needs, not just those related to the McCAP program. For these students, library mentors are able to serve as sounding boards for problems, as proofreaders and writing critics, as cheerleaders, and as friends. Some former McCAP scholars remain in contact with their library, departmental, and research mentors.

CONCLUSION

Since funding has been awarded through 1999, the future of McCAP at Central is assured for another four years. By the time the next few classes of McCAP scholars complete the program, statistics will be available regarding the numbers of former McCAP scholars who have completed master's and doctoral degrees. At present, the results look very promising. To date fourteen out of twenty students, or 70 percent of the 1991-1992 class; thirteen out of twenty-four students, or 54 percent of the 1992-1993 class; eleven out of twenty-five, or 44 percent of the 1993-1994 class have entered or completed a master's degree graduate program. None have completed a doctoral program yet. These numbers exceed the program's goal of 35 percent of the participants continuing their studies at the graduate level.[28]

Library participation will continue to be an important element of the program. For the 1995-1996 class, some redesign of the library seminar sessions occurred. Group sessions were reduced from three to one, and all library mentors participated in the session. Another goal of the restructured library component was to involve students with their individual library mentors throughout the program. Each library mentor scheduled a joint meeting with the student and the research mentor soon after the library seminar was held in order to create a more cohesive team approach to the research project. The one part of the library's participation in the program that will not be changed is individualized assistance to the students. These students are indeed special, and they require special assistance to ensure their academic success. Librarians at Central Missouri State University are committed to providing for their special reference and research needs.

NOTES

1. Carol Hammond, "Non-traditional Students and the Library," *College and Research Libraries 55*, no. 4 (1994): 323.
2. *Digest of Education Statistics 1994*, (Washington: Bureau of the Census, 1994), 167.
3. "Table 272–College Enrollment, By Sex, Age, Race, and Hispanic Origin: 1972 to 1992," in *Statistical Abstract of the United States 1994* (Washington: Bureau of the Census, 1994), 179.
4. Rebecca R. Martin. "Changing the University Climate: Three Libraries Respond to Multicultural Students," *Journal of Academic Librarianship* 20, no. 1 (1994): 2.
5. "Undergraduate Fall Student Enrollment by Selected Characteristics," *Central Fact Book 1995* (Warrensburg: MO: Office of Institutional Research, Central Missouri State University, 1995), 3.
6. "Total Undergraduate Fall Student Enrollment By Selected Characteristics," *Central Fact Book 1995*, 5.
7. Barbara Mayfield, Director of Accessibility Services, Central Missouri State University, telephone conversation with the author, December 14, 1995.
8. Martin, "Changing the University Climate," 2.
9. Mary Alice Lyon, telephone conversation with author, December 7, 1995. This estimate was based on earlier Trio-Student Support Services Performance Reports compiled by Mary Alice Lyon, the Director of Federal Trio Programs at Central, including the McNair Central Achievers Program.
10. "Financial Aid," *Central Missouri State University Facts Fall 1995* (Warrensburg, MO: Office of Institutional Research, Central Missouri State University, 1995).
11. "Table 273–College Population, By Selected Characteristics: 1987 and 1992," in *Statistical Abstract of the United States 1994* (Washington: Bureau of the Census, 1994), 179.
12. "Table 204–Disabled Students Enrolled in Postsecondary Institutions…: Fall 1986" in *Digest of Education Statistics 1993* (Washington: U.S. Department of Education, Office of Educational Research, 1993), 209.
13. Alexander Astin. *Four Critical Years: Effects of College on Beliefs, Attitudes, and Knowledge (San Francisco, CA: Jossey-Bass, 1977)*, 223.
14. Julia J. Boucher and Keith Curry Lance. "The Roles of Libraries in Education." ERIC Document ED354919. (Denver, CO: Colorado State Department of Education, 1992, microfiche), 6-7.
15. Hannelore B. Rader. "Reference Service As a Teaching Function," *Library Trends* 29 (summer 1980): 95-96.

16.   William W. Bishop. "The Theory of Reference Work," *Bulletin of the American Library Association* 9 (July 1915): 134.

17.   Rader, "Reference Service," 96.

18.   Kathleen Bergen and Barbara MacAdam. "One-on-one: Term Paper Assistance Programs," *RQ* 24, no. 3 (spring 1985): 334-335.

19.   Joan C. Durrance. "The Generic Librarian: Anonymity Versus Accountability," *RQ* 22, no. 3 (spring 1983): 281.

20.   Bergen, "One-on-one," 336.

21.   Mignon Adams. "Individualized Approach to Learning Library Skills," *Library Trends* 29 (summer 1980): 88.

22.   Marilyn Parrish. "Academic Community Analysis: Discovering Research Needs of Graduate Students at Bowling Green State University," *C&RL News* 50, no.8 (September 1989): 646.

23.   "Mentoring Orientation Brochure 1995, McNair Central Achievers Program" (Warrensburg, MO: Central Missouri State University, 1995), 1.

24.   Stephanie G. Adams and Howard G. Adams. *Techniques for Effective Undergraduate Mentoring: A Faculty/Student Guide.* (Notre Dame, IN: National Consortium for Graduate Degrees for Minorities in Engineering and Science, 1993), 2.

25.   "McCAP's First Four Years," *McCAP Journal* 4, no. 1 (fall 1995): 9.

26.   Rader, "Reference Service As a Teaching Function," 97.

27.   Rader, "Reference Service As a Teaching Function," 101-102.

28.   Lyon, telephone conversation.

THE CHANGING FACE OF THE COLLEGE STUDENT:
THE IMPACT OF GENERATION X ON REFERENCE AND INSTRUCTIONAL SERVICES

Catherine A. Lee

ABSTRACT

Today's students, members of Generation X, are in many ways different from the baby boomers who, for the most part, design and provide most academic library services. Xers have a fundamentally different world view that is being explored in marketing research but has been virtually ignored in the education and library science literature. Recognizing a few major cultural differences will help librarians to better meet the changing needs of today's students.

INTRODUCTION

When academic librarians think of their special user populations, they typically think of commuters, remote users, foreign or minority students, or the disabled. Their assumption that only user populations that are small are deserving of special study or consideration is reinforced by the subject headings used in *Library Literature* and *Education Index.*[1] Few librarians would identify the traditional eighteen to twenty-one year-old college student population as a user group with distinct characteristics and special needs. While librarians spend time and effort identifying and designing services for their smaller special populations, marketing experts for business and industry have set out to reach another group called Generation X.

Although "Generation X" may seem like an Americanism, coined and hyped by Madison Avenue, it is an imported term. *Generation X* was the title of a book by Charles Hamblett and Jane Deverson, published in London in 1964, about sex, drugs, and rock 'n' roll among England's hippie population. In the mid-1970s, the term was adopted as the name of a British boomer punk rock band fronted by Billy Idol. Canadian novelist Douglas Coupland brought the term into more popular use with the 1991 publication of his youth cult classic, *Generation X: Tales for an Accelerated Culture.* Coupland, himself born in 1961, employed the term to describe his age mates born between 1961 and 1964. This quasi-generation did not fit in emotionally with the boomers that preceded them or demographically with the baby busters that followed.[2] Since then, the term Generation X has been loosely adopted by the media to refer to everyone born between 1961 and 1981, and it has been featured on the covers of popular periodicals such as *Newsweek* and *U.S. News and World Report.*

In 1991, *Generations: The History of America's Future, 1584-2069* by William Strauss and Neil Howe was published. Strauss and Howe coined the term "13ers" to describe those born between 1961 and 1981, referring to the fact that this is the thirteenth American generation, counting back to the peers of Benjamin Franklin. Strauss and Howe argue that this post-boom generation is actually bigger than the baby boom, 79 million compared to 69 million boomers. No matter what this generation is called, Xers, 13ers, Baby Busters, or Twentysomethings, they will become the nation's largest voting block by 1998.

THE PROBLEM FOR ACADEMIC LIBRARIANS

Many higher education professionals have already noticed that something is different about the current generation of traditional college students. Much has been noted in the literature about their diverse racial makeup, yet surprisingly little has been written about the changing attitudes and character of these students. What has been published portrays a young adult wasteland full of students who are ignorant, lazy, apathetic and directionless.

As early as 1983, the U.S. Department of Education issued the report, *A Nation at Risk* which lamented the "rising tide of mediocrity" in the schools. Its conclusion was that, "for the first time in the history of our country, the educational skills of one generation will not surpass, will not equal, will not even approach, those of their parents."[3] Many books followed that report, reinforcing this image of today's students. In 1986, Litwin concluded that "it now takes another decade to grow up in our culture."[4] Stockman[5] and Sheehy[6] both arrived at the same conclusion in their respective works.

In 1987, Allan Bloom's best-selling *The Closing of the American Mind* and E.D. Hirsch's *Cultural Literacy* blamed a lax education system for the lack of a shared national knowledge and vocabulary. In 1988, Ravitch and Finn were commissioned by the National Endowment for the Humanities to assess *What Do Our 17-Year-Olds Know?* Their conclusion was that the younger generation "is ignorant of important things that it should know".[7] Comedian and entertainer Steve Allen went so far as to coin the word "dumbth" to describe the general stupidity and ignorance afflicting the American people.[8] Educational psychologist Jane Healy proposed the theory that Xers are a generation of "different brains" created by electronic media, fast-paced lifestyles, unstable family patterns, environmental hazards, and current educational practices.[9]

Clearly, much has been written about what is wrong with this generation of students. Rather than continuing to denigrate an entire generation, it would be more useful for educators and librarians to try to understand this population in order to better serve them. Before librarians can understand these students, they must recognize that a generation gap exists between academic librarians and this large group of the students they serve. In 1994, the average age of librarians working in research libraries was forty-six. A full seventy-seven percent are age forty or over.[10] In order to bridge this gap, librarians need to think of Generation X students not as younger versions of themselves but as a special population with its own unique characteristics and needs.

X FACTORS

David Cannon, director of research for the London-based firm **PRL** Consulting, is an authority on the behavior of this generation of young employees. He posits the thesis that today's students, Generation X, are fundamentally different from the baby boomers. Through extensive focus group research, Cannon has identified eight representative characteristics of this population, which he calls "X" factors.[11]

- *Craving for stimulation.* Xers have grown up in an age of media sound bites and infotainment. They want variety. They are looking for work, education, and recreation that stimulates, entertains, and is meaningful. Boring, routine, or monotonous activities are the ultimate turn-off to Xers.
- *Need for personal contact.* Xers are culturally independent, yet demand personal attention and feedback from supervisors, faculty, and other professionals such as librarians and advisors.
- *Preference for concrete, specific information.* Xers want an information service that provides accurate, up-to-the-minute information. They would like their information packaged in a concise, laser-printed format that they can take with them to view at their convenience.
- *Desire to learn leading-edge technology.* Xers are always on the lookout for new skills which will add to their knowledge and their resumes. They are attracted to cutting-edge technology and to professionals with technological expertise. Xers like jobs and activities where they can continue to learn.
- *Searching for traditional goals.* Once an Xer's career is on track, he or she will put great effort into personal affairs, striving for a good marriage and home life. Xers refuse to be workaholics at the expense of quality time devoted to family and recreation.
- *Looking for the good-looking job.* Xers are interested in work that is exciting, unique or worthwhile. Xers will avoid the trap of entry-level or service sector jobs.
- *Emotionally repressed.* Xers are pragmatic and realistic with exceptional coping skills. They may seem superficial because they tend to keep deep emotions to themselves, trusting few people. On the other hand, they are fascinated by the exaggerated emotions in television programs such as soap operas and "Thirty-something," which went off the air just as the first wave of Xers turned thirty.
- *Keeping options open.* The single most recurring statement made by the students in Cannon's focus groups was, "I want to keep my

options open."[12] They are postponing any commitments such as marriage or full-time employment, and are taking longer to finish college. College completion rates, seven years after high school graduation, fell from 58 percent for the boomer class of 1972 to 37 percent for the Xer class of 1980.[13] They are also going to graduate schools in record numbers. Between 1970 and the mid-1980s, the percentage of freshmen planning to pursue graduate or professional degrees remained fairly stable at near 50 percent. In 1990 it exceeded 60 percent.[14]

IMPLICATIONS FOR LIBRARIES AND LIBRARIANS

If librarians accept Generation X as a distinct user population, they must consider the idea of providing special services or enhancing existing services to meet its particular needs. Librarians already do this for other special user groups with programs, policies, or services benefitting adult students, disabled users, foreign or minority students, honors, and remedial students. Accommodating the needs of so many distinct groups without alienating any individual user may seem an unachieveable goal, but it is one that has been pondered by many librarians who are rethinking current reference practice.

During the last few years, much has been written about changing the traditional reference service model to be more efficient, effective, and user-centered.[15] Campbell has rightly observed that "all librarians have been accustomed to serving up information on our terms and expecting our users to meet those terms" while at the same time lacking basic knowledge about how these users would prefer to get their information.[16] None of the proposed new reference models specifically mention Generation X, but they all point to the need for change in order to ensure the relevance of reference services for the next generation.

A dramatic philosophical shift in the traditional reference service paradigm is not required for libraries seeking to better serve Xers. However, careful consideration of Xers' characteristics most directly influencing their interactions with reference librarians will lead to more pragmatic means of serving this diverse group.

A craving for stimulation. Most students do not find the idea of library instruction stimulating. Librarians complain that Xers are bored, have very short attention spans, do not retain anything, and cannot apply what they have been taught. The majority of traditional students who participate in library instruction programs are compelled to do so. Instructors arrange for course-related instruction during class time or require attendance at out-of-class workshops. Library studies credit courses may be required for a major or strongly recommended by an advisor. Library instruction can be embedded in required classes, such as English composition or freshman orientation. Since students generally do not choose to receive library instruction, its presentation must be both entertaining and meaningful in order to capture and keep students' interest.

Teaching techniques that worked in the past are not necessarily going to work for today's students. Library instruction should be related to a specific class assignment or goal. If at all possible, generic presentations covering "everything-they-need-to-know-about-the-library-in-fifty-minutes-or-less" should be avoided. Librarians can set their own manageable goals for each session. Short, focused, interconnected lessons delivered throughout the term may be needed in order to integrate library skills with the subject matter of the course. Active learning experiences should be planned for even short, one-shot lectures. Utilize technology to enhance the classroom experience. Eye-catching presentations can be created using one of the many software presentation packages available. Even simple transparencies or other visual aids illustrate and reinforce basic concepts. Lastly, librarians should not be discouraged when the Xers they have instructed come to the reference desk asking basic questions. No form of group instruction is entirely successful for every student.

Need for personal contact. With increased discussion about remote users, librarians might begin to wonder what kind of future there is for the physical library. Although Generation X will continue to access more resources and services remotely, they still crave the human touch. Campbell's assertion that reference librarians could be answering "no less than 75 percent of the questions that currently come to our reference desks using computers…without human intervention"[17] disregards this important X factor. Later, focus group research at Campbell's institution illustrated that students considered a good information source as one that "includes human help on demand."[18] Clearly, librarians can provide greater convenience to their users by using FAX, E-mail, and distance learning technologies. However, this does not minimize Xers' need for personal contact.

Cannon found that with each and every focus group, Xers were impressed by people and organizations which they felt cared about them.

Students respond to facial expressions, eye contact, body language, verbal cues, use of personal names, and the general physical appearances of staff and facilities. Xers value personal contacts and retain vivid impressions of interactions and surroundings. However, research has revealed that the traditional reference desk configuration makes it difficult for patrons to establish a relationship with library staff and actually discourages the formation of stable client-professional relationships similiar to those valued by other professionals. Additionally, the same researcher has found that a majority of librarians and staff members lack the interpersonal and interviewing skills necessary to conduct a successful reference transaction.[19] Extensive staff development is needed in this area.

This research raises many issues for librarians. While the question of the use of name tags stirs debate among librarians, name tags represent a simple means of establishing a more personal relationship between the student and the professional. The traditional reference configuration should be examined in a new light. A high and wide counter, a librarian on an elevated chair or stool, or a ringing telephone can be physical barriers, real or perceived, between librarians and students that should be minimized or eliminated.

In the process of reengineering reference, librarians who wish to streamline to be more efficient and cost-effective may consider eliminating one-on-one services in favor of group programs and instruction. However, Xers' desire for personal contact, coupled with their demonstrated need for quick information, suggests that librarians must continue to provide reference services on demand. Reference by appointment is an excellent way to meet students' craving for personal attention, but not at the expense of having a professional at the reference desk when one is needed. Planned group instruction will reach some students, but the majority of Xers will continue to expect individual instruction on a need-to-know basis.

Another way that librarians can meet the needs of Xers is to establish or strengthen departmental liaison programs. Each academic department and many support service areas, such as career development, academic computing, and off-campus services, could have a librarian liaison. In addition to normal liaison responsibilities for collection development, bibliography, and library instruction, this librarian would serve as a link in a referral chain. A referral process between departments could be established to provide Xers with personal attention and contacts, as well as to identify the liaison librarian as a "specialist" in a particular subject area.

Xers will seek out a professional with expertise in their area of need or interest.

Persuading this generation of college students to use the library will require the adoption of traditional customer service concepts. Librarians need to establish direct personal relationships, develop effective networking and referral systems, and staff public service areas with those who interact well with and genuinely enjoy working with customers. Staff development programs focusing on basic interpersonal skills and customer service concepts are essential. It is unrealistic to think that technology will eliminate the need for personal interactions in the near future.

Preference for concrete, specific information. Cannon made the observation that in general, "Xs are not crazy about libraries."[20] Serving this reluctant constituency means breaking with old traditions and rules. One tradition in dire need of rethinking is the tendency to view the reference encounter as an opportunity for librarians to teach students how to find information. Academic librarians are reluctant to simply give information to students for fear of "handing it to them on a silver platter." This inordinate emphasis on teaching at the reference desk is still another barrier between students and the information they seek.

When considering alternative reference models, Mood describes the ultimate Generation X-centered service. Patrons could leave a request and come back at a later time to find a "neatly organized file of material," consisting of a printout of citations on the subject, downloaded documents from full-text databases, photocopies of articles, and relevant books.[21] Xers, as well as many other students and faculty, would certainly welcome this level of service. However, Mood's paradigm represents more of a special library philosophy that may not be feasible at most academic libraries.

A dramatic shift in reference philosophy is not necessary for librarians to better serve Xers. Instead, they should anticipate the needs of patrons and create concise and practical guides. Handouts should be prepared in response to the most frequently asked questions. The traditional pathfinders and bibliographies can be redesigned to be more appealing to Xers. Handouts should be limited to one page of the most useful and current information. Long, narrative descriptions should be avoided. Headings, subheadings, and bullets make handouts more attractive and readable. Lastly, display handouts where students want them. The neat display in the catalog area or lobby is of little use if students are asking for this information at reference desks or in the computer labs. This prepackaged information should be distributed in as many alternative ways as possible: in the campus newspaper, on the on-line catalog, via E-mail and fax on request, and in the residence halls.

A desire to learn leading-edge technology. Many articles and books on Xers have made note of this generation's affinity and aptitude for technology. A common lament of librarians is that students expect everything to be on the computer. Equally frustrating is the average student's inability to make critical judgements about the quality of information they retrieve.

Librarians can make use of Xers desire to learn cutting-edge technology only after they have convinced students that there is technology in the library worth learning. Libraries which are physically aligned with academic computing services can take advantage of technology by association. When there is a computer lab in the library, students will naturally associate the library with technology. More often, students will have access to only library computing facilities and services, such as on-line catalogs, CD-ROMs, and networks with bibliographic or full-text databases. It can be very difficult to get library-phobic Xers to enter the library to see what is available. Librarians may have more success attracting users if they take technology to the students. Librarians should take their presentations to the locations where students congregate, such as dormitories, student unions, cafeterias and classrooms.

Demonstrations and workshops conducted in the library can be successful if marketed properly. Workshops should be offered on topics such as using the World Wide Web or other Internet navigating tools. Partnerships can be established with the career development office or academic computing center for team teaching such workshops as job hunting on the Internet or using E-mail. Because Generation X students prefer a hands-on learning environment, librarians should limit workshop attendance to the number of computers available. Lectures should be brief with most of the time allotted for hands-on practice. Other students or library staff can act as floating trouble shooters to answer questions and keep students focused on specific activities.

Keeping all staff current on the latest technology is a constant challenge. While many libraries have added systems and computer specialists to the staff, this does not relieve other reference librarians of the responsibility of remaining computer literate. To keep Xers coming to the library, everyone at the reference desk must have a working knowledge of new information technologies in order to effectively assist students with problems and questions.

CONCLUSION

There is ongoing debate about whether the characteristics of Generation X discussed above are actually unique to this current generation of college students or simply the characteristics of young people in general. Certainly there are common traits; however, librarians must recognize real cultural differences resulting from the environment in which Generation X has come of age. Librarians should be aware of Xers' affinity for and familiarity with technology, acceptance of diversity, savvy consumerism, and desire for instant gratification. Attempts to define the character of a generation may be perceived as stereotyping or labelling, but such information can be useful. The argument might be made that it is part of the academic librarian's role as educator to acclimate students to the higher education culture rather than adapting to each new generation passing through the library's doors. This argument was more successful when generations of students literally were required to visit the library in order to identify and use information.

Without some adaptation on the part of librarians, Generation X may become another lost generation: lost to the joys of academic libraries and their information culture. If librarians believe that acclimating students to this culture is an important goal, and that the library serves as a vital part of the campus educational mission, then they must effectively communicate the library's relevance. Just as marketers are trying to learn the language of Generation X to sell cars, jeans, and soft drinks, academic librarians must also learn the language if they expect to sell libraries and information literacy to this, their largest and most important market.

NOTES

1. *Library Literature* (H.W. Wilson) identifies a number of special population groups, but not Generation X. *Education Index* (H.W. Wilson) added Generation X as a subject in 1995 but has since indexed only reviews under this heading. There are no subject headings or subdivisions in either index reflecting services aimed exclusively at traditional aged college students.

2. Demographers use the term "baby busters" to refer to those born between 1965 and 1976. This is a smaller generation born right behind, and in the shadow of, the massive baby boom. See William Dunn, *The Baby Bust: A Generation Comes of Age* (Ithaca, NY: American Demographics Books, 1993) for a profile of the baby busters.

3. National Commission on Excellence in Education, *A Nation at Risk: The Imperative for Educational Reform* (Washington, DC: Author, 1983).

4. See Susan Littwin, *The Postponed Generation* (New York: William Morrow, 1986) for an attempt at explaining why today's young adults in their twenties and early thirties mature later than earlier generations.

5. Larry Stockman and Cynthia S. Graves, *Adult Children Who Won't Grow Up* (Chicago: Contemporary Books, 1989).

6. In this sequel to *Passages*, Gail Sheehy, *New Passages* (New York: Random House, 1995), takes a renewed look at young adulthood and old age and concludes that people are taking longer to grow up, thereby shifting all the traditional stages of adulthood by up to ten years.

7. Quoted from page 201 of Diane Ravitch and Charles E. Finn, *What Do Our 17-Year-Olds Know?* (New York: Harper & Row, 1988).

8. Steve Allen, *Dumbth* (Buffalo, NY: Prometheus, 1989).

9. For her insights on the plasticity of the brain and how the brain can be affected by environmental and experiential stimuli, see Jane Healy, *Endangered Minds* (New York: Simon & Schuster, 1990).

10. See Stanley J. Wilder, *The Age Demographics of Academic Librarians: A Profession Apart* (Washington: Association of Research Libraries, 1995) for demographic information supporting the notion of an age/generation gap between librarians and students.

11. David Cannon, "Generation X: The Way They Do the Things They Do," *Journal of Career Planning and Employment* 51 no. 2 (1991): 34-38.

12. Quoted from Cannon, 36.

13. College completion rates quoted from William Strauss and Neil Howe, *Generations: The History of America's Future, 1584-2069* (New York: Morrow, 1991), 325.

14. Eric L. Dey and Alexander W. Astin, *The American Freshman: Twenty-Five Year Trends, 1966-1990* (1991 ERIC Document ED 340 325). This report summarizes trends identified in twenty-five years of the Cooperative Institutional Research Program's annual surveys of college freshmen.

15. For an overview of opinions on reengineering reference services see: Virginia Massey-Burzio, "Rethinking the Reference Desk," in *Rethinking Reference in Academic Libraries*, ed. Anne Grodzins Lipow (Berkeley, CA: Library Solutions, 1993), 43-48; Douglas Herman, "But Does It Work? Evaluating the Brandeis Reference Model," *Reference Services Review* 22 no. 2 (1994): 17-28; Keith Ewing and Robert Hauptman, "Is Traditional Reference Service Obsolete?," *Journal of Academic Librarianship* 21 (1995): 3-6; Jennifer Cargill, "The Electronic Reference Desk: Reference Service in an Electronic World," *Library Administration and Management* 6 no. 2 (1992): 82-85; Beth Shapiro and Kevin Brook Long, "Just Say Yes: Reengineering Library User Services for the 21st Century," *Journal of Academic Librarianship* 20 (1994): 285-90; and Lizabeth A. Wilson, "Building the User-Centered Library," *RQ* 34 (1995): 297-302.

16. Quoted from page 10 of Jerry D. Campbell, "In Search of New Foundations for Reference," in *Rethinking Reference in Academic Libraries*.

17. Quoted from Campbell, "Shaking the Conceptual Foundation of Reference," *Reference Services Review* 20 no. 4 (1992): 31.

18. Quoted from Campbell, "In Search of New Foundations for Reference," 12.

19. For research on librarian-patron interaction at the reference desk see Joan C. Durrance, "Reference Success: Does the 55 Percent Rule Tell the Whole Story?," *Library Journal* 114 no. 7 (1989): 31-36 and Durrance, "Factors that Influence Reference

Success: What Makes Questioners Willing to Return?" *Reference Librarian* 49/50 (1995): 243-265.

20.   Quoted from Cannon, 36.

21.   Terry A. Mood, "Of Sundials and Digital Watches: A Further Step Toward the New Paradigm of Reference," *Reference Services Review* 22 no. 3 (1994): 27-32, 95.

PART III

THE IMPACT OF CHANGING TECHNOLOGIES ON REFERENCE SERVICE

INTERNET USE PATTERNS AND THE SCHOLARLY RESEARCH PROCESS

P. Warren-Wenk and Vivienne Monty

ABSTRACT

The incursion of the Internet into library services is changing the way information professionals view the world of information and the role they perform in support of research activities. Large-scale marketing studies show patterns of Internet use among the general population, but few studies have explored scholarly usage and perceptions of Internet services. A 1994 Canadian investigation suggests that academics are beginning to use the Internet to underpin their research activities; as a consequence, the traditional research process in the social sciences and humanities is gradually changing. As resource persons for bibliographic research activities, academic librarians can act as Internet mediators for their user communities.

ITERNET USE PATTERNS AND THE SCHOLARLY RESEARCH PROCESS

The incursion of the Internet into library services is changing the way information professionals view the world of information, the skills they employ, and the role they perform for their user communities. Librarians no longer front a single collection but a global information environment. Seasoned researchers struggle to acquire Net-savvy surfing skills. University students hasten to incorporate Internet-based sources into their bibliographies, often blithely substituting data of questionable validity and provenance for more trustworthy information published in traditional venues. Librarians question the role they play in a world where users have a panoply of networked resources on their desktops. While librarians know that students are using it and teachers are teaching with it, what of the impact of the Internet on the scholarly research process itself? Scientists have long used the Internet to ship data, share expensive software packages, and collaborate from a distance. But what influence, if any, has the Internet had on the research work of social scientists and humanists?

Charles McClure laments the lack of "formal efforts to…develop techniques to assess the impact of networked information services on academia,"[1] suggesting that the usual measures of an information service, such as extensiveness, efficiency, effectiveness, and impact, could be applied to the Internet. In 1994, the first small studies of faculty use and perceptions of Internet benefits began to appear and, in 1995, large-scale marketing studies of Net users were published.

INTERNET USAGE SURVEYS

In 1994-1995, O'Reilly and Associates, in conjunction with Trish Information Services, conducted large-scale mail and telephone surveys to compile demographic data on United States Internet users and their patterns of use. This study, claiming to be the first statistically defensible survey of use and users, was intended primarily as a marketing research tool aimed at identifying the features necessary to transform a Web surfer into a Web buyer. The study found that 5.8 million American adults had direct Internet access in 1995 and projected that, in 1996, 15.7 million American adults would have either direct or subscription access to the Internet and its services.[2] Also in 1995, the A.C. Nielson company, sponsored by the nonprofit CommerceNet, conducted a large-scale random telephone survey to measure Net usage. This statistically rigorous study painted a demographic profile of users and defined usage patterns in order to plan future Internet business activities.[3] This study determined that 37 million North American adults had some Internet access, 31 percent of whom reported daily use.

A CANADIAN STUDY OF FACULTY INTERNET USE

Although the Nielson and O'Reilly marketing research studies offered the first reliable picture of Internet users and use patterns throughout the general population, neither focused on Internet use in academia. The authors of this paper, interested in gauging how scholars in the social sciences and humanities were using the Internet in their research, interviewed forty faculty members and self-professed Internet users at different universities and colleges in Canada and the United States in 1994. Working from a list of pre-established questions administered by telephone, E-mail, or in person, they sought to investigate how this admittedly self-selected group incorporated the Internet into their daily activities and what impact these users believed it had on their research work. In most cases, the interviews ranged well beyond the initial list of prescribed questions. In addition, enquiries were posted to the memberships of two electronic discussion groups, P.O.R. (public opinion researchers) and METHODS (a discussion of research methodologies). The authors also subscribed to the electronic journal PSYCHOLOQUY to see how scholarly communication took place in a field outside of library science. Though not aspiring to scientific rigour, this sweep of the field did yield lists of projects, impressions, and themes from which the authors distilled a preliminary analysis of the impact of the Internet on the research process.[4]

Though lacking in the formal qualitative and quantitative indicators rightly called for by McClure and others, this preliminary exploration does show emerging patterns in faculty Internet use that suggest future changes to the traditional research process. This inquiry highlighted a number of patterns of Internet use by social scientists and humanists, since corroborated by other studies. Of those usage patterns, electronic mail, or E-mail, was the only function used consistently by all respondents. E-mail actually performs four functions in aid of research. It serves to generate links with other researchers, acting as a nexus to join people or information relating to the research activity. It facilitates trouble-shooting by enabling scholars to ask questions or seek help. E-mail plays a role in project administration, as remote teams work and communicate in tandem. Finally, E-mail functions as an agent of democratization, providing a forum where explorers of all types share equal access to each other by virtue of their equal membership in a virtual environment.[5]

Second to E-mail, respondents cited discussion groups as the next most frequently used Internet function. Those working at small institutions found the collegial exchange of discussion groups especially important. Faculty working in multidisciplinary fields enjoyed a new ease in gathering information from outside fields. Many respondents appreciated the ability to sound out a project informally in its early stages before a large audience. These uses of discussion groups suggest that the pretest stage of the traditional research process appears to be augmented and expanded in cyberspace.

While survey respondents considered discussion groups to be a new forum for exchange among colleagues, electronic journals supplemented, but did not supplant, print journals as a mechanism for monitoring developments in a field. At present, the major advantage of electronic journals over their print counterparts lies in their speedy publication, which accelerates communication between authors and readers. In the future, one hopes that other advantages of electronic journals will include innovative ways to present research results, interactive multimedia, and peer review.[6]

Many respondents expressed pleasure at the ability to connect to library catalogues and archival collections worldwide. Scholars whose institutions had mounted networked bibliographic databases were especially grateful for dial-in access. A small number of respondents cited direct access to union catalogues or to census and other numerical data as a benefit. One respondent customarily explored a multitude of on-line catalogues, using their value-added features to map the scholarly landscape of a subject area.[7] Though faculty do not appear to expect existing networked resources to displant the major indexes in their fields, it is clear that the Internet already plays a significant role in secondary research activities.

In 1994 few respondents made use of full-text data or image transmission. None listed multiuser simulation environments, but several mentioned potential uses for these services. Medievalists are interested in electronic facsimiles of manuscripts; linguists, in new possibilities for textual analysis; performance artists, in virtual reality experiments and performance spaces; educators, in simulation activities. Those actually using the Internet for document transmission tended to exchange non-published material or work-in-progress—grey literature that suddenly becomes more accessible within the virtual world. This electronic sharing of ephemera suggests that the invisible college shows signs of metamorphosing into a virtual college.

AN AUSTRALIAN STUDY OF FACULTY INTERNET USE

Another 1994 study of Internet use and perceptions by faculty, undertaken in Australia, reported similar usage patterns. A survey of approximately eighty Australian academic users found that E-mail was used most frequently, followed by remote login and then file transfer protocol (FTP), while fewer respondents used gopher or wais. This study, part of a larger investigation incorporating quantitative, qualitative and longitudinal segments, identified a strong faculty perception that Internet use benefits research. Australian academics claimed that their use of the Internet increased efficiency and access to data and collaborators.[8]

THE ADVENT OF THE WORLD WIDE WEB

Since the 1994 Canadian and Australian studies of faculty use patterns and perceptions, the World Wide Web has surpassed other Internet protocols in popularity. The advent of the Web, with its myriad search engines, hypertext links and user friendly point-and-click browsers, has brought about a number of significant changes in Internet use, making it a more viable research tool.

Organization

Web sites are increasingly well-organized. Many have logical subject trees, thoughtfully constructed menus appropriate for an electronic medium, and visually pleasing layouts. An excellent example is YAHOO, a popular web site organized by broad subject categories (URL: http://www.yahoo.com). Moreover, standards are developing naturally, as evidenced by naming conventions and Universal Resource Locators (URLs).

Simplicity

High-end Web browsers ease the technical challenges and make Internet navigation simple. Suddenly, social scientists and humanists find themselves able to explore the Internet with little or no training.

Searching Tools

The search engines themselves are increasing in number and improving in quality. OpenText is especially noteworthy. It offers both neophyte and expert search levels, uses advanced Boolean operators, and qualifies searching by field. Most significantly, it weighs search results and sorts them by relevancy in ranked order. Though it stops short of using controlled vocabulary terms, OpenText is a serious and exciting Internet-wide information retrieval system (URL: http://www.opentext.com).

Self-Publishing

The Web opens possibilities for self-publishing. Faculty can, with relatively little effort, mark their own texts with markup language (SGML or HTML) tags or use an software editor to do it for them. Many establish their own homepages, making it easy to disseminate work or share works-in-progress with colleagues.

CHANGES TO THE TRADITIONAL RESEARCH PROCESS

Research can be defined as a process of systematic inquiry, using a methodology that is either qualitative, quantitative, or historical. The traditional research process comprises four stages: project design, experimentation or data collection, analysis, and the dissemination of results. As social scientists and humanists factor the Internet into their research work, elements of the traditional research process begin to change.

Stage 1—Project Design

Discussion groups represent one of the most frequently used Internet services, and faculty report using them to solicit advice in the early stages of a project. In effect, the Internet opens the project design stage to preliminary scholarly criticism. Surveys, questionnaires, and other data-gathering mechanisms can benefit from an expanded pre-test, potentially resulting in more accurate data collection methods.

Stage 2—Experimentation or Data Collection

Social scientists gather data through interviews, surveys, standardized tests, observation, experimentation, or simulation. These methods of data collection are possible on the Internet; indeed, surveys appear frequently. The Internet offers considerable advantages for data collection:

sample size can easily be increased; freed from a geographical base, studies can incorporate an international perspective; experimenter bias may be reduced as the participants become invisible; and the Hawthorne effect, whereby subjects react positively to observation, may be tempered. However, gathering data on the Internet generates some concerns. Data collection methodology derives its validity from two essential variables: sample size and sample randomness. With networked sampling, researchers lose control over how many people received a questionnaire and therefore cannot calculate a response rate. In addition, Internet users represent a self-selected group, thereby compromising the notion of randomness. The ethical use of human participants in research must also be considered. Most universities obey ethical guidelines based on the Nuremberg Code, but these may prove difficult to apply uniformly without taking into account the unstable nature of groups in cyberspace. Robert Alun Jones suggests that social scientists need to carry out their research with "respect for human subjects as well as for the differences between virtual communities and their more traditional counterparts."[9]

Stage 3—Data Analysis

The analysis of data presents new challenges. Because control over sample size is relinquished, researchers may find themselves inadequately prepared to evaluate the flood of responses which data collection on the Internet can generate. Social scientists typically rely on statistical packages to tabulate results of pre-coded questionnaires, but Net-encoded data may require the development of new tools of analysis. Humanists, whose work may depend on an original manuscript or a specific edition of a classic text, may find their choices of electronic facsimiles determined by copyright or by mere availability in digital form. Often, an electronic text is inextricably bound to a particular search engine. Current Internet endeavours may alleviate some of these problems. For example, standard general markup language (SGML) allows a text to exist separately from a search engine. And the Text Encoding Initiative (TEI) is working to develop standards for the markup of scholarly information in SGML.[10]

Stage 4—Dissemination of Results

Academe is observing developments in electronic publishing with special interest. Cash-strapped universities have been accustomed to handing over the results of faculty work freely to publishers, only to buy it back in the form of expensive journals. Recently, universities have experimented with electronic publishing, thereby maintaining ownership of the work of their faculty, as in Johns Hopkins University's Project MUSE (URL: http://muse.jhu.edu). Because outcomes can be disseminated rapidly on the Internet, researchers no longer need to wait for print publications to share results, significantly shortening the timeframe of scholarly communication. Nevertheless, the electronic dissemination of research raises issues of concern. Scholars seeking academic recognition must, at present, continue to publish in accredited print sources, at least until academic standards and rewards are applied to work disseminated in cyberspace. In addition, authors might well be concerned about a potential loss of control over their texts, which are all too easily manipulable by others in electronic form.[11] The development of graphical viewing programs such as Adobe Acrobat, which enable writers to determine how readers view an electronic document, holds promise in leaving some control over text presentation in the hands of its author.

CHANGING PATTERNS

The element of scholarly research most affected by the Internet is that of communication at all stages of a project, from study design and data gathering to project administration and the dissemination of outcomes. Search engines indexing full-text discussion groups open up scholarly discussion to a broader assembly. Because of the ease of conferring with wider audiences, problems can be subjected to group-think more than ever before, while pretests and pilot studies can be substantiated before larger gatherings. Moreover, Internet communication facilitates crossing boundaries of discipline, geography, and culture. Scholars seem to be using the Internet as a current awareness service, both formally, using current contents databases and publishers' catalogues, and informally, through discussion groups and E-mail. Researchers appreciate both the timely nature of Internet-based activities, as well as its low cost to individuals who recognize the cost-saving possibilities of virtual conferencing and electronic publishing. The Internet permits secondary research activities through access to myriad bibliographic databases, from open-access library catalogues to union catalogues such as OCLC and RLIN, journal indexes, and even specialized databases such as the *English Short-Title Catalogue*. Finally, the Internet plays a role in document delivery through free full-text data transmission and through fee-based services such as CARL Uncover's article delivery service, as well as through library-sponsored services such as the ARIEL transmission of materials requested through interlibrary loan.

IMPLICATIONS FOR REFERENCE SERVICES

Although the Internet may be, at present, a more viable communications tool than an information tool,[12] librarians are already discovering ways to incorporate Internet-based resources into ready reference services. For example, Internet-based newswire services can serve as partial indexes to current events until a library's newspaper indexes are updated. A panoply of full-text information on world events is readily available (e.g., *Jerusalem Post's* coverage of the Rabin assassination), while small libraries enjoy access to selected electronic reference tools previously out of their price range. Indeed, the expansion of a library's collection to include electronic materials at remote sites has corollary repercussions for reference librarians who, though always responsible for knowing collections beyond their own, must now broaden their collection expertise considerably. The increasing availability of archival materials and manuscript facsimiles for historical research allows world collections to be brought together. No longer can it suffice to refer researchers to guides to archival collections or interlibrary loan services when the Internet may provide immediate, if only partial, access to electronic archives. Accessibility also becomes an issue. If librarians are to direct patrons to URLs for electronic resources, libraries must provide access to the Internet. Many materials, such as selected Canadian and U.S. government publications, are now available only in electronic format, lending a new spin to depository programs. The failure to incorporate relevant Net-based data and tools along with traditional resources and levels of service may soon come to signal inadequate or incomplete reference service. Just as reference services evolve and collections expand, so qualitative measures of reference services must change. The expanding requirements for collection expertise and technical skills give rise to professional development issues as librarians struggle to become proficient in this new arena.

The impact of the Internet extends from reference services to bibliographic instruction services. Reference librarians, accustomed to teaching patrons to do bibliographic research and evaluate information sources for accuracy, must help patrons put the Internet and its resources in context with other information tools. More than ever before, librarians need to help patrons develop the requisite critical thinking skills when evaluating Net-based information, since the usual library and publication filters are notably absent.[13] The Internet is rarely the first, the best, or the only place to turn for information. Situated on the cusp of both traditional and new information sources, librarians are perfectly placed to assist patrons to view the Internet and its resources in a broader context. As such, the Internet provides yet another opportunity for mediation with library user communities, and it can even play a role in how librarians liaise with patrons. For instance, library Web pages provide a vehicle for delivering whole new outreach programs.

As the Internet gives rise to changes in the traditional research process, so the role of the librarian as resource person for bibliographic research activities must evolve. Academic librarians can serve as Internet mediators for faculty on an individual level, an institutional level, and a network level. On an individual level, researchers should be able to rely on librarians to assist them in devising search strategies, identifying valuable Internet sites and sources, and acquiring Internet literacy skills. On the institutional level, researchers need to depend on the library to provide some Internet access and to incorporate networked sources into the provision of reference assistance, collection development activities, and archival functions. Librarians can lend their professional skills to help organize network sites in order to facilitate user access to information. OCLC, longtime vendor to the library community, has developed NETFIRST, a selective bibliographic database of Internet resources (URL: http://www.oclc.org/oclc / netfirst/netfirst.htm) with current URL information. The education community benefits from an Internet-based question and answer service, the AskERIC Web site (URL: http://ericir.syr.edu/), where researchers in education request assistance in use of the ERIC database and ERIC Clearinghouse studies. Some library reference departments are setting up electronic mailboxes and offer ready reference assistance via E-mail or via their Web page. These Internet projects represent value-added services. They are examples of electronic resources with a human component, prototypes for future Internet services.

NOTES

1.   Charles R. McClure, "So What ARE the Impacts of Networking on Academic Institutions?" *Internet Research* 43, no. 2 (1994): 2.

2. O'Reilly and Associates/Trish Information Services, "Final Study Results," *Defining the Internet Opportunity 1994-95.* (October 1, 1995). [electronic summary files] Available at URL: http://www.ora.com/survey/.

3. Donna L. Hoffmann and Thomas P. Novak, *The CommerceNet/Nielsen Internet Demographics Survey.* (November, 1995.) [electronic summary files] Available at URL: http://www2000.ogsm.vanderbilt.edu/ Also available at: http://www.commerce.net and at http://www.nielsenmedia.com.

4. Vivienne Monty and P. Warren-Wenk, "The Impact of the Internet on the Scholarly Research Process in the Social Sciences and Humanities," in *Continuity and Transformation: The Promise of Confluence* (Proceedings of the National Conference of The Association of College and Research Libraries, Pittsburgh, PA, March 1995), 284.

5. See note 4.

6. F.W. Lancaster, "The Evolution of Electronic Publishing," Library Trends 43, no. 4 (Spring, 1995): 523.

7. Peter Roosen-Runge, *Interview,* (York University, Toronto, Canada. September, 1995).

8. Harry Bruce, "Internet Services and Academic Work: An Australian Perspective," *Internet Research* 4, no. 2 (1994): 29.

9. Robert Alun Jones, "The Ethics of Research in Cyberspace," *Internet Research* 4, no. 3 (1994): 35.

10. Stuart L. Weibel, "The World Wide Web and Emerging Internet Resource Discovery Standards for Scholarly Literature," *Library Trends* 43, no. 4 (1995): 638.

11. Clifford Lynch, "Rethinking the Integrity of the Scholarly Record in the Networked Information Age," *EDUCOM Review* (March-April, 1994): 30.

12. Roma Harris, *Restructuring in Canadian Libraries.* (Presentation to York University Librarians' Group, Toronto, Canada, March 2, 1995).

13. Judith M. Pask and Carl E. Snow, "Undergraduate Instruction and the Internet," *Library Trends* 44, no. 2 (1995): 307.

REFERENCE SERVICES IN HIGHER EDUCATION:
INSTRUCTIONAL MULTIMEDIA, SOFTWARE, COURSEWARE, AND NETWORKED RESOURCES

Carol Ann Wright

ABSTRACT

As interest in multimedia resources and distributed education technologies become more widespread in higher education, teaching faculty need significant assistance in developing an understanding of underlying pedagogical principles, new teaching styles and methodologies, and also in identifying and selecting existing software, courseware and multimedia, relevant, high-quality web sites, and, when necessary, appropriate software authoring tools. Librarians in higher education have a dual role to both serve education as an academic discipline and also to be a resource and partner in the instructional mission of the university. Libraries should broaden their traditional references services to include these resources and thereby continue to respond to changing campus environments.

FORCES OF CHANGE IN REFERENCE SERVICE

Most reference librarians would agree that current reference services and collections in academic libraries bear slight resemblance to those even a decade ago. A librarian who has not actively participated in the profession over the last few years would hardly recognize the current reference environment.

New and emerging technologies are at the root of the changing landscape of reference service. Technology has altered communication patterns, shifted student and faculty perspectives regarding information access, retrieval and management, and changed the process of teaching and learning. Electronic databases, on-line retrieval, and networked and Internet resources have expanded the range and nature of materials and services that academic libraries are able to provide. External pressures from patrons, both faculty and students, with demands for electronic access, full text retrieval, and document delivery, drive the selection and design of modes of information delivery. These trends have expanded the traditional definition of reference.

Librarians have responded to the challenges of this new information and educational environment. They have enthusiastically assumed the role of information managers and expanded reference services and instructional roles to accommodate ever-changing databases, interfaces, platforms, resources, and patron needs. They have formed significant campus partnerships within the university community, extending their expertise to academic departments and colleges. Because of their common interests in technology, librarians have often teamed with the computer professionals in centers for academic computing, where librarians are recognized as experts in database content and discipline-specific resources. They fully participate in the teaching mission of their institutions through credit courses and through partnerships with the teaching faculty in the course development and delivery of credit instruction in all academic programs.

The new environment is also a direct reflection of the broad sweeping changes across higher education. Librarians in higher education have a dual role to both serve education as an academic discipline and also to be a resource and partner in the instructional mission of the university. Dramatic changes in the delivery of instruction are possible because of new and emerging technologies. These changes are desirable because of changing student demographics and institutional economics. Distributed learning systems are being developed and implemented. They include synchronous and asynchronous presentation and discussion, interactive exchanges between students and faculty, and instructional opportunities in non-centralized locations. Both faculty and administration recognize that the lecture method, the most predominant teaching style in higher education today, is not necessarily the most effective, most efficient, or the most welcomed by students.[1] Interactive and collaborative learning, often dependent on technologies, is rapidly capturing the attention of the academy. Many faculty are interested in exploring this brave new world of instructional technology, but they recognize that a large commitment of time and effort is necessary to make a successful transition to new delivery modes.

Some faculty are discouraged from exploring the implementation of instructional technologies because they assume that they will need to author their own programs. Lack of time, inadequate expertise, and minimal academic and professional rewards are all inhibitors to the process. A 1993 study at the University of Southern California (USC) indicated that among more than 1,000 colleges and universities surveyed, 53 percent have no support for faculty developing courseware, 71 percent have no formal plan for integrating computers into the curriculum, and, perhaps most importantly, 86 percent have no policy of rewarding faculty for developing courseware or a royalty-sharing program for faculty-developed courseware.[2] The traditional academic reward structure which values theory above application is a major impediment to innovation in instructional technology applications.[3] Support and assistance are needed in order to develop new teaching styles and methodologies that reflect a deeper understanding of pedagogical principles related to individual learning styles. Promotion and tenure criteria, academic reward structure, and appropriate evaluation criteria must be applied to those engaged in the use of emerging technologies in teaching and research.[4]

The Institute of Academic Technology (IAT) at the University of North Carolina argues that the scholarly community needs heavy involvement with the commercial sector to ensure the creation of high quality educational materials. If higher education does not become involved as partners with the commercial sector, the creation of materials for general education will likely pass to those who control the mass media.[5]

Recent advances in authoring software for multimedia are providing a more conducive environment for those who wish to proceed in this direction. Authoring products such as Astound, Action!, Asymetrix Multimedia Toolbook 3.0, AT&T Multimedia Designer, and Digital Chisel 2.0, enable faculty to move more easily into product development. These authoring programs require little or no scripting, and many incorporate the Web, thereby supporting cross-platform functionality and the opportunity for commercial distribution.[6]

Authoring tools, existing courseware packages, and relevant, high quality Internet sites and networked resources must be identified and selected. Academic librarians have historically supported the instructional mission of the university through traditional reference services, collection development, and bibliographic instruction. It is now appropriate for them to broaden their base of services and collections to respond to new instructional models. The accelerating influence of the Internet, the World Wide Web, and the movement toward distributed learning environments may serve to encourage educational partnerships. As technologies change, librarians must draw on their organizational and information-finding skills to create a new reference paradigm based on electronic resources.

THE LIBRARIAN–FACULTY INTERVIEW–
DEFINING THE INSTRUCTIONAL PROBLEM

Providing reference assistance for identifying and implementing software, courseware, and networked resources differs substantially from more traditional materials. Although the subject focus of the search is discipline specific, the technology places the faculty member outside of her area of expertise, working with unfamiliar databases and resources. A steep learning curve for technological applications can be a frustrating and humbling experience for faculty. In this situation, effective communication between the librarian and the faculty member is critical for a successful interview.

Before the search begins, the faculty member must convey to the librarian the exact nature of the instructional problem to be solved. Does she wish to simulate actual phenomena which can not be replicated in the classroom? Chemical experiments, reconstruction of historical events, or observation of multiple variables that impact on an event may all be developed with software. Other examples of simulation might include the movement of glaciers, the effects of global warming on shorelines, or the rapid eradication of tropical rainforests. Often a professor wants to integrate multiple art forms, so that students can study works of art, listen to music contemporary to the work, and read works reflecting the historical context of the time. Should drill, practice, and repetition be provided to support the learning process? The instructional application must also be considered. Software used as part of a classroom presentation will differ from that which will be used by students individually at their own computer's. Answers to these important questions will direct the results of the search.

GATHERING BACKGROUND INFORMATION

The Literature Search

Once the faculty member decides to investigate the implementation of instructional technologies, the librarian can provide expert reference guidance through a literature search and an investigation of various electronic and print resources. The faculty member may be tempted to proceed directly to a vendor catalog to search for existing software and courseware, or conversely, to develop her own software. Rather, her first step must be a thorough literature search, which will identify peers, colleagues, and potential collaborators with similar instructional needs and related prior experiences. The literature may provide a range of possible solutions beyond the one she first considered, a sense of what fails as well as what succeeds, and discussions of the pitfalls to avoid during the process. *ERIC*, the Educational Resources Information Clearinghouse, sponsored by the United States Department of Education, is the major database for this search. Other related sources include *Higher Education Abstracts*, and *Instructional Technology Abstracts*. The OCLC bibliographic database allows keyword searches to be limited to computer software as a publication type. This powerful keyword searching ability supports a very narrow, targeted, and efficient search for specific products.

Valuable information can also be gathered by searching a table of contents database or scanning past issues of educational technology journals such as *Syllabus*, *T.H.E. Journal*, *EDUCOM Review*, or *Multimedia Review*. Discipline-specific journals such as *Computers in the Humanities* or *Physics Teacher* should be considered. General interest computing magazines such as *Wired*, *Internet World*, *Multimedia World*, and *Software Digest* may also be of interest. Many of the above titles are available on the World Wide Web.

EDUCATIONAL TECHNOLOGY SUPPORT GROUPS

Several professional and consortium groups are important because they provide leadership for the implementation of instructional technologies in higher education. They can be a valuable source for the use of these technologies. One of the best known, representing a partnership of academic and commercial interests, is IAT at the University of North Carolina. Partially sponsored by IBM, IAT is "...dedicated to the proposition that information technology can be a valuable tool for improving the quality of student learning, increasing access to education, and containing the costs of education."[7] IAT offers workshops and seminars, produces publications, videos, and authoring software, promotes faculty training, and supports teleconferences dealing with leading edge issues. IAT's web site provides faculty position papers, newsletters, resource guides and bibliographies, reviews of new software, an IAT listserv, and a research library for visiting scholars. It also maintains an anonymous FTP site.

Another organization is EDUCOM, which sponsors conferences and seminars and supports awards for instructional innovation for undergraduate education. It established the National Learning Infrastructure and participates in national initiatives such as The Association For Managing and Using Information Resources in Higher Education (CAUSE), the Coalition of Networked Information (CNI), and the Networking Telecommunications Task Force.

Many listservs are useful forums for posting theoretical or practical questions, and exchanging ideas. The Directory of Scholarly Electronic Conferences website, edited by Diane Kovacs lists the range of groups available.[8] Selected groups from that directory include ACSOFT, whose members discuss all aspects of academic software development; EDTECH-L, a group that focuses on education technology and multimedia; INFOBITS, which is IAT's electronic service that monitors and evaluates current resources; and INTECH-L, a group which discusses instructional technology and instructional systems.

The searches of journal literature, support groups, and listservs can provide valuable insights during the planning process. Careful preparation can lessen the chances that the researcher will be surprised and/or disappointed later in the process. Often this background investigation helps the faculty member decide whether existing software will meet her instructional need, or if authoring her own software is required.

SOURCES OF MULTIMEDIA AND SOFTWARE[9]

Instructional Technology Web Sites

Web sites devoted strictly to instructional technology vary in content, scope, purpose, and subject orientation. They may include a wide range of resources, including sample syllabi, course lecture outlines, virtual scientific experiments, and virtual reality rooms. Embedded hot links support further exploration. Collectively these sites represent the extensive potential of instructional technology applications in higher education.

An excellent starting point is a site created by the University of Maine Libraries called *Courseware for Higher Education on the World Wide Web*. This site provides discussion of traditional and Internet strategies for identifying courseware, links to demonstration sites, and checklists of courseware evaluation criteria. An educational technology site maintained by TECFA, University of Geneva, Switzerland supports links to virtual reality sites, technology implementation, muds, moos, software, and more.

For many years, the largest sources of higher education software and courseware were shareware and freeware. These resources played a significant role in making electronic instructional materials available to faculty members who may not have been able to author their own software to incorporate into their instruction. Shareware and freeware still represent a large portion of available academic level courseware. They are available from software repositories and archive sites which are maintained by universities and educational consortiums. The largest of these is the Virtual Software Library (VSL). VSL describes itself as the most powerful tool available for finding software on the Internet. It maintains over 16,000 files available for searching, browsing, and downloading. IBM, through its Solutions for Higher Education Program, and IKE (IBM Kiosk for Education), sponsors an archive at the University of Washington with downloadable software with reviews and descriptions.

Once software is identified, the faculty member may need assistance with downloading and decompressing files and scanning for viruses. The librarian should be able to guide the faculty member to sites that support these technical activities. An excellent introduction to networked multimedia is found on a web site entitled "Multimedia File Formats on the Internet," which includes compressed files, sound, graphics, movies, and foreign languages. Another site that provides a variety of assistance on compressing, such as decompressing, and encrypting files is at the Pennsylvania State University. The Virtual Software Library includes links to survival kits for its software. These contain links to decompression software, step by step instructions, and virus-scanning software.

By their nature, shareware and freeware programs and archive sites often represent academic exchange and collaboration at its best and are responsible for significant advances in instructional technology applications. However, they sometimes lack the necessary support, infrastructure, field testing, debugging, product documentation, and upgrades necessary to allow the products to become broadly accepted and implemented. The presence of a file at the site does not always imply recommendation or judgment concerning the file's value, quality, or suitability of purpose.[10]

COMMERCIALLY AVAILABLE SOFTWARE

Commercial software for higher education applications has traditionally been less available and more elusive than instructional software for other audiences, such as children in grades K-12, vocational-technical students, adult education students, and business and commercial groups. However, in the last five years there has been a dramatic increase in the interest in and supply of academic software. This can be attributed to advances in the personal computer hardware and software market. Graphical interfaces are easier to use, processors are faster, and CD-ROM drives and software are more affordable. The Internet and the World Wide Web have stimulated interest in electronic access and shifted attention to alternative methods of teaching, learning, and publishing. Textbook publishers are diversifying publishing formats and exploring multimedia because students resist paying high prices for textbooks, and professors increasingly create customized course packets. Professors notice that multimedia, which supports interactivity and creativity, engages students more deeply in the learning process. Just as professors author textbooks, they must also become content experts and partners in the production of multimedia to ensure that product's meet instructional goals.[11]

Recent releases of commercial multimedia show that products often cross the artificial boundaries of academic study to serve indisciplinary or professional purposes. Educational programs are increasingly being correlated to various curriculum standards, such as the National Council of

Teachers of Mathematics standards. Programs that meet such standards help ensure evenness in content, support and reinforce learning in the classroom, and assure the marketability of a product.[12]

MULTIMEDIA PUBLISHERS AND VENDORS

Multimedia is defined as "...the use of a computer to present and combine text, graphics, audio, and video, with links and tools that let the user navigate, interact, create, and communicate."[13] Without linkages to other information sources, and without the ability to create and communicate, software is simply a computer program, not multimedia. Some software publishers are traditional textbook publishers who have integrated software and Internet publishing into their textbook divisions. Some are stand-alone products; others supplement existing products. They may be available as CD-ROM, floppy disk, or password-accessible Web sites. For example, Prentice Hall publishes *Chemistry Multimedia Presentation Manager*, *Multimedia Study Guide for Psychology*, and several authoring programs. William C. Brown has a large selection of courseware in subjects such as life sciences, physical sciences, psychology, sociology, music, art, humanities, and language study. HarperCollins College Publishers offers software in management and organizational behavior. Some publishers collaborate with other corporations or academic institutions to form new product lines. For example, West Publishing and Intellimation jointly produced materials in political science and government, and Wadsworth Publishing worked with San Francisco State University to produce materials in the area of video production, and multimedia design and careers.[14] A few new publishers specializing in software are the Bureau of Electronic Publishing, whose Great Literature Plus, offers over 1,800 works, and Multimedia World History, with over 300 titles. Trinity Software offers Hypersign, an interactive American Sign Language Dictionary, Speech Works, the Accent Reduction Tool, and Chemistry and Life Science programs. Voyager offers packages such as Amnesty Interactive, an interactive history and atlas of human rights. The last category of software publishers are those affiliated with universities or with academic professional associations. Examples are Physics Academic Software offered by the American Institute of Physics and the Computer Based Learning Software Database offered by the American Medical Informatics Association and the Health Sciences Libraries Consortium.

Librarians should maintain files of software vendor catalogs. They need to be familiar with publishers Web pages, which may provide reviews of product's, as well as relevant links to related content, sample screens, interactive product demonstrations, and embedded order forms for immediate delivery. An excellent starting point for these publishers is the Publishers Catalogs Home Page (URL: http://www.lights.com/publisher/).

CRITERIA FOR SOFTWARE SELECTION

In making a final decision for software selection and purchase, the librarian can assist the faculty member in evaluating the materials using instructional design criteria.[15] Because many students are expert visual learners and are often sophisticated computer users, amateurish multimedia with blasting sounds and annoying graphics will distract rather than enhance learning. Media should be integrated meaningfully; text and graphics should be used appropriately. Special effects, animation and sound should be substantive, not superfluous. Graphics should illustrate and enhance meaning; if they do not, text often may be a less flashy but more effective approach. The program should include information mapping, where links build upon prior knowledge so that students understand the relationships among concepts. Passive time should be incorporated into the product so that students are able to absorb new knowledge. Screen design should include icons, navigational tools, and colors which are used consistently to enhance meaning and make the program intuitive. User manuals should not be required for operation.[16]

Technical support considerations should include the hardware compatibility requirements and additional software requirements as well as requirements for future upgrades. Questions about cost should include considerations about numbers of concurrent users, and potential licensing restrictions for distance learners. Ultimate ownership of the software will depend on its implementation. Software purchased for use in the libraries can become part of the permanent collection. Software residing on the computer center's course server or the academic department's server will most likely be purchased and owned by one of those groups.

ASSISTANCE WITH USE

To be fully integrated into new learning environments, librarians need to extend reference and support services for software and courseware to assist faculty in reviewing, demonstrating, and teaching with new technologies. Facilities for this purpose may be shared with electronic classrooms already in place in libraries. Cooperation with university computing centers is an efficient and effective approach for reviewing and demonstrating software and can result in integrated services and support for faculty and staff. Cooperative efforts avoid duplication of materials and resources, and promote appropriate referrals, resulting in a more seamless service. Either the library or the computing center may be the initial contact for the faculty member. Appropriate referrals can be made after the need is assessed. At Pennsylvania State University, for example, faculty who contact Educational Technology Services in the Center for Academic Computing for support in developing courseware are referred first to the libraries to check for existing resources. Seminars and workshops are offered each semester by the libraries to introduce these reference services and resources to faculty. Michigan State University Libraries and the MSU Computer Laboratory have developed a cooperative computing center.[17] Their jointly sponsored Instructional Software Collection and the Computer Resource Center provides opportunities to preview software, videodiscs, CD-ROM products and new and emerging technologies. Another excellent program is offered by the University of Iowa Libraries through their Information Arcade. "The Information Arcade provides access to a wide range of electronic source materials, with an emphasis on textual and multimedia databases,...to equipment,...to advanced-level instructional software and specialized tool software...to support independent learning, classroom instruction, and research.[18]

Reference service for instructional software, courseware, and multimedia resources is not simply another subject area for which librarians provide information to faculty members. It requires a commitment to purchase the computer hardware and software infrastructure that is required to support the services. It also demands expertise. Librarians who provide this service must continuously upgrade their skills to remain proficient in working with new technologies.

There is much to be gained in extending reference services to include instructional multimedia. Librarians will have a broader understanding of how students and faculty use other technologies and how these technologies can be integrated into the higher education environment. At the university level, librarians who work with these new technologies can become active participants in the campus-wide electronic access and implementation. Further, there is an opportunity to integrate librarians' expertise with other faculty, collaborating in the educational process and becoming an integral part of new campus learning environments. From these services and levels of expertise, academic librarians will be well positioned within their institutions and within higher education in general for managing and teaching information technologies into the twenty-first century.

APPENDIX: SELECTED INTERNET SITES

Instructional Technology

"Courseware for Higher Education on the World Wide Web." Presented by Kim Amato and Sharon Fitzgerald, University of Maine Libraries.   URL: http://libinfo.ume.maine.edu/Courseware/outline2.htm

"Educational Technology." Maintained by TECFA (Technologies de Formation et d'Aprentissage), a unit within the School of Psychology and Education, University of Geneva. URL: http://tecfa.unige.ch/info-edu-comp.html

"Innovative Internet Applications in Libraries." Todd Library, Middle Tennessee State University. URL: http://frank.mtsu.edu/~kmiddlet/libweb/innovate.html

"Instructional Technologies at San Francisco State." San Francisco State University. URL: http://itec.sfsu.edu

"Apple Virtual Campus." URL: http://hed.info.apple.com/home.html

"World Lecture Hall." University of Texas at Austin. URL: http://www.utexas.edu/world/lecture/

Software Archives

"Merit Software Archives." University of Michigan. URL: gopher://gopher.archive.merit.edu/1/.software-archives

"Multimedia Archives." SunSite Singapore. URL: http://sunsite.nus.sg/ftpmultimedia.html

"Virtual Software Library." URL: http://www.shareware.com

"OAK Software Repository." Office of Computer Information Services, Oakland University, Rochester, MN, URL: http://www.acs.oak land.edu/oak/

"IKE: IBM Kiosk for Education Worldwide." URL: http:// ike.engr.washington.edu/ike.html

"HENSA/micros archive." Information Systems Services Department, Lancaster University, United Kingdom. URL: http:// micros.hensa.ac.uk

File Formats on the Internet

"Common Internet File Formats." Compiled by Eric Perlman and Ian Kallen for Internet Literacy Consultants. URL: http://www.mat isse.net/files/formats.htm

"Shareware Survival Kit." Virtual Software Library. URL for Macintosh version: http://www.shareware.com/macsurvival.html; URL for Windows version: http://www.shareware.com/pcsurvival.html

"Multimedia File Formats on the Internet." By Allison Zhang. URL: http://rodent.Lib.rochester.edxu/multimed/contents.htm

NOTES

1. Alan E. Guskin, "Reducing Student Costs and Enhancing Student Learning. Part II: Restructuring the Role of Faculty," *Change* 26 (September/October 1994): 16-25.
2. Kenneth C. Green, *Campus Computing 1993: The USC National Survey of Desktop Computing in Higher Education* (Los Angeles, CA: University of Southern California, 1994): 12.
3. James Noblitt, "Exploring Interactive Technologies in Higher Education," *IAT Briefings* 5 (Summer 1995): 2-3.
4. Modern Language Association, Committee on Computers and Emerging Technologies in Teaching and Research, "Evaluating Computer-Related Work in the Modern Languages: Draft Guidelines," (Modern Language Association, June 1995). URL: http:// jefferson.village.virginia.edu/mla.guidelines.html (January 5 1996).
5. Noblitt, 2-3.
6. "Multimedia Authoring Products," *Syllabus* 9 (November/December 1995): 48-52; Patrick J. Lynch, "Entry Level Multimedia Authoring Tools For Education," *Syllabus* 8 (May 1995): 10-18.

7.   Institute for Academic Technology, "IAT Web Overview," URL: http://ike.
engr.washington.edu/iat/general/about.html (December 12, 1996).

8.   *Directory of Scholarly Electronic Conferences,* edited by Diane K. Kovacs (URL:
http://www.n2h2.com/Kovacs).

9.   See "Appendix: Selected Web Sites" for URLs of resources discussed in this section

10.   Noblitt, 2-3.

11.   Noblitt, 2-3.

12.   Multimedia Source Guide, Special Supplement to the T.H.E. Journal, 1995-
1996. "Introduction," (Special Issue, December 1995): 8.

13.   Sylvia Charp, "Editorial," *T.H.E. Journal,* (February 1995): 6.

14.   "Textbook Publishers Prepare New Electronic Products For The Curriculum,"
Syllabus 9 (1995): 36-40.

15.   Kim Amato and Sharon Fitzgerald, "Courseware for Higher Education on the
World Wide Web," University of Maine, http://libinfo.ume.maine.edu.Courseware/
outline2.htm (May 5, 1996).

16.   Ronald D. MacFarland, "Ten Design Points For the Human Interface to Instructional Multimedia," *T.H.E. Journal,* 22 (1995): 67; John P. Campbell, *Evaluating Software: The Process,* (University Park, PA: CBEL Teaching and Learning Technologies
Group, 1992), 1-11.

17.   Nancy A. Lucas and Kathy D. Stuut, "Cooperative Instructional Computing
Resource Centers," *EDUCOM Review* (November/December 1992): 32-37.

18.   University   of   Iowa   Libraries,   "The   Information   Arcade."   http://
www.lib.uiowa.edu/arcade/ (May 15, 1996).

DESIGNING CUSTOM COMPUTER APPLICATIONS FOR REFERENCE

Stephen Sottong

ABSTRACT

The personal computer, (PC) has changed the face of reference. From its earliest days, use of the PC has been pioneered by reference librarians. This chapter suggests the possibility of using the library profession's own internal pool of programming talent to write software which could be shared with other libraries. The author uses as an example the ready reference software which he wrote during a library school internship and has distributed to libraries throughout the country. This chapter also discusses some of the latest tools that simplify the process of writing software.

Reference in the days before computers was paper and memory based. The venerable card catalog provided access to books and journals, while print indexes were used to find articles in journals and proceedings. A mass of factual data was found in encyclopedias, atlases, gazetteers, handbooks and the like. The most frequently used data was stored by reference librarians either in their memories or in manual ready reference files. All of these sources are still used today, but many have been converted from print to computer files. This shift has made a profound change in the face of reference. Along with all of the traditional and still useful skills, today's reference librarian must be the master of a hundred computer interfaces (most not as simple or intuitive as their print predecessors), a speedy typist and a wizard of Boolean logic. Librarians have fostered and adapted to these changes because they have increased the quantity and quality of available information and the speed of delivery.

The advent of the microcomputer a mere fifteen years ago increased the pace of these changes in library reference. Librarians are at the forefront of an information revolution created by this new technology. In the early days of Apple and Commodore computers, there were no ready-made applications, so ingenious and industrious librarians wrote their own. Today, most of those early applications are mere memories. Commercial catalogs are filled with library software, and, like a person with wide feet trying to wear stylish but narrow loafers, librarians tend to shoehorn their needs into the limitations of existing applications. Like that foot-sore person, librarians may find it painful to force their software needs into available packages. It may be time for them to follow the examples of our colleagues in earlier computer times and write their own custom applications.

Programming is not an end unto itself for reference librarians. It is simply a tool to increase or improve services to users or the efficiency of staff. The many possible custom applications include, databases, interfaces to programs or databases, information packages, automated tours, and library statistics packages. One example of an interface program is a shell written for the computers in the Georgia Tech online public access catalog (OPAC) terminal area. These computers needed to run the Netscape^{TM} World Wide Web browser so patrons could access the school's web-based catalog, and databases provided by the school and the state of Georgia. The shell prohibits software other than Netscape^{TM} from being used on these computers. This example points out one of the key advantages of a reference librarian writing custom software. Since the reference desk overlooks the OPAC terminals, problems with the software can be detected and changes implemented quickly. This also can be a disadvantage for a reference librarian who writes software since the programmer can readily see problems and receive feedback from colleagues and users, the possibilities are endless. Nearly twenty revisions to the software have been made in four months with no end to the changes in sight.

For the individual with programming experience, designing custom library software provides opportunity to use old skills in new and useful ways. For inexperienced people, it can be an opportunity to develop new skills and broaden their horizons. Even those who do not wish to learn how to program can encourage others and help to provide them with the time and resources needed.

PROGRAMMING TOOLS

There has never been a better time to begin or resume programming. A wealth of tools are available to ease the work of application development and to make the end product both powerful and polished. More than ever before, the amateur programmer can produce interesting and useful custom applications. With as little as one course in Basic or a good introductory book on programming, the librarian can now write quality software and develop database applications.

One common misconception is that programming languages and tools are expensive. Many, in fact, are provided as part of other software packages. For example, QBasic^{TM} is included with MS-DOS^{TM}. It can be used to make simple presentations and perform essential number crunching. More useful to reference librarians are the development tools included with many database programs. These tools can be used to design sophisticated database handling programs and to automatically generate reports and statistics. Development tools, included in such database software packages as dBase^{TM}, Paradox^{TM} and Access^{TM} are an underutilized resource that can be exploited with a little study. Documentation for the programming languages is included with the software, and excellent books that will speed the process of learning the intricacies of programming with these tools are also available.

The latest development in programming tools is the reemergence of the once maligned language, Basic. Basic was the staple language of personal computers in the 1980s. It came loaded on most computers and was used to write many early applications including some of the early library programs. It fell out of favor for serious developers with the advent of C and C++. Its return to favor is due to the development of structured Basic languages such as Visual Basic^{TM} in the early 1990s which made code more readable without sacrificing the simplicity of the language. Visual Basic^{TM} is the backbone of Microsoft's tool development strategy. Besides the Visual Basic^{TM} compiler, it is used as the automation tool in the Access^{TM} database, Excel^{TM} spreadsheet, and Word^{TM} word processor. The latest version of the ready reference software was written in Visual Basic^{TM}.

Visual Basic^{TM} is one of a family of similar products that can be used to develop Windows applications. Others are Visual App Builder^{TM}, Delphi^{TM}, and Power Builder^{TM}. Most of these languages cost between $100 and $200 for the entry-level package. Libraries may get substantial, educational discounts that bring the prices of these products down to $60 to $100. These packages are capable of full applications and database development.

BUILDING THE READY REFERENCE FILE

During library school, the author[1] interned at a large California public university. Because of his computer background, the librarians asked him to automate their ready reference file. This file served as a repository for the reference department's collective wisdom. It was a place to store and share hard-won answers to difficult questions that could not be readily answered with standard reference tools. Whenever a reference librarian answered such a question it was logged in a notebook. On a regular basis, these notebook entries were manually transferred to card stock and filed them in a card drawer at the reference desk. There were several hundred of these cards when the automation project began

The DOS Version

Every programmer has a different style and every situation demands a different approach. In this case, the available tools and the librarian's needs were analyzed. Once the database had been designed, the software was written and tested. After receiving feedback, the programmer repeated the process.

The first task in the project was to determine the best tool to use for automating the system. The reference desk had a PC in place running DOS^{TM}. The university library had not yet begun its transition to Windows^{TM}, so Visual Basic^{TM} could not be used. It did have multiple copies of dBase III+^{TM}, so this was the logical tool.

The next task was to determine the needs of the librarians. Their foremost concern was ease of use. Within steps of the reference desk were the OPAC terminals, an OCLC terminal and twenty or more CD-ROMs. Adding another complex interface to this mix of computer terminals was out of the question, the ready reference database had to be user-friendly. The interface of the database needed to mask the fact that it used the dBase program since many librarians were intimidated by dBase's complexity.

In addition to simplicity, the electronic database needed to preserve all of the information in the card file and to present it in a manner that was as straight-forward as the original version. More than this, the electronic database needed to add value to the information. If automation merely replaced the card file with an electronic one, it would not be worth the effort. The card file was easy to use and relatively quick, so the speed of the computer was not a significant advantage. The automated ready reference file had to do more.

With these factors in mind, some of the cards were examined. Each card had a subject heading at the top that was used for filing. The cards contained two types of information. Some were brief answers to questions, others supplied titles of sources where answers could be found. Some cards were dated, and most had the initials of the librarian who had provided the information.

Transactions at the reference desk tend to be brief explanations of how to locate sources of information rather than the answers themselves. This is in keeping with the teaching philosophy of the library and with the fact that the university has a single library with a single reference desk staffed by two librarians. The automated ready reference file had to speed up these transactions and provide more useful information.

Taking all of this into account, a simple database was designed with ten fields. In place of the single subject heading on the cards, the database has seven Keyword fields. This gave the database added value, since there are now seven points of entry into any record rather than the one. This enabled librarians to find records more easily since they did not have to know the category the original filer had used to index the entry. It also meant that the database needed fewer records than the original card file since it was not necessary to create multiple records in order to provide multiple access points.

The largest field is called the Source field. It contains the answer or source information from the body of the card. A Librarian field provides space for the initials of the individual responsible for either creating or maintaining the record, and a Date field to keeps track of when the record was last updated. The Librarian and Date fields also add value to the automated ready reference file because the database can be sorted by these fields and records that have not been recently updated can be reviewed for accuracy by the appropriate librarian.

The last design question was how to implement the database manipulation functions. The card file required four basic operations: proposing new entries; inputting entries; making inquiries into the file; and editing old entries. One idea was to combine the proposing and inputting functions and let every librarian create new entries in the database as interesting questions arose. Since a controlled vocabulary for this database was not desirable, entries would be in natural language. For instance, the Watts Towers is a folk art landmark in Los Angeles. If a patron were looking for information using the term "Watts Towers," they would find very little since they are formally classified as the "Simon Rodia's Towers (Los Angeles, CA)." So an entry in the ready reference database might have Watts Towers as a keyword and "see: Simon Rodia's Towers (Los Angeles, Calif.)" as the Source field.

The idea of letting every librarian input records into the database was rejected for two reasons. First, there was a possibility of duplication, and second, it was decided that some controlled vocabulary was needed in order to group similar concepts. For example, a number of the entries in the card file told librarians where to find Supreme Court cases. These cards were filed by the common names of the court cases and provided the formal name of each case, its legal citation, and library call number. For each of these entries in the electronic database, the librarians decided to add the common keyword "court case." This meant that all Supreme Court cases in the database could be brought up by searching on that particular phrase. To maintain some control over the vocabulary, the number of persons performing input to the database had to be limited. Therefore, the notebook for proposing entries was retained, and the input module of the software was password protected. This was a local decision; the ready reference software is flexible enough to be used in many configurations depending on librarians' needs.

Input and editing could have been combined into one module, but this was deemed too risky. Editing in dBase is very powerful and, if it not done properly, can damage records or change the entire structure of the database making the data unavailable to the programs. Because of these possible problems, the two functions were kept separate. The input module of the program only allows the librarian to add new records onto the end of the database. The program presents the user with a template where he or she fills in the blanks. The most damage a librarian can do to the database using this program is to add a few bad records. Editing is left to one person who knows dBase well enough to perform that task without programming help.

The inquiry module is open for anyone to use. Since all input and editing functions are separate from this module, it can be safely used by the public without possible damage to the database. For simplicity's sake, there was only one search strategy, this found a user's word or phrase anywhere in keyword fields. For example, when a person types in the word "arch," the program finds records with Keywords such as "pointed arches" or "architecture." Because it also retrieves records with keywords such as "golden arches" or "monarchy," a certain number of false hits was to be expected. The trade-off of false hits for overall simplicity was deemed acceptable as long as the database did not become too large.

More than half of the project time was spent analyzing the needs of the librarians and the original card file before any programming was attempted. The ready reference project required coding two modules, an input module and an inquiry module. The dBase™ language has extensions that make it easy to design on-screen forms and menus. The display for the inquiry module was designed (see Figure 1) and eventually the same layout was used for the input module. This not only made programming easier, but also meant that the records would look the same in both modules so a librarian could align text in the Source field to improve readability.

After the first draft of the program had been written, the ready reference file was demonstrated to the librarians. They liked the speed and simplicity of the program and thought it would be an improvement on the card file. The additional access points for the database records were espe-

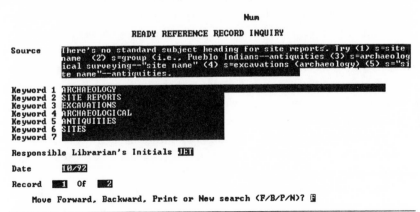

Figure 1. Ready Reference Inquiry Module

cially appreciated. The librarians made several useful suggestions, such as the addition of a print function so they could give the information to students quickly and more search options that would eliminate false hits. Two more search options were added. The first search option finds a word or phrase only at the beginning of keywords. This option would find records with the keyword "law cases" but not with the keywords "common law" or "design flaw." The second search option also find a word or phrase at the beginning of keywords, but finds the first record containing that word or phrase rather than all records containing it. This options speeds searching if the librarian is sure there is only one record in the database with a particular keyword. Testing also showed that the database could be destroyed if input or editing was interrupted by power failures or other system glitches. To protect the information in the database, an automated backup procedure was added.

At the end of the semester, the database handling programs were completed. The software ran on any DOS-based machine with dBase III or higher. Response time depended on the speed of the computer and the size of the database. Several librarians have begun the task of converting the card records into the database. Retrospective conversion of a large ready reference file has proven to be a very labor-intensive project, and at this writing, the process has not been completed.

The Windows Version

While the first version of the ready reference database was an improvement over the card file, it had three disadvantages. First, it required that the user own a copy of dBase. This could be an expensive hurdle for a small library, since the program retails for around $500. The second disadvantage was that at the time the original ready reference software was written, there was no version of dBase for Windows. Since Windows was rapidly becoming the operating system of choice, it made sense to have a version of the software that would run in that environment. Finally, because DOS is not a multi-tasking environment, running the ready reference software required leaving other applications such as the online catalog in order to search the ready reference database. This was a major inconvenience.

Moving the database handling software to Visual Basic would take care of all of these disadvantages. Visual Basic^{TM} lets the programmer create "standalone" programs that do not require users to own Visual Basic^{TM}

which cuts costs. Visual Basic^{TM} also has a built-in database search engine that makes it possible to search and manipulate databases created with other programs such as Access^{TM}, Paradox^{TM}, dBase^{TM}, or Btrieve^{TM}. Therefore, the Windows^{TM} program could use the same database created for the older DOS^{TM} program. This meant that databases could be shared within and among libraries with different computer configurations. Windows^{TM} is a multi-tasking environment, so a number of programs can be run simultaneously. One computer could access the OPAC, CD-ROMs, and the ready reference file simultaneously.

Just as the original database manager insulated the user from the complexities of dBase, the new one insulates the user from Structured Query Language (SQL). SQL is the language used by Visual Basic and many other database programs to format searches. The program transparently creates a properly formatted search query from the user's input. When a librarian types in the search term "law," the program creates the SQL inquiry statement:

select * from **READYREF** where (Keyword1 LIKE "LAW" or Keyword2 LIKE "LAW" or Keyword3 LIKE "LAW" or Keyword4 LIKE "LAW" or Keyword5 LIKE "LAW" or Keyword6 LIKE "LAW" or Keyword7 LIKE "LAW")

Search options were kept to a minimum to avoid cluttering the screen presentation. The only search strategy initially implemented in the Windows^{TM} version of the ready reference database was to find the user's word or phrase anywhere in the keywords.

The concept of splitting the functions into separate programs for security was retained in the Windows version. The inquiry and input modules were similar to their DOS counterparts, but editing for the Windows version was assigned to a third program. The original search screen was simple: it contained boxes to display the data in for each of the fields in the database, a box to input a search term and buttons for moving between records.

Once the librarians became familiar with the Windows version of the database handler, they began to request added features such as different search methods, the ability to search the Source field, and Boolean searching. Adding search options proved very simple, and there are now four: one can: (1) find the user's search term anywhere in any keyword field (if the word "law" is entered, the keywords "law," "law cases," "common law" and "design flaw" would be found); (2) find it at the start of any keyword field (from the previous example, "law" and "law cases" would be found); (3) find it at the end of any keyword field (here "law," "common law" and "design flaw" would be found) ; or (4) find only an exact match to a keyword field (using this search method, only "law" would be found).

Some librarians believed that occasionally it would be useful to query the information in the Source field. In this way they could find records that they partially knew the answer for. Adding the Source field to the search options was not difficult, so it was included.

There was no elegant way to implement Boolean logic in a timely fashion. Since it was necessary for the program to compose the SQL search command, users could not simply place an "and," "or," or "not" within their search term since the Boolean connector would not occur in the correct place in the final SQL statement. To perform Boolean logic, the user must type in their first search term, click on the "AND" or "OR" button and then type in their second term. So to restrict a search to California law, the librarian would type "law," press the "AND" button, type "California" and then press the "Make an Inquiry" button. "Not" in SQL performs a simple negation of one term and does not join two terms together as it does in many on-line systems. To "not" a term, the user must click the "NOT" button before inputting a term. To search for law

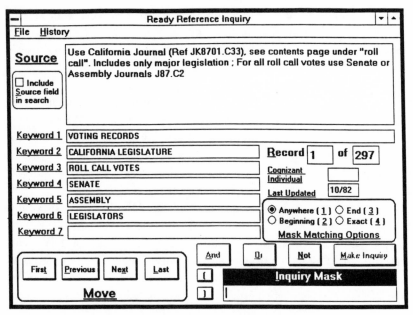

Figure 2. Ready Reference Inquiry Module

that does not relate to California, the user would type "law," click the "AND" button, then click the "NOT" button, type "California" and then press the "Make an Inquiry" button. The same type of placement problem that occurs with Boolean operators also happens with parenthesis, and buttons were created for them as well. This solution to the Boolean logic problem complicated the screen design. The final page on the inquiry module appears busy (see Figure 2), but all the testers agreed that it was vital that all searching options be displayed on one screen.

The input and edit modules are nearly identical in appearance and closely resemble the inquiry module (see Figure 3). This makes it possible to format the Source text for greatest speed of comprehension or create small tables in the Source field. Both modules allow the user to automatically backup the database both before and after editing to minimize the possibility of data loss caused by power failures, computer viruses, accidental or intentional deletions or tampering with the database.

The final version of the Windows database handler is fast, flexible, powerful and relatively user-friendly. Both the DOS^{TM} version of the ready reference software and the Windows^{TM} version use the same data-

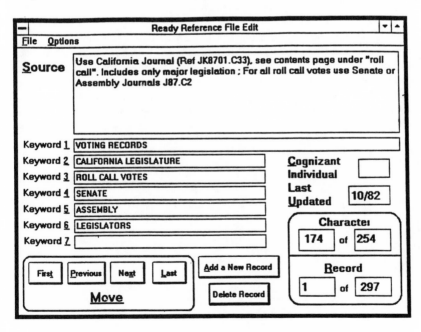

Figure 3. Ready Reference Edit Module

base file, so libraries can upgrade to the Windows^{TM} version without losing their ready reference data.

CONCLUSION

Many librarians could learn how to program using the new, simplified tools. There is a waste of potential talent that could be used to design computer software that would make libraries more efficient and productive. The author's experience designing programs for reference departments has shown that there are tasks that can be usefully automated if someone would write a customized program. Libraries do not have the market clout to get these programs written and marketed at a reasonable price, so they need to make use of home-grown talent and then share their applications with other libraries. Embracing the concepts of shareware and freeware would expand the range of software available to libraries without straining budgets; but to do this, libraries must provide those who can write software with the necessary time and resources.

NOTE

1.   The author studied programming in the early 1970s before training in the Navy as an electronics technician. After a number of years as a technician, he went back to college and got a bachelors degree in electrical engineering. He worked for ten years as an engineer before earning a master's degree in library science. He had always used programming skills to develop small applications for himself and in his work as an engineer, but didn't develop an application that was distributed to other people until he wrote his first ready reference program in library school.

DEVELOPING ELECTRONIC LIBRARY SERVICES AT THE UNIVERSITY OF NORTHERN COLORADO

Lisa Blankenship and Jane Smith

ABSTRACT

The University of Northern Colorado Libraries developed electronic library services in order to increase patron access to library staff, services, and information. This chapter describes the process of implementing this service from the genesis of the idea to its realization in a World Wide Web-based format. The role of librarians in the project is demonstrated in conceptualizing the system, designing the service in cooperation with many service units with the libraries, and programming for successive generations of campus computer networks. The University of Northern Colorado Libraries experience shows that a willingness to take risks with new technologies in order to meet patron needs and expectations is an important step in successfully creating dynamic library services.

BACKGROUND

When the James A. Michener Library at the University of Northern Colorado (UNC) was recarpeted in the summer of 1994, various departments in the library were relocated. During the three months of upheaval, the Circulation Department was in a basement alcove outside the Government Publications area, the Interlibrary Loan (ILL) Department was in a hallway in the Video/Film area, and the Reference Department was relegated to a single desk on the second floor amidst the bound periodicals. Despite the UNC Libraries Administration's best efforts to assure the university community that Michener Library was open and fully functioning, patronage of these service areas decreased dramatically. The library users who did find the Circulation, Reference, or ILL departments were quite pleased with themselves, though the questions "Isn't there an easier way to do this?" and "could I just E-mail it (whatever 'it' was) to you?" kept surfacing. In thinking about those questions, the librarians realized that there were alternative ways to conduct library/user interactions, and that perhaps technology could help expand and improve services.

The UNC Libraries has had an on-line catalog since the early 1980s, when several Colorado libraries jointly established the Colorado Alliance of Research Libraries (CARL) for the purpose of creating on-line access to their catalogs. Over the years, CARL has grown to include other databases such as the Academic American Encyclopedia and several periodical indexes, as well as many other catalogs from libraries throughout the country. At the time the UNC Libraries began to consider expanding its electronic services to include more than just access to CARL, Internet connectivity was slowly becoming available across campus in computer labs, dormitories, and offices. More students were coming to college equipped with computers along with stereos, bicycles, and skis. As ownership of personal computers became more common, and as campus Internet access from faculty and staff offices improved, remote use of CARL increased. The reference desk received increasing numbers of questions from patrons interested in searching CARL from their homes and offices. Calls for assistance from the Automation Manager in connecting to CARL also increased, with many of the voice mail messages left on weekends and late at night. The Bibliographic Instruction Librarian had been thinking about how to reach these invisible library users with assistance in searching CARL and with advice about using the information from CARL efficiently and effectively when they visited one of the UNC Libraries.

Investigation into how other libraries were reaching out to remote users revealed that some were establishing services such as on-line reference or interlibrary loan. Others were putting their handouts and other information on campus gophers. These text-based Internet browsing tools made library information easily accessible on-line and eliminated the need for the patron to travel to the library. Gophers, unlike most libraries, are open twenty-four hours a day every day. UNC's Information Services had recently set up a gopher, and librarians wanted to take advantage of it.

PLANNING THE PROGRAM

Two UNC librarians, the Bibliographic Instruction Librarian and the Interlibrary Loan Coordinator, started talking about designing a program to provide as many library services as possible to remote computer users. They were familiar with ZAP, Colorado State University Library's electronic interlibrary loan requesting system. ZAP is a simple menu driven program that lets the user request an item from ILL, ask for a status check on a previously requested item, or ask for a renewal of ILL material. Using ZAP, the library patron can carry out any ILL task without going to the library. One of the best features of ZAP is that anyone who has a computer and modem or telnet capabilities can access it.[1]

The summer of recarpeting gave the librarians time to think about designing a program that would provide a wide range of reference services for remote users. Through informal discussions, it was agreed that the program would include informational components and also provide a variety of interactive functions that mirrored services provided in the libraries. The program would offer:

- information about collections and policies,
- information about connecting to CARL remotely,
- CARL searching tips,
- answers to frequently-asked reference questions,
- the ability to make renewal and hold requests to circulation,
- the ability to make interlibrary loan requests,
- information about the Off-Campus Library Programs office and the ability to request its services,
- an on-line reference question service.

As the project was discussed with other library staff, it became apparent that this type of system was an important avenue to providing the type of service patrons deserved. At this point, the libraries might be a step or two ahead of user demands, but it would not be long before this type of service would be expected. It was time to begin.

Initially, the two project coordinators identified three constraints to the program's design. First, the program had to be easy to use. There had to be a simple way to exit every screen, with as many screens as possible allowing the user to quit the entire program with one command. A second constraint was that the program must consist of text only. The UNC Libraries did not have its own server or a local area network, so the new program would reside on one of the University's Information Services computers. At the time, Information Services staff was still organizing its gopher, and was only experimenting with establishing a World Wide Web site. Some of the faculty and staff offices were still not connected to the campus backbone and only had dial in access to the gopher. The libraries' program needed to be easily accessible to as many people in the UNC community as possible, many of whom did not have the equipment necessary to use a graphical World Wide Web browser such as Mosaic or Netscape. Lastly, because each screen held a limited number of lines and scrolling through pages of long sections of plain text on a computer screen was not appealing, the amount of information to be included in each section was limited.

Ideally, when taking on a project like this, a library should have access to the programming expertise and appropriate software and hardware needed for development. UNC's Information Services did not have the staff to offer assistance to the libraries for the development of projects like this. The only person in the libraries with appropriate programming experience was the Interlibrary Loan Coordinator, who had a limited amount of experience with shell programming in Unix. The program would be written in Unix shells, and would be accessible as a menu item on the University's gopher. Even though the libraries were able to devote only limited programming time and experience to the project, the librarians were excited about the possibilities and decided to move forward.

STAFF INVOLVEMENT

In order for the program to be successful, it was important that the entire staff know about the project and understand its possible impact. Fred

Roecker writes that when an innovation is being introduced, people will be concerned about its impact on them. Staff need to be involved in the planning and development of the program.[2] The project coordinators could simply tell staff that the program would provide better service or that patrons would find it useful, but the specific advantages to staff also needed to be delineated and discussed. In this case, the ability to receive requests for certain services on-line would allow staff to handle the requests at their convenience instead of on demand. It would also be an efficient and cost effective way to publicize library services and collections and offer basic library instruction.

The project coordinators met with the libraries' administrative staff to introduce the idea. The administrative staff endorsed the project and agreed to schedule meetings with the department managers to be followed by a meeting with all library faculty and staff. At this meeting, the project coordinators distributed a flyer introducing the project, presented background information about how the idea was developed, and showed sample screens of the proposed program. The coordinators pointed out the value of this service to patrons and discussed how it could help library staff. At the conclusion of the faculty and staff meeting, comments were solicited by distributing sheets with two statements to complete: "My hopes for this program are..." and "My concerns about this program are...."

Although the project coordinators heard many positive comments, only a few written responses were received. The positive responses focused on the public relations value of the project, and hopes that it could expedite work flow in some departments. One concern was that electronic advertising might increase demands for services to such an extent that the libraries would be overwhelmed with requests. The project coordinators addressed this concern by gathering information from other libraries that offered E-mail reference services and by posting a query on a reference listserv. Several libraries that offer electronic services reported that it has great public relations value. The people who take advantage of the service really appreciate it, although the actual numbers of requests are not overwhelming.

The other concern was the lack of library automation staff to maintain the program. This was a legitimate concern. The project coordinators could perform initial planning and programming, but adding new screens or significantly changing the structure of the program would require a significant ongoing commitment of staff time and specialized knowledge.

The hope was that eventually, as the Library Automation Department expanded from the existing staff of one person to the planned staff of two or three, the responsibility of maintaining the program could be shifted to that department.

Not everyone on the libraries staff was interested in being actively involved in the project, but there was at least one person in each department willing to help contribute information and handle the various patron requests once the program was running. After enlisting administrative support and acceptance from the staff, the libraries held a contest to choose a name. The winning entry was UNC Libraries Expressway (UNCLE).

DEVELOPING THE PROGRAM

From an earlier joint project with the University's Educational Technology Department, the librarians learned that the development team of a complex project requires input from several people. In general, a development team should include a team leader, subject matter experts who provide information for the content, a designer who works on screen design and the flow of the program, and a programmer. The UNCLE team was not formally structured with several people as the team had been in the earlier project. The two project coordinators acted as co-team leaders and designers. Several subject matter experts, who were department heads or other representative staff members, provided material for their departments' sections of UNCLE. The project coordinators met with the department representatives to discuss the possible approaches and came to consensus about the content of the screens. After gathering input, the coordinators shared in the work of designing the screens and the Interlibrary Loan Coordinator wrote the program.

The overall organization of the program was based on the departmental structure of the libraries. Using information gathered from librarians and staff members, the coordinators pseudocoded modules for each of the different departments by writing descriptions of the functions that each module would perform as well as the menu structure. The programmer scripted the Unix shells in an account on one of the university mainframes.

THE UNCLE PROGRAM

When a user first entered the original version of UNCLE, an opening screen gave a welcome message that could be changed to notify users of

UNCLE – UNC Libraries Expressway Main Menu

1. Library Information
2. Circulation
3. Interlibrary Loan
4. Electronic Databases & Reference Assistance
5. Government Publications
6. Video/Film Services
7. Off-Campus Library Services
8. Archives and Special Collections
Q to Quit

Enter your selection:

Figure 1. The UNC Libraries Expressway Main Menu

new library policies, services, or exhibits. This was followed by the Main Menu, shown in Figure 1.

The menu items led to further menus, text screens presenting information, or interactive sessions in which a user could request a service. Information entered in these requests was automatically sent to the appropriate destination via an E-mail message. Each screen included simple instructions for continuing or quitting.

The first item, Library Information, included basic information about the libraries' collections, services, and policies that was found in printed information packets traditionally offered to new faculty, staff, and students. The electronic version of this information would allow the libraries to eventually discontinue the paper version of these packets. Also under the Library Information section was an Administration subsection that included an on-line suggestion box and information about student employment in the libraries.

The Circulation section allowed users to send messages requesting that checked out materials be recalled or held for them upon their return. Choosing the Interlibrary Loan menu item took a user directly to the ZAP program which let the user perform any ILL function electronically.

The Electronic Databases & Reference Assistance menu item included many more information screens than any other part of the program (see Figure 2). This section duplicated some of the handouts provided in the libraries, answered common reference questions, and provided an interactive on-line reference service.

UNCLE – UNC Libraries Expressway Electronic Databases and Reference Assistance

1. Electronic Information Sources
2. Library Survival Skills
3. Find a Librarian in Your Field
4. Ask a Reference Question
5. How to Get Further Library Instruction
6. Request Materials for Purchase Consideration

Enter your selection (or B to go Back):

Figure 2. The UNC Libraries Expressway Electronic Databases and
Reference Assistance Menu

The Electronic Information Sources subsection included information about CARL and the CD-ROM databases available in the Libraries. The CARL sections covered instructions on how to access the system from outside the libraries, search tips, information about available search features that are not clearly described on the screens, and database descriptions. Library Survival Skills covered some of the questions that were asked repeatedly at the reference desk. Users could learn what UNC Libraries collections contain, how to find periodical articles, and how to read a variety of basic citations. They could also learn to distinguish a popular magazine from a scholarly journal and how to evaluate information sources. Find a Librarian in Your Field offered a list of subject librarians and their subject specialties. How to Get Further Library Instruction gave information about the libraries' Bibliographic Instruction Program. Request Materials for Purchase Consideration allowed users to send collection development suggestions to librarians through the Acquisitions department. Ask a Reference Question led to a message that described the service and outlined the types of questions that could be handled (see Figure 3). Users entered brief questions that were automatically sent to the E-mail address of the reference librarian on duty to answer electronically transmitted questions.

The main menu selection Government Publications offered basic information about collections and reference services offered by the Government Publications Department. Its subsections included Hot New Documents and On-line Services and a list of handouts. Video/Film Services and Archives & Special Collections provided descriptions of their collections and policies, and the Off-Campus Library Programs section,

UNCLE – UNC Libraries Expressway Ask a Reference Question

A reference librarian will answer your question if it can be easily answered from materials in the ready reference collection. If your question is more involved, we will send
you information about how to begin a search and how to receive further assistance.
We will check for questions once a day Monday through Friday and will try to send
your answer within 24 hours of our receipt of your question.

To ask a reference question, type R
To go back (without asking a question) type B

Enter your selection:

Figure 3.   The UNC Libraries Expressway
Reference Question Menu

like the Electronic Databases & Reference Assistance section, replicated
many on-site services. Students enrolled in off-campus programs could
request reference assistance and order library materials.

LESSONS LEARNED

The design and creation of the UNCLE screens went smoothly. However, the actual implementation of the program was plagued with problems. There were limitations on the number and size of files that could be
loaded. A forced move to a machine which ran a different version of
Unix required extensive reprogramming. When UNCLE finally found a
home on the same computer that ran the University's gopher, the Information Services staff could not get the shell scripts to execute within the
gopher environment. Information Services was also concerned about the
possible security breach that UNCLE might cause. The final disaster was
a lightning strike that hit the gopher machine and erased everything.

When the project was finished, the coordinators realized that if the
project planners do not have control over the system that will run the program, there can be problems. In this case, permission to point to
UNCLE from the gopher was not enough. The project coordinators
should have been in close communication with Information Services
from the planning stage, discussing ideas and working out hardware
issues. UNCLE was not a top priority project for Information Services, so
progress on the project did not move forward as quickly as originally
planned. In addition, any complex project like this takes longer than esti-

mations of time for completion. A team leader for the UNCLE project would have helped organize and maintain the project's schedule.

TRANSITION TO THE WORLD WIDE WEB

A year and-a-half after the idea for UNCLE was born, and several months after UNCLE finally found a home on the gopher, Information Services decided to offer space for university departments, including the libraries, on their World Wide Web server. Having had the experience of assisting in the creation of UNCLE, the Bibliographic Instruction Librarian and one of the reference librarians worked to transfer the program to the Web. At that time, the World Wide Web had clearly superceded gopher as the Internet browser of choice. Hypertext Markup Language (HTML) was fairly easy to learn, and maintenance of the Web site would require less specialized knowledge than maintenance of UNCLE, a Unix program.

During a month-long term break, the two librarians learned HTML by attending an afternoon workshop offered on campus and reading Laura

UNIVERSITY OF NORTHERN COLORADO

Welcome to the UNC Libraries

James A. Michener Library

Hours and Telephone Numbers

Collections and Services—visit the web pages for the departments located in Michener Library

Mari Michener Art Gallery

Music Library

Laboratory School Library

Finding Information

Reference Services

Learn about Library Research—UNC Libraries Instruction

Links by Subject—Links Organized by College, Division, School, or Department

Connect to CARL PAC—Our on-line catalog

Figure 4.   The UNC Libraries World Wide Web Home Page

James A. Michener Library

Collections and Services

Administration–Including an on-line suggestion box and student
job information

Archives and Special Collections

CARL PAC–Our on-line catalog

Cataloging–Including requests for rush cataloging

Circulation–Policies and procedures for check-out and renewal, overdue fine information, and information about the circulating collection

Copy Center

ERS Curriculum Collection

Government Publications

Interlibrary Loan–including on-line ILL requests

Library Instruction–including requests for instruction sessions and guides to using
the Libraries and CARL PAC

Off-Campus Library Programs

Periodicals Department

Reference–Including an on-line reference question service

Reserve–Information on the required readings area

Services for Faculty

Video/Film Collection

Figure 5. The Michener Library World Wide Web Page

Lemay's book *Teach Yourself Web Publishing With HTML in 14 Days.*[3]
Within the same month, they developed the UNC Libraries web site.
Many of the Web pages were taken directly from the UNCLE screens, and
most of the same services were offered. Although the opening screen was
changed to feature the branch libraries more prominently (see Figure 4),
the list of menu items under the Collections and Services section of
Michener Library resembles the UNCLE main menu (see Figure 5).

One advantage of the new platform was the ability to offer longer pages
than had been practical in UNCLE. The forms capability of the Web was
used to make the electronic reference question page, as shown in Figure
6. The Web hypertext links offered patrons the flexibility to move easily
from one page to another. Because there were still a large number of
users on campus without access to a graphical Web browser, the librarians were very careful to make sure that the pages worked well in Lynx, the
text based browser available on campus.

UNC Libraries Electronic Reference Service

You may request information using this form. This service is available to UNC faculty, staff, and students, and members of the Friends of the UNC Libraries. The service provides:

- replies to requests for brief factual information found in our Ready Reference collection,
- information about how to begin researching your topic or how to receive further assistance,
- referrals to subject librarians or other persons who can suggest resources.

We will reply within 24 hours of our receipt of the request, Monday - Friday. Twenty-four hour service is not available on weekends.

Please enter your name:

Enter your phone number or E-mail address:

Type in your reference question:

Submit Query   Reset

Figure 6.   The UNC Libraries Electronic Reference Service Page

Although the original UNCLE program never moved beyond its test phase, the ZAP interlibrary loan portion received enough positive patron response that the libraries staff was already convinced of the advantages of offering information and services electronically. The procedures for handling requests were already in place. UNCLE provided a wonderful beginning that allowed movement to a more sophisticated program with relative ease.

None of the librarians who created UNCLE and the web site were programmers, but they were interested in exploring new ways to use technology to help librarians do their jobs better. They were willing to invest time in learning something new, and library administrators were willing to support these efforts. Other librarians interested in developing programs like this should not be reluctant to tackle what may at first seem to be an overwhelming project. They should observe technological initiatives at other libraries and learn from other librarians who have worked through similar projects. They need to take advantage of educational opportunities such as computer programming workshops offered on many campuses. Cooperation with other units and departments on campus is essential when their goals are interconnected with the library's. Most importantly, librarians must be willing to take risks with new technologies in order to create new reference services.

NOTES

1.   Jane Smith, "Internet Access to ILL at Colorado State University" In *The Internet Library: Case Studies of Library Internet Management and Use,* ed. Julie Still (Westport, CT: Mecklermedia, 1994).

2.   Fred Roecker, "Basic Foundations for Creating an Effective Computer Information System." *Journal of Academic Librarianship* 21 no. 3 (1995): 167-174.

3.   Laura Lemay, *Teach Yourself Web Publishing With HTML in 14 Days.* (Indianapolis, IN: Sams.net Publishing, 1995).

PART IV

REFERENCE SERVICE BEYOND LIBRARY WALLS

UNDERSTANDING REMOTE ACCESS AND ITS IMPORTANCE FOR REFERENCE SERVICES

Pamela Snelson

ABSTRACT

The widespread use of telecommunications technology has a major impact on the ways in which library users access information. As libraries redesign and improve services, they must take into consideration the habits and usage patterns of remote users who access library resources via on-line services. This chapter defines the remote user of libraries and traces the development of services to this user population. It presents the results of research studies on remote use and users, and discusses the implications for reference services.

INTRODUCTION

Although it appears that the arrival of computers and networks encouraged remote access to libraries, the idea of remote access is not new. Book catalogs, decentralized libraries, microform catalogs—these are all examples of a steady movement toward increased remote access. In fact, one can view the card catalog, a monumental achievement of the late nineteenth century, as a step backward! Brian Aveney[1] recounts the story of a Harvard College Library user who complained that the new card catalog required a visit to Cambridge to find out if the college had needed material. Before this new enhancement, a user could sit at home and consult the old book catalog to find out whether Harvard had a book. While one can argue that centralized libraries are less costly to maintain, there are costs to library users in terms of time, energy and decreased use. These costs result from locating a library farther from its potential users.

BACKGROUND

Print Era

Branch libraries of public library systems are also examples of remote access. Early in this century, researchers found supporting evidence for the usefulness of these decentralized facilities. When individuals reside farther than one mile from a branch library, there is a decline in the number of borrowers.[2] In a similar examination of the relationship between nearness and access, Horowitz noted that patrons beyond a radius of two miles used the library infrequently.[3]

In the academic arena, faculty members have argued that their work requires unlimited access to library materials and that these materials should be physically situated close to the greatest number of potential users. As a result, remote access in the form of subject-oriented libraries is common on both university and college campuses. In a finding comparable to that of public libraries noted above, the distance from researchers' offices to libraries housing documents of interest influenced their choice of libraries.[4] While studying the use of personal collections, Soper found that personal collections accounted for the largest number of cited works.[5] In addition, as the distance of the author from a location increased, the proportion of works cited in that location decreased.

Connecting to an information source from a remote location did not begin with on-line catalogs. Commercial businesses established on-line database services over twenty years ago. Bibliographic utilities, which made information about the contents of library collections available, emerged in the late 1960s and early 1970s. However, these services were designed for remote access expert users. No one went to Palo Alto, California or Dublin, Ohio to use these systems. Librarians began to experience remote use when the on-line searching of large bibliographic databases and commercial databases became important library services. While acting as mediators for their users, librarians themselves were remote users. With the emergence of new services, these library patrons have now become remote users in their own right. Today's remote access issue for both on-line database services and bibliographic files is the provision of direct access to the library patron rather than through an intermediary. Although remote access now occurs without the mediation of library staff, this does not preclude (and sometimes demands) support from the library.

Impact of Telecommunications

While the historical trend toward remote access can be documented, today's telecommunications abilities require that librarians take a new look at the provision of remote services. For on-line catalogs and other information systems designed for naive users, an important issue centers on the increased availability of access outside the physical confines of the library building. Telecommunications technology easily supports this availability to the point that there now exist many remote users.

How might librarians define the remote user in terms of current library services? Stated most broadly, a remote user is anyone who gains access to a library's on-line catalog or other services from a location outside the library building. At some academic institutions, remote users may be defined as those students, faculty and others who do not reside on campus. If one uses this narrower definition of remote user, anyone connected through a campus network is seen as within the boundaries of the library and is not considered to be a remote user.

As more and more libraries make their databases available over the Internet, the boundaries separating user categories become blurred and confusing. A common situation is for a user, let's call her Susan, to sit in the Drew University Library and search a library catalog in New York City. To Drew, Susan is an in-house user; to Columbia University, she is a remote user. Next semester, Susan enrolls in an off-campus program in Washington, D.C. Through the university sponsoring the program, she connects to her Drew account and searches catalogs and databases as if she were in her previous semester's dorm room. Using this scenario, when is Susan my remote user? When is she your remote user? When does she become *our* remote user?

REMOTE USERS TODAY

Categories

As libraries extend reference services to remote users, it is important to know who these users are and whether their information use differs from traditional in-library users. Remote users as an overall group can be simply defined as persons who gain access to a library's information system from locations outside the library. Buckland[6] identified four types of access to on-line catalogs: first, by dedicated terminals located in the library; second, via telecommunications technology; third, by a computer network functioning as a virtual terminal; and fourth, through a database server. Less than a decade later, this list of access options must be modified to reflect today's reality. While many libraries still depend on dedicated terminals to service in-library users, the growing trend is for computers to replace terminals and utilize client-server architecture. Although the differences among telecommunications technology, computer networks, and database servers have blurred, there is some use in retaining certain distinctions. For example, in the case of an academic institution, on-campus users who connect to a library database through a campus network may have more familiarity with searching protocol than those who connect from a geographically distant site. This familiarity can result in different service needs, especially for those enrolled in distance education programs.

Demographics

Computer monitoring and transaction log analysis, combined with user surveys, are the most common methods for gathering data about remote users of on-line systems. This type of monitoring produces large datasets which can be analyzed with regard to pattern, error, or time. Variables such as instructions per second or minute, query complexity, learning curve for terminal users, and most likely path of next actions in a search session can be explored. It is also possible to look at user behavior in an individual session or to look for comparisons across systems or tasks. Monitoring data is used to corroborate survey data about system use, and vice versa. A linked on-line questionnaire and transaction file can provide data for a comparison of users' attitudes about the on-line catalog with what they did during their sessions. Three sites provide most of the data on remote users: Drew University, the Pennsylvania State University, and the University of California (UC), Berkeley.

The earliest report on remote use of on-line catalogs was published in 1984; it discusses remote access to LIAS, an integrated, on-line catalog designed and produced by the Pennsylvania State University Libraries.[7] A one-week transaction log revealed that remote use was heaviest between 2:30 P.M. and 5:00 P.M. Although no formal survey was conducted of remote users, 73 percent of the phone calls about the remote service came from university faculty. Another survey a few years later confirmed these initial findings: remote users differ from typical library patrons at Penn State.[8] Resident undergraduates are the typical in-library user while remote users tend to be faculty members, graduate students, and professionals. Using a mailing list of all inquiries concerning remote use of the MELVYL[9] catalog, 1986-1987 surveys disclosed heavy use of the catalog by a wide mix of UC Berkeley faculty, staff, research personnel and graduate students.[10] Over 50 percent remotely accessed the catalog six times or more in a three month period; 97 percent of the users lived within fifteen miles of Berkeley. Reports from a more recent on-line survey of remote users of MELVYL indicate that the percentage of non-UC users has increased.[11] Frequency of use is comparable between the two surveys. In the 1991 survey 47 percent of all users and just over half of the UC users used the system weekly. Contrary to previous reports, Snelson found that remote users were overwhelmingly undergraduate students.[12]

Growth

Remote use is growing dramatically at public and academic libraries. Cuyahoga County (Ohio) Public Library averaged 7.5 calls per hour when it introduced dial-up service in 1989; in 1991 the average was twenty-five calls per hour with busy hours reaching one hundred calls.[13] Between 1986 and 1993 the percentage of Association of Research Libraries member libraries providing remote access increased 26 percent.[14] Remote users account for one-fourth of the MELVYL system usage at the UC Berkeley during a typical high-use period;[15] in 1988 only 9 percent of use was remote. During a six-day period in 1994, a countywide library system received over five thousand logins through dial access to local databases such as on-line catalogs and two-year college course descriptions. In the same period, the public accessed Gopher menus close to eight thousand times.[16]

Casual monitoring of the library system at the University of Norwich indicates that two-thirds of the connections to the on-line catalog emanate from other parts of the campus.[17] However, library use, measured by attendance, circulation and interlibrary loan requests, has risen despite a decline in student population. The author attributes this growth to the introduction of an integrated system with remote access.

ACCESS AND USE

As remote use of library systems continues to grow, there is a need to explore how these developments affect traditional notions of information behavior. A radically decentralized information process is being created; however, librarian's perceptions of users' behavior is still limited by their experience with patrons within the traditional library context. Understanding and evaluating accessibility are essential to designing information systems.

Indications that accessibility can affect information system use predate the widespread use of computerized systems. Twenty-five years ago Allen proposed a model of information channel selection in which channel selection is based solely on accessibility, the most accessible channel being used first.[18] This model relates to Zipf's law of least effort,[19] and there is empirical evidence to support it.[20] Zipf explained that:

> an individual estimates the probable eventualities, and then select(s) a path of least average rate of work through these.[21]

Using an information system requires considerable effort for the average user. In most cases, an individual must expend effort to merely arrive at the physical location of the library. Rosenberg[22] further extended Allen's model and found that preference for an information gathering method reflects the estimated ease of use of the method rather than the amount of information expected.

Recent studies of the relationship between accessibility and use confirm previous work done in this area. Variations in the reported frequency of use of four information sources (handbooks and procedure files, memos and newsletters, peer and supervisor work-group information, and external sources) were primarily a function of the rated physical accessibility of the sources.[23] Culnan established a positive relationship between perceived access and selection of an information source.[24] Nickerson speculated that accessibility is a major impediment to use of inter-active computer systems.[25] Users would like to work on a problem whenever, and for however long as, they have the inclination to do so. The ambient atmosphere probably has an influence on the user's decision to continue or terminate an interactive session.

Volume of use is directly related to the convenient placement of the terminal in the work place. Rice and Shook found that closer proximity to a terminal is associated with greater usage of an electronic messaging system, and greater usage leads to reported increased effectiveness.[26] When a terminal was no longer convenient to clinical pharmacy students, end-user searching of National Library of Medicine databases dropped substantially.[27]

Accessibility encompasses a wide range of qualities that include convenience, distance, and individual perceptions. These qualities can contribute to a user's perceived satisfaction of an information source. It is appropriate to quote Mooers' Law at this point:

> An information retrieval system will tend *not* to be used whenever it is more painful and troublesome for a customer to have information than for him not to have it.[28]

Increasing accessibility through technology provides closer proximity to an information resource by essentially removing distance from the library as an accessibility issue. Further, it allows users unlimited time to search without interruption from other users.

Patterns of Use

The 1987 UC Berkeley study of remote users revealed that the "Purpose" category most frequently checked was "preliminary check before going to a local library"; the second most frequent purpose was "compiling bibliographies.""[29] Remote users and in-library users answered a related question in Snelson's study.[30] A course paper or report was the number one reason for using the on-line public access catalog (OPAC) for both groups; the second most frequent task was class/course reading.

Kalin analyzed over two thousand searches of remote and in-library users using criteria such as search subjects, search type, errors made and special commands used.[31] In the analysis, the author further divided remote users into two categories: dial-access and network. Although the differences were small, Kalin argues that remote users do search on-line catalogs differently than in-library users. In particular, dial-access users and network users do not search the on-line catalog in the same way. Network users displayed the most sophisticated searches, knew what they wanted to find, and were more persistent in finding it. Dial-access users had more procedural difficulties and were the least likely of the three groups to have a successful search. In Snelson's study, there were no differences in user reports of satisfaction between remote users and in-library users.[32] After an examination of transaction logs, Millsap and Ferl concluded that if remote users do not initially find what they are looking for, they have problems effectively restating their search.[33]

IMPLICATIONS FOR REFERENCE SERVICE

As information systems that were originally designed for in-library use become available anywhere users are located, it is imperative that librarians examine and evaluate the relationship between the library and users

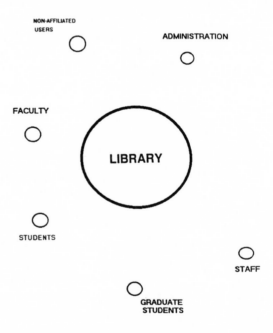

PTOLEMIAN VIEW

Figure 1. Library-Centered Model of the Information Universe

COPERNICAN VIEW

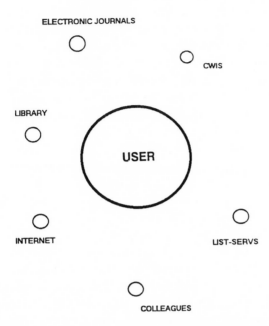

Figure 2. User-Centered Model of the Information Universe

of information. It is useful to understand this relationship in terms of the solar system models of Ptolemy and Copernicus.[34] In the Ptolemian model of information use, the library is at the center, surrounded by a varied clientele (see Figure 1).

Librarians expected users to come to the library for services and information. In the Copernican model, the focal point is no longer the library, but the user (see Figure 2).

The library's position changes from central repository to one of several options available for finding information. Users decide which information source to use at their convenience without mediation from the library. In this conceptual model, it is the library that is remote, not the user. Librarians are now challenged by the tasks of helping users navigate the multitude of information options and forging links between the options.

How can librarians identify the service needs of remote users who are now working in a Copernican, user-centered model? There have been few attempts to gather information from the users themselves. Much of the literature is based on librarians' experiences. Kalin[35] was the first to speak to the public service needs of remote users. Remote users, who have high expectations of fulfilling information needs on-line, experience more technical difficulties than in-library users. According to Kalin, remote users need technical advice, special instruction aids, and remote reference services. De Kock reiterates two types of problems encountered by remote users, technology and search protocols, and suggests that libraries offer different support services to remote users.[36] These users need technical advice and special instruction aids and guides. DiMattia notes that librarians have difficulty fulfilling the information needs of their users in person.[37] The dimension of distance inherent in remote access brings a new array of problems and opportunities to information provision. Adapting library services to a distance mode of education will allow libraries to play an important and meaningful role as the delivery of educational content changes and evolves.

Besides asking how well our systems support the needs of remote users, librarians need to ask, "When will remote users become primary users?" In other words, when will the balance shift so that remote users become the majority? This may have already occurred. The term "*remote user*" may already be an oxymoron; the distinction between remote user and in-library user may no longer serve a useful purpose. Whereas the virtual library received much attention in library literature and the digital library continues to dominate discussions, it is now time to focus reference services on the virtual user.

ACKNOWLEDGMENT

This chapter is based on a panel presentation, "Beam Me in Scottie: Transforming Remote Users into Primary Users," Summary in *Continuity & Transformation: The Promise of Confluence*, Proceedings of the seventh National Conference of the College and Research Libraries, Pittsburgh, PA., March 29-April 1, 1995 (p. 456).

NOTES

1.   Brian Aveney, "On-line Catalogs: The Transformation Continues," *Wilson Library Bulletin* 58 (1984): 406-410.

2.   F.M. Jones, *Library Services for Greater Wilmington: A Report on the Present Status and Future Expansion of the Wilmington Institute Free Library.* (Wilmington, DE: Wilmington Free Library, 1926).

3.   A.B. Horowitz, "Effect of Distance on Frequency of Use of Public Facilities," *City Planning* 9 (1933): 135-149.

4.   R.M. Dougherty and L.L. Blomquist, *Improving Access to Library Resources: The Influence of Organization of Library Collections, and of User Attitudes Toward Innovative Services* (Metuchen, NJ: Scarecrow Press, 1974).

5.   M.E. Soper, "Characteristics and Use of Personal Collections," *Library Quarterly* 46 (1976): 397-415.

6.   M. Buckland, *Library Services in Theory and Context*, 2nd edition, (NY: Pergamon Press, 1988).

7.   S.W. Kalin, "Remote Access to On-line Catalogs: A Public Services Perspective," *Proceedings of the Second National Conference on Integrated On-line Library Systems* (1984): 206-212.

8.   E.H. Dow, "The Impact of Home and Office Workstation Use on an Academic Library" (Ph.D. diss., University of Pittsburgh, 1988).

9.   MELVYL is the automated library system of the University of California. It provides access to monographs and periodical titles held principally by libraries of the University of California.

10.   E.M. Kirensen, "Studying Dial-up Use at UC Berkeley," *DLA Bulletin* 7 (1987): 12-14.

11.   T.E. Ferl and L. Millsap, "Remote Use of the University of California MELVYL Library System: An On-line Survey," *Information Technology and Libraries* 11 (1992): 285-303.

12.   P. Snelson, "Relationships Between Access and Use in Information Systems: Remote Access To and Browsing of On-line Catalogs," *Proceedings of the ASIS Annual Meeting* 30 (1983): 73-80.

13.   "Dial-up Access Soars at Cuyahoga," *Library Systems Newsletter* 11 (1991): 98.

14.   C. Haynes, *Providing Public Services to Remote Users*, SPEC Kit 191 (Washington, DC: Association of Research Libraries, 1993).

15.   Ferl and Millsap, "Remote Use."

16.   D. Fisco, *Quantitative Findings on Gopher and Modem Usage in the Morris Automated Information Network*, (1994). unpublished report.

17.   P. Heller, "Remote Access: Its Impact on a College Library," *The Electronic Library* 10 (1992): 287-289.

18.   T.J. Allen, "Performance of Information Channels in the Transfer of Technology," *Industrial Management Review* 13 (1966): 72-83.

19.   G.K. Zipf, *Human Behavior and the Principle of Least Effort: An Introduction to Human Ecology*, (NY: Addison-Wesley, 1949).

20.   P.G. Gerstberger and T. J. Allen, "Criteria Used by Research and Development Engineers in the Selection of an Information Source," *Journal of Applied Psychology* 52 (1968): 272-279.

21.   Zipf, *Human Behavior*, 6.

22.   V. Rosenberg, "Factors Affecting the Preferences of Industrial Personnel for Information Gathering Methods," *Information Storage and Retrieval* 3 (1967): 119-127.

23.   C.A. O'Reilly, "Variations in Decision Makers' Use of Information Sources: The Impact of Quality and Accessibility of Information," *Academy of Management Journal* 25 (1982): 756-771.

24.   M.J. Culnan, "The Dimensions of Perceived Accessibility to Information: Implications for the Delivery of Information Systems and Services," *Journal of the American Society for Information Science* 36 (1985): 302-302.

25.   R.S. Nickerson, "Why Interactive Computer Systems are Sometimes not Used by People who Might Benefit from Them," *International Journal of Man-machine Studies* 15 (1981): 469-483.

26.   R.E. Rice and D.E. Shook, "Access to, Usage of, and Outcomes from an Electronic Messaging System," *ACM Transactions on Office Information Systems* 6 (1988): 255-276.

27.   W. Sewell and S. Teitelbaum, "Observations of End-user On-line Searching Behavior over Eleven Years," *Journal of the American Society for Information Science* 37 (1986): 234-245.

28.   C.N. Mooers, "Mooers' Law or, Why Some Retrieval Systems are Used and Others are not," *American Documentation* 11 (1960): ii.

29.   Kirensen, "Studying Dial-up Use."

30.   Snelson, "Relationships Between Access and Use."

31.   S. W. Kalin, "The Searching Behavior of Remote Users: A Study of One On-line Public Access Catalog (OPAC)," *Proceedings of the ASIS Annual Meeting* 28 (1991): 178-181.

32.   Snelson, "Relationships Between Access and Use."

33.   L. Millsap and T.E. Ferl, "Search Patterns of Remote Users: An Analysis of OPAC Transaction Logs," *Information Technology and Libraries* 12 (1993): 321-339.

34.   J.R. Sack, "Open Systems for Open Minds: Building The Library without Walls," *College & Research Libraries* 47 (1986): 535-544.

35.   Kalin, "Remote Access to On-line Catalogs."

36.   M. De Kock, "Remote Users of an On-line Public Access Catalogue (OPAC): Problems and Support," *The Electronic Library* 11 (1993): 241-244.

37.   E.A. DiMattia, "Total Quality Management and Servicing Users through Remote Access Technology," *The Electronic Library* 11 (1993): 187-192.

SUPPORT SERVICES FOR VIRTUAL LIBRARY USERS

Sally Kalin

ABSTRACT

Libraries face new challenges as scholars increasingly access information resources from the convenience of their offices and homes, isolated from the very libraries that develop on-line services. On-line system designers and implementers must assure that their systems are responsive to the special needs of remote users. Libraries need to redefine their support services to include new forms of instruction and outreach. New service models that incorporate technical assistance, customer service standards, and customer feedback techniques are necessary to assure that libraries maintain their position as key information providers.

Several years ago, spurred by her experiences helping remote users, the author spent a sabbatical studying the remote use of on-line catalogs. An important part of the study involved visiting university libraries to learn about how librarians were supporting the growing number of users who were accessing catalogs and databases from their homes and offices. Most librarians were still trying to figure out what to do about remote users. One unforgettable remark, by a librarian from a high-profile, technologically advanced university, reported how her staff handled calls from remote users: "why, we all run and hide."

Five years later, academic libraries have lost their walls. Studies have found that as many as 80 percent of academic library users have personal computers in their homes.[1] Now information can be delivered to every desktop computer, regardless of where or how the information originated. This new kind of library is virtual in that it has no physical place: it depends on technology to link users from many locations to its services and collections. A new breed of patrons has abandoned traditional information channels to surf a wave of electronic information. Remote users may still be invisible, but they are important in that they are helping to push forward acceptance of the philosophy of access over ownership that is becoming prevalent in academic libraries.

John Sacks aptly describes the changes in the information world in his 1986 article in *College and Research Libraries*.[2] He sees the historical or traditional information world as Ptolemaic in that the library was the core or heart of the information universe. Universities added credence to this concept by consistently referring to their libraries as the hearts of their institutions. In the Ptolemaic definition, the scholar was a supplicant to a mortar and bricks library for his or her information needs. Today's information users have moved towards a Copernican view of libraries. The library is not a specific place, but a node in a complex web of information resources that includes the World Wide Web, database services such as DIALOG, invisible colleges, listservs, colleagues, and personal libraries. The center of the Copernican world is the scholar, not the library.

What this all means is a subtle shift in the power of the user. Prior to the change from a Ptolemaic information world to a Copernican one, librarians were in the enviable position of telling the users what was best for them. Librarians had control over information, its access, and often its use. In the user-centered or Copernican information world, libraries must address what the user wants and needs. Customer service moves to center stage in an increasingly competitive information world.

Does a library have a responsibility to remote users? Yes. These users may be invisible, but they are there, and librarians cannot afford to ignore them. When considering support services for remote users, every librarian needs to keep in mind two important concepts:

- The scholar is becoming less a patron of libraries and more a user of information.

- The term "remote user" is really a misnomer. It is the library that has become remote from the user.

Consider this scenario. A library has an information desk. A patron walks up to the desk, indicates that she wants to use a particular business reference source, and asks where it is located. The staff member directs the patron to the business library where the source can be found. Now for a second scenario. A remote user phones the information desk. The caller indicates that she has a personal computer, has heard that there is a business database available through the library's on-line system, and wants to know how to access it from her home. The staff member tells the patron that yes, he knows that the business database is available, but that he doesn't know how to access it remotely.

Is this good or appropriate service? If the staff member at the information desk had informed the walk-in patron that he didn't know where the business library was located, librarians would agree that the patron had received poor service. The remote user received this same level of poor service when she was informed that the library could not help her access the business database, even though the library had made it available via remote access.

If libraries are serious about supporting the access versus ownership model, they must address the growing remoteness of the library from users. They must ensure that users can access what they need, regardless of their location. The challenges of meeting the needs of remote users are many, but they can be categorized into four areas.

1. Getting connected. Making a clean, simple connection to the library's on-line system is the most critical need of users, and it is the one that generates the most support issues. Anne Woodsworth once wrote that if on-line public access catalogs "cannot have the same command language, so be it. That is not as critical as being able to make the connection in a relatively easy fashion."[3]

2. Searching and navigating. Once a remote user is connected, she must be able to move through the system easily and the search process should be logical and intuitive. In this process, the remote user may have to rely on specialized on-line assistance or documentation.

3. Obtaining information. Merely finding out that something exists is not enough for remote users; now they want the real documents.

Libraries are responding by making full-text information available through their on-line systems and by implementing document delivery systems.

4. Manipulating and using information. Information gathered electronically must be manipulated and organized before it can be used or applied; therefore, users that gather information through on-line systems ask the question: "Now that I've got it, what do I do with it?" Some users are establishing personal information management systems, often with the aid of commercial bibliographic software such as Library Master and Pro-Cite.

What do remote users expect libraries to do for them? They want on-line systems that are designed and marketed with the user in mind. They expect these systems to perform as advertised, and would like to have service before, during and after the sale. In a sense, they expect a business-customer relationship. They want constant and consistent access, convenient and easy to use systems, and immediate responses to their problems. In short, they want it all!

THE ON-LINE SYSTEM SHOULD PROVIDE BASIC SUPPORT

Remote users primarily interact with a system, not with the library. Therefore, most of their support should come from the on-line system they are using. The burden of accommodation should be on the system, not on the user. Isolated from the library's staff, remote users are dependent on the on-line system for guidance. They should not be forced to stare at cryptic screens and fumble around, especially since they choose to become remote users because of the availability and convenience of on-line information.

Some design principles for a good system include:

- *Easy connections.* When a system can be easily accessed, patrons will love it and think it wonderful; if they have difficulty accessing it or the connection fails, they will blame the library. For those systems that have security or licensing requirements, remote users must have an easy way of identifying themselves to the system. Dial-access users should be able to communicate with the mainframe about the compatibility of their terminal emulation. In libraries that have moved to a client-server environment, the client must be readily available and able to assist users with connections.

- *Adequate number of ports/no waiting.* The patterns of remote access are changing. Internet use is growing at an exponential rate, and many dial-access users are switching to the Internet as a means of access. Libraries must consistently monitor the contention for dial-access and Internet ports and be prepared to respond to changing demands with new or reallocated ports. To minimize the number of users encountering busy signals, some sort of time-out feature is essential to keep inactive users from tying up busy ports. If at all possible, a queuing mechanism that allows users to wait until a port becomes available would help counter user impatience.

- *Generous hours of operation.* Because remote users are seeking convenience, remote access should be available, if at all possible, twenty-four hours a day. From a public services perspective, it is far easier to have a system that is constantly operational that to have to explain to users when it will and will not be accessible.

- *Upgraded modems.* Remote users with high speed modems want to be able to "talk" with other high-speed modems. As users upgrade to 14.4bps or 28.8bps modems, they will lose patience with libraries that offer only 9,600, or even worse, 2,400 baud connections. Also, compatible modem speeds will speed up the connection process for remote users.

- *Obvious beginnings and endings.* Nothing is worse than staring at a blank screen. Users need prompts to get them started, to inform them of the basic commands, and to explain how to get assistance. They also need to know how to log off gracefully so that they can easily break their modem or telnet connection.

- *Diagnostic error messages.* The author's study of the searching behavior of remote users found that they receive more procedural error messages than on-site users.[4] This means that remote users have more difficulty mastering system commands and sequences. To be helpful, error messages should be diagnostic. Users should not only be informed of an error, but also told what to do. Error messages, especially those that are cryptic or geared toward system operators; for example, "error #49 has occurred," are especially frustrating to remote users.

- *On-line help.* Remote users are more likely to consult on-line help than on-site users. The author's transaction log study found that remote users are twice as likely to use on-line help;[5] this was supported by Sloan's finding at ILLINET.[6] On-line help messages must be clear and concise, be designed with the remote user in mind, and allow users to easily return to their workscreens. The popularity of windows and hypertext should provide system designers with the flexibility to develop help systems that are more user-friendly.

- *On-line "helpdesks."* A support service component can be built into the on-line system to allow remote users to send on-line comments or even requests for assistance. When one user encountered a problem searching the University of Texas' on-line catalog, she sent an on-line query through the system and received a satisfying response within thirty minutes.

- *Enhanced bibliographic records.* Remote users only have access to bibliographic records; they are not able to review the physical items to decide if they have found the materials they really need. The enhancement of records with tables of contents, indexes, or reviews would greatly assist remote users in determining the relevance of the information they retrieve.

- *Shortcuts.* Frequent users, especially remote users, do not want to waste time wading through menus or complicated screens. Once users have mastered a system, they want to be able to use shortcuts, abbreviations, and other techniques to reduce the number of interactions with the system. The system needs to be flexible to compensate for different searching styles and abilities.

- *Limited interfaces.* Despite users' tolerance for multiple interfaces, the onus is still on the user to learn and master the commands and searching techniques of diverse systems. This learning curve can be reduced if system designers make a conscious effort to minimize the number of interfaces available. Consideration should be given to new protocols, such as Z39.50, which allow users to employ the commands from their native system to search remote systems.

- *Printing and downloading.* Remote users want not only to access information, but also to use and manipulate it. They expect an on-line system to act like the CD-ROM they find in the library, regardless of whether they are using the on-line system in the library or from their homes. The on-line system should provide the ability to print and download, preferably with the flexibility to select citations or ranges.

- *User-centered development.* Initiating user-centered development, and including remote users in this process, is probably the best way to ensure that on-line systems are responsive to user needs. Too many of the on-line systems offered by libraries were designed by librarians for librarians. They are not intuitive. Thinking of remote users as customers, and incorporating these customers into the development process, encourages libraries to assess their needs, to incorporate these needs into the system, and to develop a continuous quality feedback mechanism. Libraries must remember that the networked world is not just a matrix of machines, but of people.

PROMOTIONAL AND INSTRUCTIONAL ACTIVITIES

There are many ways in which libraries can support remote users. Some are common sense, others are merely extensions of what libraries do for their in-house customers. Technological innovations offer libraries new possibilities for expanded and more effective support. Corporations and computing centers can serve as models of support operations.

Instructional and promotional activities for remote users are the easiest and the most comfortable support activities for librarians to implement because they can easily be blended into their traditional programs. Remote users have two instructional needs: they must learn how to access the system they want to use; and they must learn about the availability of on-line databases and services and how to use them properly. Faculty surveyed at the State University of New York (SUNY) identified more "information about databases/services" as the major factor that would increase their use of electronic technologies. The same faculty wanted more training on computer equipment, emphasizing the importance of technical knowledge to effective remote use of on-line systems.[7] Unfortunately, as most librarians will testify, faculty are not likely to seek help or attend classes despite their identified need. Despite good planning and content, many classes often reach a very limited audience. Therefore, instructional activities should not be regarded as the only level of support.

There are other activities that may be more effective in assisting remote users.[8] A news feature or an announcement screen on the on-line system or catalog can inform users about the newest databases, latest system changes, or scheduled downtime. Since remote users are wired users, libraries should make liberal use of electronic media such as newsgroups, Gopher, and the World Wide Web for announcements and news items.

Connecting to a library's on-line system is often the most pressing need of users. Instructional brochures should be produced that simply and systematically explain the different methods of access, such as dial access, telnet, or the World Wide Web. Printed information can be distributed widely on campus, and electronic versions can be made accessible via FTP servers, the World Wide Web or other on-line services.

Libraries already offer information on how to search and navigate the various databases and services they make accessible through their on-line catalogs. This specialized information should be made available both in print and on-line formats. On-line tutorials for remote databases and catalogs can be made available through the on-line catalog, services such as the World Wide Web, or through the campus network. Audio and video tapes can be developed and distributed as instructional tools. As computer networks become more widespread and able to push more information over their bandwidths, it is not unreasonable to expect libraries to develop their own mini-broadcasting stations to deliver instruction to dorms and offices.

Directions on how to print and download are especially helpful to users who are accessing systems from homes or offices and want to capture information. Since the commands to print and download vary depending on the communications software being used, libraries can create guides that provide commands for all communications software programs supported by or in common use by faculty, staff, and students.

Some libraries have had considerable success offering special classes devoted to what is available on their own on-line catalogs or via the Internet. The SUNY faculty identified small group classes or workshops as the training method they most preferred.[9] It is easy to integrate into these classes information on the technical aspects of remote access to the library's on-line catalog. An entire class can be offered on the varying ways of connecting to the library's on-line system. These classes must be generic, since each individual's technical requirements and problems cannot be addressed in a classroom situation. Some libraries also offer classes on the use of bibliographic management software such as Pro-Cite, Reference Manager, and other tools that allow users to create personal information management systems. These classes help users answer the question: "Now that I've got it, what do I do with it?"

Librarians and staff need to exploit opportunities to interact with the campus community. As library walls tumble down, librarians are free to visit offices, meetings, and other areas where their patrons congregate.

Some librarians have traveling shows that allow on-site demonstrations and presentations. This is an ideal way to show potential remote users how to access on-line systems from the convenience of their offices.

ESTABLISHING A SUPPORT SERVICE
FOR REMOTE USERS

Bernard Sloan has written that "remote users are more likely to be under-served."[10] If traditional library structures and services, which were established for walk-in customers, are unable to adequately serve remote users, then it is imperative that libraries investigate alternative means of support. Nothing undercuts a library's reputation faster than poor service. A rule of thumb for information professionals is that 20 percent of people with a bad experience with an organization will tell at least twenty others about it.[11]

If remote users' problems related primarily to the choice or even the use of on-line systems, librarians would have little problem pulling remote users into their traditional library service model or establishing a special unit to assist them. However, many remote user problems are integrated with technical issues; for example, "How do I connect?" or "How do I download the information from Medline?" A fundamental problem with microcomputers is that many users are not properly trained to use them and others are not willing to read the instructional documentation—when it is available. The challenges of coping with the various software programs, hardware platforms, and diverse means of access can be daunting. These challenges may be beyond the expertise of librarians or library staff; or perhaps more accurately, fall outside their area of interest. Many library professionals consider these concerns the domain of campus computing centers.

Generally, libraries have resisted developing in-house technical support services, instead referring these problems to computing centers where high-level support is supposed to be readily available. However, the incredible growth of networks to disseminate information and the increase in the number of users accessing library-based information on these networks may cause libraries to re-evaluate this decision. The line between content and technology is blurring. A user cannot access an on-line catalog on the World Wide Web (WWW) without understanding the functions and power of a Web browser or the concept of hyper-links.

It is not only the user that is affected by this phenomenon, but the librarian as well. An art librarian must understand WWW technology if he expects to be knowledgeable about art museums; the documents librarian knows that the most recent and popular government information is often available first on the Internet. This forces librarians who wish to maintain their subject expertise and reference skills to master the technology that too many resisted for too long.

Remote users do not care who responds to their calls for assistance. They just want assistance whenever and wherever they need it. They want one-stop shopping instead of a service desk shuffle. It is imperative that libraries decide how their remote users will be served. Many academic institutions are establishing new procedures or projects designed to move their faculty, staff, and students onto the Internet not only from their networked offices, but from their homes via dial-access. It is a logical assumption that many of these newly connected users will want to use the library's databases. Now is the time to review how libraries and computing centers can cooperate to offer the kinds of support users are seeking. There are valid arguments for one centralized support center for the entire institution, and also valid arguments for having the libraries and computing centers operating separate support services.

Keeping remote user support service under the umbrella of the campus computing center means that users should have ready access to high-level technical support. For years computing centers have run helpdesks, or dedicated service desks, for members of a campus community having problems with the mainframe or their microcomputers. A helpdesk provides one-stop shopping for users who are unable to determine whether the library, computing center, or another unit should respond to their calls for assistance. For instance, a user having problems downloading from Medline while using university-licensed software cannot determine if the problem relates to Medline, therefore necessitating a call to the library, or to the software. Also, many libraries do not have a sufficient volume of questions to justify maintaining a support desk for remote users; therefore, combining their support with an established helpdesk operation makes good economic sense.

Wielhorski maintains that the users' need for the one-stop support approach means "that librarians should develop in-house technical support for handling the needs of remote users as well as providing support for searching and using electronic information resources."[12] Libraries have always maintained reference desks, but the concept of a helpdesk, so familiar to the users of personal computers and other technologies, is new and perhaps intimidating. Helpdesks connote the idea of a service component dedicated to those with immediate needs that are primarily technical in nature. Perhaps libraries need to create a new type of help-desk that has a scope beyond technical questions. For instance, a librarian handling a helpdesk call relating to connecting to ERIC may take advantage of the opportunity to ask the user if she has any questions about the content or searching of the database. He may be able to tell her about a special seminar the library is offering on ERIC. As libraries move to rethink reference and their instructional efforts, they should be looking at their users' needs and new ways of addressing them. The helpdesk concept is one alternative that should be considered.

The concept of a library helpdesk blends easily with the functions of a gateway library. As library walls come down, the gateway concept must extend beyond the bricks-and-mortar building. Remote access to library systems is a gateway unto itself that needs specialized support. Gateway libraries that only support walk-in users are disregarding an important and growing segment of library customers.

Any library operating a support service or helpdesk for remote users must ensure that the desk is promoted in every way, and that hours are maintained not for the convenience of the staff, but for the user. The helpdesk could accept requests via phone, electronic mail, fax, or even walk-in. It is critical that the library employ the appropriate kind of staff to operate a helpdesk. Staff members who support remote users must have the technical skills necessary to handle trouble-shooting, access concerns, and consultation. They must also possess what are called soft skills, such as good interpersonal relations, the ability to communicate technical information to a non-technical audience, and patience. If the helpdesk offers even rudimentary assistance with the actual use of the databases, its staff also needs a solid grounding in reference skills. Helpdesk calls often come from patrons who are unsure or anxious about the equipment or programs that they are using; some are looking more for reassurance than facts. Helpdesk staff must be part technician, part psychotherapist. They must be well trained and consistently updated in the new technologies and electronic services that the library offers.

The use of helpdesk software, which has been popular in corporate environments and is beginning to be adopted by libraries, is another way that libraries can monitor helpdesk operations. Helpdesk software keeps statistics and information on calls, allows for the recording of calls that may need follow-up, keeps schedules of instructional classes, and can even provide the staff with canned answers to frequently requested information. It helps to track calls, thereby providing the background to queries from users such as "sometime in the last two weeks (*when?*) I talked with a woman (*what woman?*) who told me…." This analysis of helpdesk calls facilitates the sharing of information among staff and can be used to detect consistent problems that can then be referred to system developers for solutions.

Libraries and other university operations can learn some lessons and best practices in user support and helpdesk management from corporations. Many of these corporations produce and sell computer equipment and software. They find that the follow-up support they offer is critical to sales and the continued goodwill of their customers. One of the best models for user support is IBM's Helpcenter, located in Raleigh, North Carolina. In response to customer concerns and the company's desire to offer improved support for the products it sells, IBM revamped its Helpcenter operations, hired more staff, instituted a new phone system, established a training program, and made quality control measures an integral part of operations.[13]

The Helpcenter employs several hundred people who answer 20,000 phone calls a day and thousands of other queries via Internet-based services. Customer service is a major emphasis. All employees are taught and expected to adhere to established service standards. To ensure this adherence, random tape recordings are made of employee-customer interactions and the calls are checked for compliance to service standards. In addition, 8 percent of callers receive follow-up calls from IBM to check on the quality of service they received.

Helpdesk software provides support staff with detailed information on IBM products and services. Employees are also required to keep track of who is calling and the kinds of trouble calls received. Patterns in Helpcenter calls can then be detected and relayed back to product developers who can solve the problems or build improvements into future IBM products. Also, customer suggestions are noted in the helpdesk software under a feature called Voice of the Customer. Various customer satisfaction councils consider customer problems and suggestions, thus making customer feedback a formal process that is integral to all Helpcenter activities.

CONCLUSION

The tremendous growth of the Internet indicates that remote use of information systems will increase. Users' overwhelmingly positive and enthusiastic acceptance of tools such as the World Wide Web illustrates the insatiable demand for information that is accessible, convenient, and deliverable to the user's desktop. The buzzword for what is causing this phenomenon is "virtual libraries," which Kaye Gapen defines "as the concept of remote access to the contents and services of libraries and other information."[14] As everyone plugs into the ever increasing network of networks, librarians must redefine the parameters of their responsibilities. Many users of these networks will be long-distance learners or patrons that librarians have never seen. If librarians are serious about continuing to build new gateways to information, then they must commit to offering corresponding reference and support services. They must ensure instruction, not just in information literacy, but in the corresponding technology; they must help create systems that are transparent in their use and supportive of remote users' needs; and they must make themselves available to users who have trouble connecting to the virtual world or who find themselves lost in it.

ACKNOWLEDGMENT

This chapter is based on a panel presentation, "Beam Me Up Scottie: Transforming Remote Users into Primary Users," Summary in *Continuity & Transformation: The Promise of Confluence*, Proceedings of the Seventh National Conference of the Association of College and Research Libraries, Pittsburgh, PA, March 29-April 1, 1995 (p. 456).

NOTES

1. Judith A. Adams and Sharon Bonk, "Electronic Information Technologies and Resources: Use by Faculty and Faculty Preferences for Related Library Services," *College and Research Libraries* 56 (March 1995): 122.

2. John R. Sack, "Open Systems for Open Minds: Building the Library Without Walls," *College and Research Libraries* 47 (November 1986): 535-544.

3. Anne Woodsworth, "Emerging Electronic Library Services," *Academic Computing* (February 1990): 50.

4. Sally W. Kalin, "The Searching Behaviors of Remote Users: A Study of One On-line Public Access Catalog." *Proceedings of the 54th Annual Meeting of the American Society for Information Science* 28 (1991): 155.

5. Kalin, "The Searching Behaviors of Remote Users: A Study of One On-line Public Access Catalog," 155.

6. Bernard S. Sloan, "Remote Users: Design Implications for the On-line Catalog," *Cataloging and Classification Quarterly* 13 (1991): 137.

7. Adams, 127.

8. For more detailed information on providing special services to remote users, consult: Scott Davis, "Dial Access Users of On-line Catalogs: Responding to the Needs of BI's Newest User Group," *Illinois Libraries* 70 (December 1988): 638-644; Sally W. Kalin, "Support Services for Remote Users of On-line Public Access Catalogs," *RQ* 31.2 (Winter 1991): 197-213; Karen Wielhorski, "Teaching Remote Users How to Use Electronic Information Resources," *The Public-Access Computer Systems Review* 5.4 (1994): 5-20.

9. Adams, 127.

10. Adams, 136.

11. Ken White, "Customer Service—Whose Job Is It?" *Data Training* 8 (March 1989): 31.

12. Wielhorski, 11.

13. Bart Ziegler, "Help!" *Wall Street Journal.* Special Technology Insert. June 27, 1994. Information also gathered during author's personal visit to IBM Helpcenter.

14. Kaye D. Gapen, "The Virtual Library: Knowledge, Society and the Librarian," *The Virtual Library: Visions and Realities,* ed. Laverna M. Saunders (Westport, CT: Meckler, 1993), 1.

HOLDING LIBRARY OFFICE HOURS IN ACADEMIC DEPARTMENTS:
REACHING OUT TO FACULTY

Lucia Snowhill

ABSTRACT

The rapid explosion in electronic information resources and technologies challenges librarians to rethink how they provide reference services. Holding office hours in an academic department offers librarians an opportunity to take advantage of electronic technologies in order to provide convenient ways to instruct faculty in the use of on-line systems, to facilitate consultations on collections, course assignments, and research needs, and to heighten faculty awareness of the range of library services and resources.

ELECTRONIC ENVIRONMENT

Librarians are confronted with two very different changes that have had considerable impact on library information management, organization, and services. The explosion of electronic information and technological capabilities has provided tremendous opportunities to improve both management of and access to information. At the same time, libraries, facing budget cuts for materials and personnel, are reconsidering the organizational structure of reference services. These changes challenge librarians to take advantage of new technologies and organizational models in order to continue to play a viable role in the academic mission.

Electronic access to information is changing reference services in a number of ways. The range of options for accessing and providing consultation about information has been greatly expanded. The number of electronic resources is growing in all academic disciplines, and an increasing amount of information is being distributed on networks. Like print sources, electronic resources range from the general to those tailored to specific academic disciplines. Reference librarians are expected to be aware of and use electronic information in all formats in order to provide appropriate information referral services. They must know how to use a variety of system commands and interfaces, understand and interpret the elements of electronic records, and teach users search strategies and protocols.[1]

Various models of organizing reference services have emerged to adapt to both increased electronic capabilities and reduced staffing. At one end of the spectrum are those libraries opting for the Brandeis University model, which eliminates the reference desk altogether and replaces it with an information desk staffed by paraprofessionals. Librarians are available only for reference consultations.[2] At the opposite end of the spectrum are those libraries that continue to provide full reference desk services. Between these two extremes are a growing number of hybrid service models, which combine reduced or merged reference service points with increased reliance on reference consultation by subject specialists. A number of authors have suggested a tiered model for reference, which includes elements such as an information desk, reference desk, reference consultation, increased bibliographic instruction, and increased liaison with faculty.[3] These models take advantage of improved information access, concentrate subject specialists' time more effectively, and demonstrate that there can be a variety of ways to think about how and where reference consultation is done.

As libraries incorporate and adapt to electronic technologies, researchers are also coping with changing patterns of scholarly communication and research methods. Scholars are excited about the technologies that allow them to access electronic information. Library users who once would have come into the library to obtain assistance in finding information are now retrieving some of their information from workstations in their homes or offices without consulting either library resources or librarians. As a result, traditional reference services, while still important, are not providing the range of assistance that information users now need. In addition, there are varying levels of computer literacy among academic researchers. As with printed sources, researchers need assistance in identifying appropriate electronic resources and developing search strategies.

As they restructure public services and information access to adapt to these changes, reference librarians should ask the following questions. How do libraries provide effective reference service to a population of users that may not come to the library? Are librarians available where their users need assistance? Are all researchers capable and sophisticated electronic resource users? If researchers do need assistance, do they see reference for electronic information as an extension of traditional library services? It is important for these users to see the library as a service as well as a resource. If the essence of providing reference services is to survive in the electronic environment, librarians must find ways of delivering those services outside the library building.

The ability to use electronic technologies for information access frees the reference librarian from a service based on location and creates opportunities for new ways to assist patrons. Public services must be re-engineered to think less of services associated with location and more of services that can be performed both electronically and in locations remote from the library building. As Lori Goetsch writes, "Taken at its most basic element, reference is an interactive process that is not tied to an physical place, or even to a person with a particular status."[4]

CAMPUS OUTREACH

Librarians have to be more aggressive in making users aware of reference services and in providing those services where information seekers need them. One of the ways to rethink reference is to consider improving relationships with faculty, targeting a primary user clientele for information services. Anne Lipow suggests that there are several reasons to focus on outreach to faculty in the electronic library environment. Faculty need to learn new bibliographic concepts, and they act as vital conduits to students. Working with faculty in new ways will be essential to the changing role of librarians in the electronic environment.[5]

How can librarians achieve the long-term goal of ensuring that faculty perceive librarians as providers of a range of services related to the access of electronic information? One way is for librarians to provide reference service in the location where faculty need it. Holding office hours in an academic department offers librarians an opportunity to reach library users who no longer need to come into the library to fill some portion of their information needs. This new type of service has several objectives:

- to assist faculty with use of on-line catalogs and electronic information systems;
- to consult with faculty on library collections, course assignments, and research needs;
- to increase librarians' level of contact and visibility with faculty;
- to increase librarians' knowledge of academic departments;
- to heighten faculty awareness of the range of library services and resources.

In the Fall of 1993 the author began to hold regularly scheduled office hours in the Political Science Department at the University of California, Santa Barbara. She is the library's collection manager for political science and law, with a range of responsibilities including materials purchase, reference, bibliographic instruction, and faculty liaison in those academic fields. One of the library's goals for collection managers has been to increase faculty liaison and instruction. The idea of holding office hours initially came from both the pragmatic objectives listed above and a broader concern for the future of the faculty's image of library and information services. The author was not satisfied with the level of contact she had achieved with faculty through interactions in the library and regular memorandums sent to them regarding library news and the range of services available to them and their students. There was a specific need to assist faculty with effective use of the on-line catalogs and other electronic resources, but few faculty were likely to seek out assistance from librarians for that kind of consultation. The author wanted to test the possibilities for providing a range of services at a location outside the library by taking advantage of electronic technologies.

Once it was determined that office hours would be beneficial, plans were presented to the academic department chair and library administrators. The political science department chair was interested in an experiment with office hours, and library administrators were supportive of the experiment. Equipment and space were available at no cost to the department or the library.

ESTABLISHING THE SERVICE

The essential factor in making physical arrangements for office space was access to the campus network via a computer terminal or workstation, since a primary goal of holding office hours was to provide reference service and instruction for using electronic systems. In order to offer this service, the ability to connect to the library's on-line catalogs and other electronic resources was needed. By accessing the library's systems via the campus network, it was also possible to assist patrons with specific access configuration issues that they face in reaching appropriate on-line systems. In addition, it was desirable for the computer to have a graphical interface to the Internet, document management software for work on text and spreadsheets, and a modem for access to dial-up services. For the experiment in Santa Barbara, an IBM 286 with campus network access, which provided access to both the campus network and the library's on-line catalog. The computer was later upgraded to an IBM 486 connected to the campus network, with NetScape for World Wide Web access and word processing and related software.

While the most important factor in selecting office space in the political science department was the availability of a campus network connection for the workstation, high visibility and convenience to the faculty were also desirable. Although separate office space would have been preferred, the academic department did not have such office space available. Given the low number of office hours to be held, it was important for the librarian to be flexible and pragmatic about the space provided.

For this test, the librarian used the department's computer/fax room, which contained two personal computers, a fax machine, and a typewriter. The room was normally open and available for faculty, graduate students and staff to access equipment or electronic mail accounts. The room was centrally located in a high traffic administrative area of the department, near administrative assistants' offices, the department mail room, and the photocopy area. One of the computers was wired to the campus network, allowing access to the library's on-line catalog and the Internet.

This space was already available for related purposes, so it was not necessary for the department to provide additional office space for the librarian, only to allocate time in existing office space. In fact, it was beneficial to share space. Because department personnel were frequently in and out of the room, the librarian's visibility and opportunity for informal exchange were greatly increased. Traffic in and out of the office for other uses was not disruptive for the vast majority of discussions held with faculty and students. Although the office served as a home base, the librarian actually spent considerable time circulating in other areas of the department.

The setting of office hours was determined by the project's objectives, the level of the librarian's other commitments, and the availability of space. It was important to select hours when the majority of faculty and students were working in the department. For this project, the librarian scheduled two hours per week in the department, 1:30-2:30 on Tuesdays and 11:00-12:00 on Wednesdays. These specific hours were selected for a number of reasons. The librarian wanted to be available at times that coincided with both the Monday/Wednesday/Friday and Tuesday/Thursday class schedules. The morning and afternoon schedules of faculty were also considered. Mail delivery times were desirable because traffic near the office was high. For consistency, the same hours have been scheduled every term. By scheduling according to these criteria, the librarian increased opportunities for informal exchange and visibility.

Office hours can be advertised with flyers in mail boxes, posters, notices in newsletters, postings on library and librarians' web pages, and memoranda to the faculty from the librarian. The librarian may announce office hours to classes during bibliographic instruction sessions and give informal reminders when speaking to individual faculty members. Hours should be posted on the door of the office where the service is located. Using a variety of advertising techniques and repeating them frequently in the first year increased the success of office hours at Santa Barbara. Colorful flyers and posters were the most effective way of providing initial announcements of office hours. Newsletters, memos, and E-mail to the faculty served as regular reminders of the availability of the service.

EFFECTIVENESS OF LIBRARIAN'S OFFICE HOURS

It has been noted by Daniel Blewett that time spent in office hours does cover both the range of reference services and the spectrum of the academic population.[6] During office hours at Santa Barbara, as much time has been spent with students, both graduate and undergraduate, as with faculty. The librarian has given initial assistance on information resources related to term papers and other research projects. Some time has been spent consulting on the use of resources such as on-line catalogs, the

Internet, and E-mail. With faculty, the librarian has consulted about research needs, collection development requests, course assignments, and the creation of library guides and class instruction delivered by librarians for specific courses. Like reference desk service, the demand for consultation during office hours has been cyclical. The author has made use of non-peak demand periods to catch up on department news, share library news informally with individuals, and follow up on previous consultations. A portion of time each week has been spent circulating to catch people informally by dropping in on faculty, talking to people in the mail room and hallways, and getting updates on department information from administrative personnel.

For faculty, the benefits of office hours have been the convenience of assistance and consultation from the librarian. With increased visibility have come opportunities to inform faculty of the range of services the library and the subject specialist can offer. The librarian has explained library policies and recommended ways to obtain needed information. She has assisted with course-related library research projects through the development of guides and instruction for students on library resources and research techniques. Faculty have appreciated the fact that a librarian has dedicated time to work specifically on their needs and concerns.

This informal interaction has also been very helpful to the librarian, who has learned more about faculty concerns in order to better anticipate needs. It was very beneficial to establish good communication with department support staff, who have become familiar with the types of department information that were useful to the librarian in serving the faculty's teaching and research needs. The increased awareness of the librarian's role has generated more communication and referrals through other means, such as E-mail, phone, mail, and in-library consultation. At Santa Barbara, as the office hour contacts increased, so has the number of contacts and referrals for the librarian's assistance in the library. The time spent in the department has generated appointments, referrals and commitments to projects for faculty that were subsequently scheduled to take place in the library.

CONCLUSION

Advancements in electronic information technologies and information access now allow librarians to provide reference services to targeted academic populations outside the library in locations where users are doing their research. Holding office hours in an academic department complements reference and collection consultations done in the library. It does not replace in-house reference and consultation, but it can be used to reach users who may not think they need to come to the library for their research. There is mutual benefit for faculty and the librarian in information exchanged, visibility and familiarity. By holding office hours in an academic department, librarians can improve communication and working relationships with targeted academic users.

Several issues should be addressed in determining whether or not to hold office hours for faculty outside the library. Depending on librarians' current opportunities for faculty contact, adding office hours may or may not be viable or appropriate. For librarians with collection management responsibilities in large general university libraries, office hours provide librarians an opportunity to become more visible to faculty. For branch libraries located in academic departments, however, holding office hours may be redundant, since a high level of contact and interaction between librarians and faculty may already exist.

There are many options for setting up office hours in academic departments. Librarians who decide to establish office hours must determine, in conjunction with the academic department, what kind of equipment and physical space are needed, what the hours of availability will be, and how the service will be promoted. The time commited to office hours need not be large if it is scheduled for maximum visibility. In the long term, providing informational services outside the physical library location establishes a continuing presence for reference services in the electronic information environment. Departmental office hours keep the library's information services visible to the faculty and help keep the library a viable part of the academic mission.

NOTES

1.   Leslie M. Kong, "Reference Service Evolved," *Journal of Academic Librarianship* 21 (January 1995): 13-14.

2.   Jackie Mardikian and Martin Kesselman, "Beyond the Desk: Enhanced Reference Staffing for the Electronic Library," *Reference Services Review* 23 (Spring 1995): 21.

3.   Willian L. Whitson, "Differentiated Service: A New Reference Model," *Journal of Academic Librarianship* 21 (March 1995): 103-110.

4.   Lori Goetsch, "Reference Service is More Than a Desk," *Journal of Academic Librarianship* 21 (January 1995): 15.

5.   Anne G. Lipow, "Outreach to Faculty: Why and How," in *Working with Faculty in the New Electronic Library* (Ann Arbor, MI: Pierian Press, 1992): 7-13.

6.   Daniel K. Blewett, "The Librarian is In," *College and Research Library News* 56 (November 1995): 701-703.

TELEPHONE REFERENCE:
DIVISION OF LABOR VIA AN ON-LINE NETWORK

Kathryn Robinson and Sally Fry

ABSTRACT

The population of Orange County, Florida has doubled over the last twenty-five years, which has put tremendous pressure on the Orange County Library System, especially on its reference service. The yearly reference transactions increased from three quarters of a million in fiscal year 1986 to 1.7 million in fiscal year 1993. When adjustments to the reference process could no longer assure quality responses in a timely manner, the need to restructure the process became critical. This library system addressed this need by creating a separate telephone reference department. The new service is supported by an on-line database program that captures and tracks questions, documents each step of the process, and assures consistent, high quality and timely responses.

ORANGE COUNTY LIBRARY SYSTEM

The Orange County Library System (Orange County, Florida) consists of the downtown Orlando Public Library and eleven branches. Its mission is "to provide access to resources to support the informational, educational, recreational and cultural needs and interests of the members of the Orange County Library District in a financially responsible manner." Begun as a small municipal library in 1923, the system is now an independent taxing district created by community referendum in 1980 and supported through ad valorem property taxes of residents of the district. The district, which has a service area of 900 square miles, includes all of Orange County except the incorporated areas of the cities of Winter Park and Maitland. The governing board of the district is composed of the Board of County Commissioners and one member appointed by the City Council of Orlando. This board appoints the five-member Orange County Library Board of Trustees. The current library director is Dorothy Field. Ms. Field succeeds Glenn F. Miller, who retired in 1995 after serving 25 years as library director (see Appendix A for organization chart).

Orange County has grown tremendously in the last twenty-five years. The county's population which was 344,311 in 1970, grew to 746,000 by 1995.[1] The more than double growth in population has changed Orlando from a large Southern town into a major U.S. city.[2] Traffic has become fast paced and congested. Free parking downtown has been virtually eliminated. Therefore, a significant number of residents cannot or do not choose to visit the main library. This is most clearly shown by the popularity of MAYL (Materials Access from Your Library), a service which has delivered library materials such as books, videos, music cassettes, and compact discs to individual households for over 20 years. In 1995 alone, 250,000 items were sent to patrons using MAYL.

REFERENCE IN NEED OF CHANGE

The growth of Orange County, the library system, and its use put tremendous pressure on reference service. Approximately one-third of reference transactions were taken on the phone and two-thirds were from walk-in patrons. For all patrons, librarians offered readers' advisory services, assistance in reference searches, reserving materials not on the shelves, and verification of requests considered for purchase or borrowed through interlibrary loan. In addition, staff answered both ready reference and in-depth questions. In juggling these tasks, staff knew that some users were being short-changed, either in the amount of time or in the quality of reference service. Phone lines backed up and walk-in patrons competed with callers for staff attention. The library's reference standard of searching each question fully and closing a question only when all sources have been checked, all options pursued, and/or all appropriate referrals offered was difficult to uphold.

With this increased demand on staff, a more structured process became necessary to monitor and gauge the effectiveness of service. In order to gather meaningful statistics, a callback form that had been in use for a number of years was revised (see Appendix B). The forms generated statistical information that the administration could use to look at the number and type of reference transactions and identify which types of questions were difficult to answer. In addition, the use of these forms encouraged teamwork on difficult questions and gave managers specific examples for coaching staff in interviewing and search strategies. The data collected from these forms gave managers concrete information for analyzing what units were doing and how well the staff met patron requests.

By early 1991, a revised callback form was used for all questions not answered while patrons were on hold or standing at a reference desk. As new reference questions came in, the majority were answered during initial searches. However, in-depth questions written down on callback forms frequently were not answered fully or in a timely manner. Often, the questions had not been negotiated properly, or librarians had been too busy to spend the necessary time on each reference transaction. These callback forms documented an alarming trend: reference service demands had begun to overwhelm the staff's ability to consistently meet the library's high standard. A clear sign of this was the increasing number of pending callback forms extant in each reference department. The harder or more complex the question, the less likely it would be answered in a timely manner. With the steady increase of unanswered reference questions, it was time for staff to ask themselves "What are we doing?" and "How can we do it better?"

The library took several steps to address this observed need for improved service. The first step was to learn how other libraries handled difficult or unanswered questions. Phone calls were made to U.S. libraries of a similar size to learn how other libraries handled challenging reference questions. A study tour was made to several libraries in California to observe their second and third tier backup reference systems.[3] Also, a series of classes called the University of OCLS (Orange County Library System) was developed by managers and experienced librarians. These classes were refresher courses on topics which included interview skills, teamwork in reference service, common questions and sources, creative methods for handling more difficult questions, the use of indexes, verifying titles, and finding book reviews. A variety of teaching methods were used, including lectures, videos, role playing, and discussions.

Members of a special department worked a night shift at the main library for a one-year period. Among other duties, these librarians assisted with reference requests taken throughout the day and entered unanswered questions in the Question and Answer (Q&A) database newly created by the library's Data Processing Department. This uninterrupted time to study the work of the day provided another opportunity to take a careful look at the numbers and types of requests and the quality of work that went into the filling requests. Their observations revealed that reference service was inconsistent and not always of the highest quality.

The Question and Answer database could be searched by Dewey classification number and keyword. The database was first used to compile statistics on subjects that had the highest percentage of unanswered questions. For example, statistics revealed that among the most frequently unanswered questions were those requesting the addresses or phone numbers of lesser-known companies. The staff also used the Q & A database to identify categories of specific sources for addition to the collection. It was evident, for example, that additional sources of business information were needed. Later, when CD-ROM products were first introduced, unanswered questions from the database were used to test the usefulness of the CD-ROMs.

By 1993 the average number of pending or in-progress callback forms was well over two hundred and ranged from one day to several weeks in age. The need to restructure the reference process became critical. Consideration was given to three options: limiting the amount of effort and time given to each question; hiring additional reference staff; or redesigning the process to support an efficient, effective method to maintain the current reference standard. The library chose to redesign the process because this option required no reduction of service and no additional staff. The goal was to improve the efficiency and quality of service to library users. Staff would provide service on an equitable basis and in a manner which was cost effective for the taxpayer. In order to reach this goal, the library administration encouraged the staff to break public library paradigms in order to create the most effective solutions to meet the needs of library patrons.

Many unknowns existed in creating a telephone reference process in which transactions would be recorded and tracked through an online system. Therefore, it was stated clearly to all staff that there must be flexibility in developing and adjusting procedures. When procedures were established prior to the start date, managers clearly conveyed that this was how the process would start, not how the process would be finalized. It was further understood that procedures and processes would be subject to constant evaluation and adjustment as more was learned about providing the most efficient service to callers.

In order to give staff time to adjust to a new telephone reference service and to further study the reference process, nearly a year was spent in planning and preparation. System reference managers met with the administration to understand the need for change and to brainstorm on how changes could be made. Staff attended seminars which included discussion of the reasons for change, an initial look at what the changes would be, and even role-playing to help staff problem-solve anticipated situations. The head of the reference division spoke at staff meetings in each subject department, and staff training classes were held. Phone calls were also made to libraries which had established separate phone reference functions to obtain information about collections, staffing, and challenges of a phone reference service.[4]

TELEPHONE REFERENCE IMPLEMENTATION

With the decision to set up a separate telephone reference department, a Telephone Reference (TR) room was established. The room was equipped with telephone workstations, CD-ROM workstations, and print resources. The most fundamental and critical component was, and continues to be, the online database program developed by the library's data processing department. This TR database captures and tracks the questions, prompting staff to continue at each distinct step of the reference process. It documents when each step is completed and credits individual staff members' involvement. Reference managers can monitor active questions via the program's listing of all questions assigned to that department. Database information is displayed on a large screen which is divided into categories. Staff can see how many questions are pending in phone reference, how many are pending in the departments, and how may answers are ready to be delivered. The database displays information that enables managers to reassign staff and improve workflow at any time.

The unit was organized to reflect the two parts of the reference process: interviewing and research. The Interview Team staffed the phones, and the Research Team found answers to the questions. Members of the Interview Team spoke with callers, negotiated requests, advised patrons, and provided referral information. They instructed callers on how to conduct a search for information in the library and entered questions with all identified clues and necessary patron information into the online TR database. Callers with questions that could be answered within three minutes were transferred to a Ready Reference station staffed by a Research Team member. If an answer was not found, the question continued to the next stage of the answering/research process.

At this step, a reference manager reviewed the question and assigned it either to the Research Team to be searched in the TR reference collection or to a subject reference department for searching in specific sources. The reference manager also stopped any problems that had developed by this point in the process. Such problems might include questions not fully negotiated, questions that should have been answered with ready reference sources, and questions that required a patron to come to the library. This offered immediate ongoing feedback to individual interviewers in TR and generated examples for general training sessions.

Answer Delivery was identified as a separate function of the telephone reference process. As part of the interview, the method of delivery is negotiated, including alternatives if the patron is unable to be reached with a first phone call. Options now include: phone call, message or full information on machine/voice mail, fax, and mail. The staff member who finds the answer makes one attempt to deliver it and then enters the answer in the TR database. If subsequent phone calls are necessary, the answer remains active. As a result, all terminals show a message that answers are waiting to be delivered. Staff in all reference locations are responsible for delivering answers and are instructed to use any free moment to do so.

As TR developed, the most useful reference sources were moved within easy reach of the Interview Team, allowing the staff to answer ready reference questions during the interview process. This ready reference process continues today and will be expanded in the future to include the networking of selected CD-ROM products for use by the Interview Team. During the early months of TR, approximately 52 percent of all requests were completed at the time of the interview or with ready reference sources. This number has grown to 62 percent and should climb as the TR reference collection grows and access to CD-ROM products expands. In addition, TR staff answer another 10 percent of the total telephone reference questions using the CD-ROM sources, not while the patron is on hold, but during non-peak caller times. As more questions became answerable at the interview stage, the need for separate interview and research teams decreased and has resulted in a merged TR staff.

During TR's early months, all questions designated to be searched in reference departments were printed in a centralized location, separate from TR. In this temporary reference unit, dubbed the "Interrogatory Laboratory" or "Lab," a reference manager oversaw staff working on two types of reference questions: those needing to be checked in specific subject department sources and those requiring materials on specific subjects to be sent to the caller. The unit used this opportunity to discover which questions could not be answered using the TR collection, and what impact would be felt by subject departments if questions were sent to them rather than transferring phone calls. Their study revealed gaps existed in the circulating collection, in the reference sources, and in TR interviewers' knowledge of department sources. Once the study was completed, Lab staff were reassigned to subject departments and questions were routed directly to departments. Currently, questions assigned to subject departments are instantly printed at work stations in each specific location. Approximately 28 percent of the telephone reference questions are assigned to and answered by reference department staff who enter their answers at the same work station. (See Appendix C for flow chart.)

As originally planned, the TR department was to rely on CD-ROM products for its collection. This collection consisted of more than thirty CD-ROM titles, which included magazine and newspaper indexes, business and residential telephone and address information directories, unabridged dictionaries, general encyclopedias, and indexes to quotations, recordings, poetry, and biographical sources. Many of the products duplicated print sources already available in the subject reference departments. Selected electronic products, such as *PhoneDisc* and the *New York Times Index*, met our expectations for improved currency and greater access via keyword indexing. CD-ROMs of multi-volume directories and indexes such as *Columbia Granger's World of Poetry* and the *Biography and Genealogy Master Index* offered the most immediate improvement over their print counterparts. For answering simple ready reference questions, print versions of sources, such as the *World Almanac, Statistical Abstract of the United States,* and *World Book Encyclopedia* proved more efficient. It was quickly obvious that full-text indexes provided answers, while citation/abstract indexes gave only clues to where answers might be found. This was a significant factor in evaluating the future role of CD-ROMs in telephone reference. When the goal is to answer the majority of questions while the patron is on hold, citations and abstracts frustrate rather than please both patron and librarian.

The TR room was initially furnished with standard reference department tables, desks, chairs and book shelves. While staff found these furnishings suitable for several hour intervals of public desk assignments, ergonomically they did not support a full eight-hour work day. Applying what had been learned over the last year, a new unit has been ordered that incorporates adjustable work stations surrounding circular book shelves. Each shelf rotates separately, and workstations include desk and computer worktops. The unit will enable staff to safely reach all needed equipment and resources while remaining seated.

BENEFITS OF TELEPHONE REFERENCE

Both the library system and its patrons have benefited from the Telephone Reference Service. The most obvious beneficiaries of TR are the patrons who call the library. They now have the undivided attention of experienced staff members who recognize that question negotiation is the heart of the process. It is this initial communication between librarians and patrons that is critical to the success of the reference transaction. Concise instructions have been prepared to guide TR staff through each phone call. These guidelines state what information is needed, what is ready reference, and what information can realistically be delivered.

Both questions and answers now receive scrutiny that they never did or could in the past. Reference managers evaluate and turn back for renegotiation those questions which are unclear or not fully negotiated. Answers are reviewed to monitor accuracy and relevancy to the questions. This continual review of reference work results in concrete examples for the managers to use in coaching and developing staff performance. On-going evaluation results in more accurate and speedier delivery of the needed information or requested materials as well as higher patron satisfaction. Over 90 percent of the telephone reference questions, which are both ready reference and in-depth questions, are answered within twenty-four hours. Over half of the requests are handled while the patron is on hold. With the implementation of Telephone Reference, only a handful of current requests are identified as pending at any one time.

Walk-in patrons also benefit from Telephone Reference. They have better access to reference assistance than ever before. They do not have to wait for librarians to deal with ringing phones before their needs can be addressed. Librarians in subject departments are able to spend more time on readers' advisory services and on teaching patrons how to use the library and its reference sources.

The library as an organization benefits from the implementation of its new vision of reference services, as well. Librarians no longer are faced with the conflict of choosing which patron will be helped first: the walk-in or the phone-in. Both types of patrons receive a librarian's full attention. System-wide, the library benefits from this new service because staff time is used more efficiently. Increased efficiency results partly from the division of responsibility of service between phone-in and walk-in patrons. More significantly, efficiency has increased due to making some tasks, such as the delivery of reference answers, the responsibility of any available staff member.

The TR department is looking forward to continued improvement. Currently, TR calls are routed through the switchboard. In the immediate future, there will be a direct telephone line to TR so that a caller's first contact is with staff prepared to answer the patron's question. The library is upgrading its circulation and catalog system, which will allow access via the Internet. As part of this project, the reference CD-ROMs will be networked, making them available at most main library terminals. At the same time, branches will also be able to tap into TR's database, thereby referring their unanswered reference questions on-line rather than over the telephone. Because main and branches will have access to the Internet, the library plans to test some electronic subscriptions to full text periodical sources via the World Wide Web. The development of a World Wide Web home page will offer a guide to library resources and provide links to sources outside the library. Brainstorming sessions have created more ideas. A reference database of difficult-to-find answers to questions is being considered. In the future, there could be an interactive video librarian negotiating questions and advising patrons who call from a kiosk located at a mall or other off-site location's.

CONCLUSION

The goal of designing a new reference process was to improve efficiency and the quality of service to library users while providing the service on an equitable basis in a cost-effective manner. The process was to be one that would support continuing evaluation, modification, and improvement of service. It should interface with future technological and philosophical developments within the library. Already the process has passed several tests. The original design was developed under one library director and has responded well to support the vision of the current director. This is most clearly demonstrated in the meshing of TR's work with the planned enhancement of online access to the library's catalog and other resources.

By dividing the process and workload of reference service, the tiger has been tamed. Where day-to-day reference service once dominated, if not sometimes overwhelmed, reference managers, they are now able to dedicate some time to longer term projects. Now the main library can more easily address how best to accommodate walk-in patrons, whether by relocating, merging, or splitting departments, or by considering additional resources and services. With Internet access systemwide comes the opportunity for the branches and the main library to eliminate the barriers of distance and develop methods to connect patrons with information no matter where either is located.

Although not as physically imposing as the library's newly constructed city-block sized building, the design and implementation of this new reference process has affected the future of the library system nearly as much. It is as significant a foundation for the future as any building. Telephone Reference has enabled the Orange County Library System to learn "What are we doing?" and "How can we do it better?"

APPENDIX A

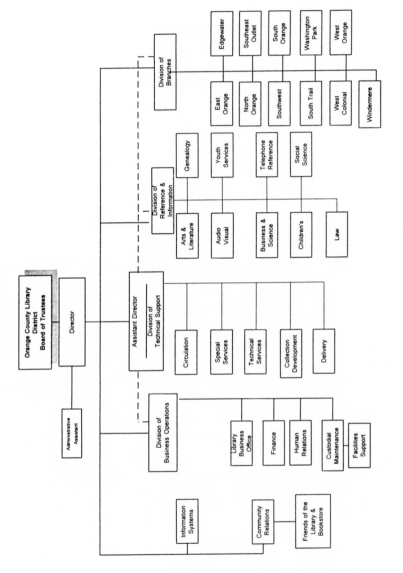

APPENDIX B

CALLBACK/SEARCH
Orange County Library System

Date _____ Dept _____ Staff _____ Deadline _____ Referred to/from _____

FOUND? No Partly Yes By _____ Date _____

Options Offered? No Yes: _____

_____

QUESTION:

Answer/Source:

SOURCES CHECKED (Give subject headings & dates, continue on back)   INITIALS

SUBJECT _____

_____

	Date & Time			
PATRON _____	No	Message to	Progress Rpt.	Patron
Address _____	Answer	Call Back	Only	Notified

DEWEY# _____

Zip _____ Card# _____

Phone: (HO) _____

Phone: (WO) _____

OCLS #89-4 (Rev. 4/92)

APPENDIX C
Telephone Reference Workflow

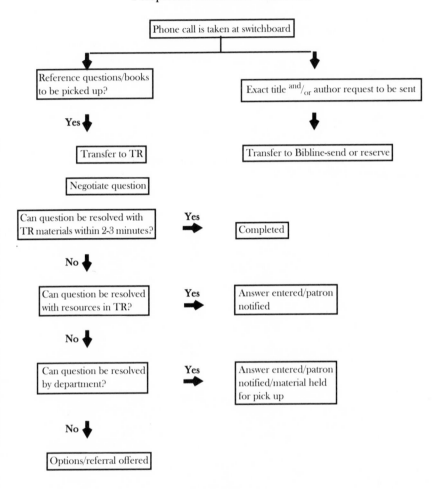

NOTES

1.   Seventy-five percent of the people live outside the city of Orlando. The library serves a young population: twenty-one percent are under fifteen, and eleven percent are over sixty-four, compared with statewide percentages of fifteen percent under fifteen and 15 percent over age sixty-four.

2.   The impact of the doubling of the population on the library is reflected in these growth figures: The main library grew from 6,700 to 290,000 square feet. Public seating at the main library increased from less than a hundred to nearly 1,000. Main library door count averaged more than 3,000 daily by 1988. Daily incoming phone calls reached 1,000.

Branch libraries grew in number from eight to eleven and in size from 6,000 to 10,5000 square feet. Total reference transactions increased from three quarters of a million in fiscal year 1986 to 1.7 million in fiscal year 1993.

3. BALIS (Bay Area Library and Information Service) and SJVIS (San Joaquin Valley Information Service) are two of the fifteen regional, second-tier reference referral centers of California. When a public library requires assistance to meet a reference need, the patron's question is referred to a regional center. Until its recent closure, SCAN was available to assist regional centers with extended reference requests. SCAN (or the State of California Answering Network) operating out of the Los Angeles Public Library, provided third-level reference service for the regional systems. Providing service for twenty-five years, it first functioned as a back up service for Southern California libraries and expanded service statewide in 1988. SCAN ceased operating early in 1996.

4. Information was obtained about San Francisco Public Library's Telephone Information Program (TIP), Infoline at Tucson Public Library, the King County Library's Answerline, and the Boston Public Library's Telephone Reference Group.

ABOUT THE AUTHORS

Barbara B. Alexander manages the federal documents unit at Illinois State University. Before moving there in 1992 to head General Reference and Documents, she worked at Texas A&M University (1987-1992) as Head, Documents/Maps; Documents Reference Librarian; Microtext Librarian; and Humanities Reference Librarian, along with teaching a semester long, two-credit course in library research from 1988-1990. She has held various offices in professional organizations, chairing the New Members Round Table, Texas Library Association; Government Documents Round Table, Illinois Library Association; and the American Library Association, Library Administration and Management Association, Library Organization and Management Section, Leadership Discussion Group among other activities. Among her numerous publications are "Maintaining the GPO Tapes: Using MARCIVE's Printout," co-authored with Laura Tull, and "Merging Federal Documents with General Reference: A Transformation in Usage and in Librarian Stature," presented with Sharon Naylor at the Seventh National ACRL Conference. In 1990, Ms. Alexander was honored as the Outstanding New Librarian in Texas and as one of those invited to attend the first annual Snowbird Leadership Institute. She is listed in Who's Who of American Women.

Inga H. Barnello is the Social Services Librarian at Le Moyne College in Syracuse, New York. She is the coordinator of the Library instruction and editor of *alphabytes*, the library newsletter. She has written several essays and commentaries on the transformation of libraries and the role of libraries in society. Her memberships include Beta Phi Mu, ALA, New York Library Association, and the Eastern New York Chapter of ACRL where she served as Secretary and serves on the Program Committee.

Lisa Blankenship is Instructional Services Librarian and an Assistant Professor at James A. Michener Library, University of Northern Colorado, Greely, Colorado. She received her Master's degree in Librarianship and Information Science from the University of Denver in 1984, and began working at UNC in 1989. She is a member of the Colorado Library Association and the American Library Association, and presented a poster session on the UNCLE project described in this book at the annual ALA Conference in 1995. Ms. Blankenship received a UNC Teaching Excellence Award in 1993 for her work with undergraduate library instruction. In addition to providing library instruction, Internet instruction, reference service, and helping to maintain the UNC Libraries' web pages, she is currently participating in the Educational Technology Improvement Project at UNC. Participants in this project are learning to use technology in the development and delivery of standard-based courses.

Kathleen M. Conley is currently an interim Assoicate Dean of University Libraries at Illinois State University. From 1991-1996, she worked as a Reference and Documents Librarian at Illinois State, and she continues to serve as the Coordinator of Library Services for Heartland Community College. Ms, Conley is a member of the American Library Association and the Association of College and Research Libraries where she serves on the Communications Committee of the Extended Campus Libraries Section and the Library Media Technician Training Committee of the Community and Junior College Libraries Section. She is a member of the Illinois Association of College and Research Libraries, chairing the Bibliographic Instruction Discussion Group. Further state activities include serving on the Alliance Library System Transition and Interim Boards and the System Advisory Council. Currently she is serving by appointment of Illinois Secretary of State and State Librarian George H. Ryan on a Regional Planning Panel charged with developing a statewide plan for universal library service. Ms. Conley has recently finished editing and indexing *A Matter of Life and Death: Health, Illness and Medicine in McLean County, 1830-1995* and has contributed three essays to the *International Directory of University Histories* to be published by Fitzroy Dearborn.

Sally Fry is Head of the Audio Visual Department of the Orange County, Florida Library System. Her work with the system began in 1985 as a reference librarian in the Business and Science Department followed by positions as the library's Community Relations Coordinator, head of a special projects team that worked throughout the night at the Main Library, and a manager in the Telephone Reference Department. Prior to coming to the Orange County Library System, Ms. Fry worked as a reference librarian with the Chicago Public Library. She received her Master of Library Science Degree from Florida State University and is a member of the American Library Association.

Jessica George is a reference librarian in the General Reference and Documents Department at Milner Library, Illinois State University, Normal, Illinois. She is actively involved in professional development and continuing education with the Illinois Association of College and Research Libraries. She is committed to the development of a philosophy for academic librarianship which will give young librarians better direction in their life's work, and to that end she is involved with several research projects on the role of the university library in student life and campus development.

Dena Holiman Hutto is Documents/Social Sciences Librarian at Reed College, Portland Oregon. She began reference work at Pennsylvania State University's Documents and Maps Section and has worked closely with electronic government information at a time of exponential growth in the field. An active member of the American Library Association's Government Documents Round Table, she is co-author of "Gopher for Reference Service: Organization and Use," presented at the seventh Association of College and Research Libraries conference, and has published several articles on government information and bibliographic access. Ms. Hutto received an M.S. in Library and Information Science from the University of Illinois at Urbana-Champaign in 1988.

Sally W. Kalin is Acting Assistant Dean for Collections and Reference Services, Penn State University Libraries. Most of her career has been devoted to work in public services librarianship. Her interest in remote use of library information systems began in 1984, the same year that Penn State began offering remote access to LIAS, its OPAC, and she was given responsibility for providing assistance to off-site LIAS users, and also did a sabbatical study in 1991 on the searching behaviors of remote users as compared to in-house library users. In 1994 she was awarded the Reference Services Press Award for her *RQ* article on "Support Services for Remote Users." A graduate of Penn State and the University of Pittsburgh, Ms. Kalin has been active in the American Society for Information Science and the American Library Association.

Mollie D. Lawson is Associate Professor of Library Services and Coordinator of Technical Services at Ward Edward Library, Central Missouri State University, Warrensburg, Missouri. She holds her M.L.S. from George Peabody College (Vanderbilt University) in Nashville, Tennessee, and an Education Specialist degree from Central Missouri State University. She is active in the Missouri Library Association and the American Library Association. She is currently Vice-president of the Missouri Chapter of Beta Phi Mu and President of the CMSU Chapter of Phi Kappa Phi National Honor Society. She is a member of the American Association of University Women, Warrensburg Branch. Her research interests are in the areas of Bibliographic Instruction and Library Materials Budgeting. She is a co-author of a textbook *Academic Libraries and Research: Mastering the Maze* used in Central's two-hour credit University Studies course on library research and information resources.

Catherine A. Lee is currently Head Librarian at the Penn State DuBois Campus Library in DuBois, Pennsylvania. Her former positions include Public Services Librarian at Eastern Kentucky University, Richmond and Library Director of the Greenbrier Community College Center, Lewisburg, West Virginia. Lee earned her M.L.S. in 1990 from the University of South Florida and an M.A. in English from Eastern Kentucky in 1993. Lee is an active member of the American Library Association and the Association of College and Research Libraries. She is involved with the Extended Campus Library Services Section and Community Junior College Library Section of ACRL and is a member of the ECLSS Planning Committee of the CJCLS Instruction Committee. She is also a member of the National Council for Learning Resources and is editor of the organization's *NCLR Newsletter for Presidents*. Ms. Lee has published several articles on Generation X in such journals as *The Reference Librarian* and *Research Strategies* and has made numerous presentations on the topic at state and national library conferences. Her most recent focus is on managing Generation X employees.

Vivienne Monty has published three books on Small and Medium business in Canada. Her latest was published this year. She is the author of numerous articles on various aspects of government documents, business, and currently, the Internet. She has just completed a detailed index to the *Monetary Times of Canada, 1867-1935* on a grant received from the Social Sciences and Research Council of Canada. She is about to undertake the indexing of *Maclean's Magazine* 1905-1976. These indexes will be Internet accessible. Ms. Monty is a former President of the Canadian Library Association and is active in SLA, ALA, and the Ontario Library Association. She has recently been appointed to the ALA Committee on Accreditation.

Robert L. Mowery is Archivist and Special Collections Librarian at Illinois Wesleyan University, Bloomington, Illinois. An alumnus of three Big Ten universities, he has a B.S. in Mechanical Engineering from Purdue, an M.S. in Library Science from the University of Illinois at Urbana-Champaign and a Ph.D. in Early Christian Life and Literature from Northwestern University. Besides two articles on the subject cataloging of Chicano literature, he has published articles on the Cutter Classification and the subject cataloging of African literature, African history and Women's Studies. He has also published articles on the books of Matthew, Luke and Acts in various American and European scholarly journals. He has held offices in the American Library Association, the Illinois Association of College and Research Libraries, the Society of Biblical Literature, and the Chicago Society of Biblical Research.

Roberta Pitts is Library Director at Texas A&M University—Kingsville. Prior to her current appointment she worked in Reference Services and Personnel Operations at Texas A&M University in College Station. She was selected to set up an international library at Texas A&M University's former Japan campus. She holds a Master of Library Science degree from the University of North Texas.

Kathryn Robinson is Head of the Division of Reference and Information at the Orange County, Florida Library System and is responsible for the nine Reference and Programming Departments at the Main Library. Her work with the system began in 1985. Recent projects include developing a Telephone Reference Department, a Storytelling Troupe, establishing goals and objectives for the library's five Year Plan, revising the Reference Policy, and setting up the selection of, and staff training on, electronic resources. She received her Master of Library Science degree from Florida State University and is a member of the American Library Association, Southeast Library Association, Public Library Association, Florida Library Association, Central Florida Library Consortium Reference Interest Group, and the Orlando Women's Executive Council.

María de Jesús Ayala-Schueneman is currently Associate Professor and Head of Public Services at the James C. Jernigan Library, Texas A&M University–Kingsville. A native of Mexico, Ms. de Jesus Ayala-Schueneman was educated in Mexico City, Texas, and California. She holds a Master of Library Science degree from San Jose State University, an M.A. degree in Spanish from Texas A&I University, and is working on a dissertation at Texas A&M University–Kingsville concerning bilingual education and libraries. Her interests range from Internet instruction to nineteenth century Mexican novelists.

Jane Smith is the Head of the Interlibrary Loan Department at the University of Northern Colorado. She has participated in poster sessions at ALA and LITA, has given presentations at conferences for LITA, ALA, CIL, and IFLA, and has published numerous articles addressing interlibrary loan and document delivery issues. Ms. Smith serves on several Colorado state committees and has serves as a consultant on interlibrary loan workflow. The primary focus of her work, in addition to interlibrary loan duties is the design, development, and implementation of software for a variety of library projects such as UNCLE. Ms. Smith is a professional scuba diver, has a bachelor's degree in English, and is currently completing her Master's degree in Educational Technology.

Dr. Pamela Snelson is Assistant Director for Automation and Public Services at Drew University Library, Madison, New Jersey. Currently, she is chair of the College Libraries Section of the Association of College and Research Libraries Association (ACRL), and chair of the *College and Research Libraries News* Editorial Board. In addition she is a member of the *New Jersey Journal of Communication* Editorial Board and the PALINET Board of Trustees. She has made presentations on the concept of access at the ASIS Annual Meeting and the ACRL National Conference; a book on the topic is underway.

Lucia Snowhill is the Social Sciences Collection Coordinator at Davidson Library, University of California, Santa Barbara. In addition she has collection responsibilities for Political Science, Law, and Foreign Government Documents. She has published articles and made presentations on topics such as access to federal government information, Z39.50 databases, teamwork, and holding academic office hours. She has been active in ALA Government Documents Round Table, ACRL Law and Political Sciences section, and the Librarians Association of the University of California.

Stephen P. Sottong is a native of Indiana and a graduate of Purdue University and San Jose State University. For a decade he worked as a California aerospace engineer on the global positioning satellites. He heeded the call of librarianship in 1992. He bagan his library experience as an engineering libarian at Georgia Institute of Technology and is now Science Librarian at Pepperdine University in Malibu, California. His hobbies include studying anthropology and creating software, about which he has previously written for the library literature. A compulsive "fixer," he has remedied most of the software problems mentioned in his chapter in this volume.

Lynne M. Stuart is a Humanities Librarian in the General Reference Section at the Pennsylvania State University Libraries. She also has extensive experience in fine arts and government documents reference, and is a member of the American Library Association's Reference and Adult Services Division, Bibliography and Reference Publishing Advisory Committee. Ms. Stuart and Dena Hutto have co-authored a paper on using the Internet Gopher as a reference tool, which was presented at the seventh national conference of the Association of College and Research Libraries, and an article on Internet health policy resources. Ms. Stuart received her library degree from Simmons College.

Gary B. Thompson has been Head of Information and Instruction Services at Cleveland State University in Cleveland, Ohio since 1989. Prior to that he managed reference and instructional services at Hobart and William Smith Colleges and Ohio Northern University. He has served as a member of the Choice Educational Board and the College and Research Libraries Editorial Board. His other professional activities and interests include customer service, customer usage, and customer satisfaction studies, reference management, library instruction, book reviewing, indexing, and electronic product design and evaluation.

P. Warren-Wenk, Associate Librarian at York University Libraries, Toronto, Canada, is a reference librarian and educational biographer. She has designed and led Internet training programs for faculty, teachers, and librarians, and writes in the area of bibliographic instruction and new technologies. Most recently, she is co-author of the book *A Guide to the Bookstores of Toronto*, ECW Press, 1996.

Carol Wright is an Educational Librarian at the Pennsylvania State University Libraries, with responsibility for Education Policy Studies, including Higher Education, Educational Administration, and Educational Theory and Policy. Ms. Wright is a recent recipient of a grant from Penn State's Department of Continuing and Distance Education to develop instructional materials to support library and information research skills for distance education students. Ms. Wright is the University Scholars Librarian, and through that program has supervised honors student research projects in London, England. Ms. Wright is responsible for coordinating the delivery of basic library instruction to freshman composition students. In partnership with Penn State's Center for Academic Computing/Educational Technology Services, Ms. Wright assists faculty in identifying existing software and multimedia for instructional applications. She is active in the American Library Association and holds an M.L.S. from Syracuse University and a B.S. from the State University of New York at Plattsburgh.

INDEX